A HISTORY OF THE
REGIMENTS & UNIFORMS
OF THE BRITISH ARMY

First published in 1950
Second Edition 1951
Third Edition 1954
Fourth Edition 1957
Fifth Edition 1962

PLATE I   THE HORSE GRENADIER GUARDS   1750

FIRST TROOP: GRENADIER

Their uniform and equipment were a mixture of cavalry and infantry. They were dressed like dragoons but wore the infantry grenadier cap, and carried carbines, pistols, swords, bayonets and grenades. The heavy and light dragoons and the Dragoon Guards were issued with bayonets (presumably a relic of the origin of the former as mounted infantry) until well into the 19th century, but it appears that latterly they were kept in store.

The Horse Grenadiers belonged to the Household Cavalry, and in addition some of the Horse regiments had a troop of them. They were in existence for nearly a hundred years, being finally disbanded in 1788.

A HISTORY OF THE
REGIMENTS & UNIFORMS
OF THE
BRITISH ARMY

By

Major R. Money Barnes

Illustrations by the Author

FIFTH EDITION

LONDON
Seeley Service & Co.
Limited

Printed in Great Britain

This book is dedicated to British soldiers who have served all over the world during the last three centuries

By the same author

THE UNIFORMS & HISTORY OF
THE SCOTTISH REGIMENTS

MILITARY UNIFORMS OF
BRITAIN & THE EMPIRE

INTRODUCTION

'God and the soldier we alike adore,
In time of danger, not before.
The danger past and all things righted,
God is forgotten, the soldier slighted.'

Thomas Jordan, 1612-1686

A record such as that of the British Army, which for centuries has been unsurpassed by that of any other nation, cannot fail to be common knowledge, in some degree, to all who pride themselves on having British blood. But in many cases the details are vague and nebulous and consist mainly of half-forgotten bits of history, imperfectly understood at school.

We are all aware that the Services saved us from the two great German efforts, of recent years, to ruin and enslave us, and most of us can see that their task is nowhere near completion yet. But many are inclined to think of the British armies of this century as quite different from those of earlier periods. They think of them just as collections of men from all the families of the Empire, who left their peaceful homes for a time to become temporary parts of a machine, until the job was done, when they could (if they survived) return to normal occupations.

What is, perhaps, not so clear to everyone is the wonderful spirit of the old army which possessed these men, moulded. trained and inspired them to go through every kind of ordeal and set-back, to endure delays and frustration which had no clear meaning and yet to be fresh and keen for battle, until finally they were victorious. They do not all appreciate that these temporary warriors are the successors of the soldiers of Cromwell, Marlborough, Wellington and innumerable less-distinguished figures, but for whom there would have been no Empire to fight for, and without whose prowess Britain would have been just a province of France, or at best a tenth-rate power.

Some may not know that until these years of universal service, when it would be absurd for each family to look down on its own relations who join up, the soldier had, except in war-time, always been treated as an outcast; that our governments had always been

7

rabidly opposed to 'the standing army' and had dealt with it abominably as regards pay, food, quarters, and all its conditions of life (yet often expecting it to do the work of two or three times its numbers) and after every war had done their best to abolish it.

But, in spite of all discouragement, small numbers of British men—many from the lowest grades of life, without education and with no background except what was acquired in the army—have, with the leadership and care of good regimental officers, given the country a centuries-old fighting reputation and a position which are the envy of the world. Not only have they been feared and respected in war, but in peace their good nature and fair-mindedness have made friends for them and for the nation wherever they have served.

Unimaginative people say that all tradition before 1914, or even later, is forgotten, and therefore no longer worthy of study. But actual experience of warfare proves this to be altogether wrong. Every battle from the earliest had its lesson and the great majority of these still apply. Tools and tactics change, but the principles do not; and as regards a regiment, it is more than likely that if it distinguished itself at Minden or Waterloo, it did so again at Alamein or in Normandy, the latest exploits having a definite connection with the successes of former centuries.

The first-class soldier, besides developing his mental and physical alertness and toughness and acquiring the technique of using his weapons, learns to subjugate the body to the mind to such an extent that it becomes his machine. By his own willpower he can drive it through the most terrifying ordeals and hardships, if necessary until it is physically incapable of further movement.

There are innumerable instances in the annals of British regiments, some of which are mentioned in this book, where individuals or whole units have reached this highest possible standard and have not broken even during the process of complete annihilation. Each one of these has enriched the army's history, and has enhanced the high reputation it must maintain.

A soldier does not do these things because he likes them more than any other man; he learns to attain these heights through discipline, resulting from the schooling which has come down to him from many generations of his own people who have served before him. Their experience, gained in all parts of the world, much of it won in the hard way, through numerous defeats to final victory, is by no means dead. It lives on, not only in the spirit of the army, but in its methods and science, where every detail of the past has been assimilated in its development into the complex and highly mechanized force it is to-day.

8

Introduction

It is impossible to think that the armies of temporary soldiers, which saved the existence of the Empire in the last two wars, could have been built up of civilians in so short a time, without the knowledge, the organization and, most of all, the high morale and tradition which the regular army has been storing up from all its varied experiences since 1660. These it had all ready, processed and labelled, and prepared to hand on to its brothers from 'civvy street'.

This book attempts to give some impression of the men, as far as possible pictorial and colourful, and of the way in which the invaluable traditions of regiments and the team spirit of the whole army grew up between the Civil War and the Second World War.

The uniforms in the illustrations are accurate, as far as years of painstaking research can make them. But to avoid being wearisome to those who want only a general impression, the recitation of the details in the text has been cut to a minimum. For those who like to go deeper there is much detail in the drawings, and the notes about them have been carefully sorted out and provide an authentic view of the main features throughout the period to which they refer. To give an account of every regimental difference in dress would, of course, need a book many times the size of this, but each figure illustrated can be taken as a representative type and (allowing always for regimental eccentricities) the tables in the appendices will provide more ample information.

As regards the dates of changes of the uniforms, allowance must be made for the slow circulation of orders in the early days —by horse and sailing ship—and the fact that even up to the present day the superseded uniform is nearly always allowed to be worn out before being replaced. Another point is that in many cases, e.g. the bearskin Grenadier cap of 1768, the chevrons of 1802, etc., some regiments had anticipated the order, perhaps by several years.

CONTENTS

LIST OF ILLUSTRATIONS

Regimental Titles are given in full in the Appendices

12

List of Illustrations

REGIMENTS & UNIFORMS
OF THE
BRITISH ARMY

CHAPTER I · 1642-1758

The history of the regular army dates from the restoration of the monarchy in 1660. Before the Civil War there had been no standing army, apart from a small force of the Yeomen of the Guard, which then comprised active units of cavalry and infantry.

Previously armies had consisted of men recruited specially to deal with a national crisis or an overseas expedition. The great majority of the troops had been raised by the feudal lords and landowners, who formed units from the retainers on their estates and usually commanded them in person. These men fought under the banners of their masters and, in most cases, wore their livery or uniform. The continuance of this tradition can be traced up to the middle of the eighteenth century, when regiments were still known as Colonel ———'s, and the Colonel's coat of arms or crest was emblazoned on the colours and on the Grenadier caps of the men.

For home defence the Militia or Trained Bands had been in existence from Anglo-Saxon times and training with the bow or 'hand-gonne' had, at various periods, been compulsory for fit men, who could all be called up in a national emergency. Many Irish and Scots took service as mercenaries under the Kings of France, but this type of career does not seem to have appealed so much to the English.

In addition to these comparatively small armies raised at home, considerable use was made of foreign mercenaries—mainly Germans, Dutch, or Swiss. At a later date the early Georges who, besides being Kings of England, were also Electors of Hanover, kept a number of Hanoverian regiments which were uniformed and equipped similarly to the British.

COLOURS

Banners or Standards had been found necessary in very early times (e.g. the Roman Eagles) to show the position of the commander and to form rallying points. The Colours of British regiments became something like the Ark of the Covenant, and were

19

invested with a more than earthly significance. They were symbolic of the very spirit of the regiment, and were carried into battle in the centre of the line, always closely guarded by the Ensigns and an escort of specially chosen non-commissioned officers. Where *they* stood, there the regiment stood, come what might, and if necessary the last man would be expected to give his life to keep them from the enemy.

It was always tangible evidence of victory to bring home an enemy's Standard, as it proved beyond doubt that he must have been demoralized and routed and, conversely, to lose a Standard was almost the lowest disgrace which could befall.

In the seventeenth century every company of infantry and every troop of cavalry had its own Colour in addition to the regimental ones which, in the case of infantry, were usually three in number—one each for the two wings of musketeers and the wing of pikemen. They were reduced to two when the pikes were abolished at the end of the century. Company Colours bore heraldic difference marks to distinguish those of the Majors and each of the Captains in order of seniority. These did not survive long except in the regiments of Foot Guards, to whom Charles II gave a distinctive badge for each company.

ORIGIN OF UNIFORMS

Apart from the obvious purpose of distinguishing friend from enemy—the red cross of St. George on a white ground was the traditional English device—and differentiating one corps from another, sumptuous and awe-inspiring uniforms were designed to raise the morale of the troops, to impress the enemy with their martial prowess and to demonstrate the importance of the power which sent them into the field. (This was, of course, a later development than the purely ferocious aspect of military dress, which dates back to the woad of the Ancient Britons, and the hideous facial disfigurements of primitive tribes in North America, Africa, the Pacific, etc.) An equally important point is that uniform is an aid to establishing discipline, which is the essential beginning of efficiency. Men all dressed alike get the feeling of being parts of a machine and experience a great pride and satisfaction in the precision of really good drill. Moreover, it is of great value in keeping them smart and clean, and absolutely up to standard, as any man on parade who has been at all slack about his dress becomes conspicuous. Incidentally, a smart turn-out impresses the other sex and thus gives the soldier an additional cause for self-confidence, and helps to attract recruits.

A further point is that small distinctions, which mean a great deal to the wearers, can be added to the men's uniforms as rewards for exceptional service, which give them something to be proud of when among men of other units or civilians. Examples of these are—the red hackle of *The Black Watch* (*Royal Highland Regiment*), which was given as a regimental distinction in recognition of their conduct at the battle of Guildermalson, in Holland, in 1794, and as a personal one the ribbon of the V.C., or the D.C.M.

THE 'NEW MODEL ARMY'

At the beginning of the Civil War men enlisted on either side without uniform. As long as they could raise some fairly useful weapons, that was good enough to start with and, apart from some issues of sashes of distinctive colours (then worn by all ranks), nothing much was done about it until Cromwell raised the 'New Model Army' in 1645. This consisted at first of eleven regiments of Horse, twelve of Foot, a thousand Dragoons, and some artillery. They were uniformly dressed in red, and regularly paid (a great innovation), and discipline was exceedingly strict.

RANKS OF GENERAL OFFICERS

An interesting point is that this force was commanded by Captain-General Sir Thomas Fairfax. The cavalry was under Lieutenant-General Oliver Cromwell, and the infantry under Sergeant-Major-General Skippon. This is the explanation of the familiar conundrum, 'Why is a Lieutenant-General senior to a Major-General?' The answer is (*a*) The Major-General was originally a Sergeant-Major-General; and (*b*) the first Lieutenant-General commanded the cavalry, which was the senior branch of the service.

ORIGIN OF DESIGNATIONS OF RANKS AND UNITS

The following are the derivations of the ranks below those of General officers:

COLONEL: From Italian *colonello* = a little column. So called because he led the 'little column' at the head of the regiment—presumably the Regimental H.Q.

MAJOR: A 'greater' or more important one than the company officers. The lowest rank of field officer.

CAPTAIN: From French *Capitaine*. Means simply 'the head' of a company or small unit. A very similar rank to that of the Roman Centurion, or commander of a hundred.

LIEUTENANT: French = 'one who acts as a substitute' for a Captain, Colonel, General, etc.

ENSIGN: From French *Ensigne*. The junior commissioned rank of infantry and, in early times, of dragoons. Named from the Ensign or Colour, which was carried by them.

CORNET: Equivalent of Ensign, in the regiments of Horse and later all types of cavalry. Named from the Cornet (Standard or Guidon). Both of these ranks were changed to 2nd Lieutenant in 1871.

SUBALTERN: Officers below the rank of Captain. 'Inferior to, or subordinate.' From French *Subalterne*.

ADJUTANT: From Latin *adiutans* = assisting. Not a rank, but an appointment. (French platoon commanders are called *ajutants*.)

SERGEANT: From French *Sergent*, derived from Latin *serviens* = serving.

CORPORAL: From French *Caporal*, originally from Italian *capodi* = 'head of' a section, etc. No connection with corpus.

SOLDIER: Originally meant a mercenary, or man who served for *solde*. Derived from Latin *solidus* = a shilling. (In the nineteenth and early twentieth century a soldier's pay was a shilling a day, and enlisting was known as 'taking the Queen's shilling'—the first day's pay, handed out by the recruiting sergeant.)

PRIVATE MAN: Meant a man who was responsible only for himself. Up to the end of the seventeenth century a soldier was described as a 'private centinel', i.e. one of a hundred, which was the normal strength of a company. This word survives in corrupted form and meaning as 'sentry'.

Many of the names of arms and units and sub-units are self-explanatory, but the following are a few of the less obvious ones.

CAVALRY: From Italian *cavallo* = a horseman, also Spanish *caballero* and French *chevalier*.

INFANTRY: Origin doubtful. It appears to have been a word used by the Staff, to describe the troops who, though they formed the battle line, could only move at a foot's pace, and could not carry their own baggage or supplies to last any length of time, and were therefore given the technical description of infants. It may also have been a term of abuse or condescension, used by the more fortunate mounted men when on the march.

ARTILLERY: From French *artillerie*. Derived from old French *artiller* = to equip or fortify, which in turn came from low Latin *artillare* = to make machines. The term originally meant the provision and maintenance of all types of weapons, but later came to apply only to guns and their personnel.

BRIGADE: From Italian *brigata*, from *brigare* = to fight.

REGIMENT: From Latin *regimen* = a rule or system of order. Some confusion arises between regiments and battalions, as regiments which were amalgamated in 1881 often still refer to their own battalion as 'the regiment', and many of them continue to use their old numbers.

BATTALION: From Latin *battuere* = to strike. Connected also with *battalia* = an army in battle array. Thus means a battle unit.

SQUADRON: From Latin *quadra* = a square. French *escadron*.

TROOP: Means literally a collection of people. From French *troupe*, probably derived from Latin *turba* = a crowd.

COMPANY: This also meant a collection of people. The word was used by mercenaries and 'soldiers of fortune', in the Middle Ages, and had a commercial meaning, rather on the lines of its present one in civilian life. Its members were out for pay, loot, and ransoms for wealthy prisoners.

WEAPONS AND TACTICS

At the time of the Civil War the recognized arms of the service were Horse, Foot, composed of pikemen and musketeers (known as 'the shot'), Dragoons (mounted Infantry), and Artillery. The normal battle formation consisted of pikemen in the centre of each battalion, and musketeers, in three ranks, on the flanks, cavalry in rear ready to move out quickly on either flank, and the guns, usually in pairs, posted in the intervals between the infantry regiments.

The pikes were used either in pushing home an attack or in resisting one, and they must have been a very serious obstacle to cavalry when formed up six deep with the butts of the sixteen-foot staves held firmly into the ground. Halberds, which were a modification of pikes, were also used. They were about eight feet long, with various types of heads, which usually combined an axe and spear, or in some cases resembled a billhook or a boat-hook. (There was a tendency to reduce the length of pikes and to use four ranks instead of six, as being less unwieldy.)

Muskets were very primitive—so heavy and recoiling so violently, that they had to be fired from a rest driven into the ground, very slow to load, extremely inaccurate and possessing a very short range. They were described as harquebuses or cullivers—a corruption of calibre, a name acquired when the bores were to some extent standardized. A slow match or smouldering fuse was used for firing (replaced by the flint-lock about 1675), which in rain went out, and at night glowed and so prevented the possibility of a surprise attack. There is no comparison between the smokeless crack of a modern high velocity rifle and the heavy

23

shattering roar of one of these weapons, with its flame and cloud of foul smoke. That they were, however, improving is shown by the fact that in 1600 musketeers formed one fourth of a battalion, but by 1670 they accounted for five-sixths of its strength. (In order to reduce the time taken in loading, musketeers used to hold one or two bullets in their mouths. Hence the expression 'to bite on the bullet', which was the old equivalent of 'taking it'.)

The sword was common to all branches of the service, in addition to any other arms, and was the principal weapon of the cavalry, who were taught never to rely on their carbines unless they were attacked when dismounted. A 'Horse' pistol of large dimensions, with a flint-lock, was also used, but once it had been fired in a cavalry engagement, it could not be reloaded until leisure was obtainable to carry out the lengthy process involved. It did, however, form a handy and heavy missile to throw in the face of an opponent and was often used for this purpose.

There were also a few lances among the cavalry, but this weapon was considered merely a survival from the 'knightly years' and was thought to be cumbersome and more or less useless. It was discarded during the Civil War and was not revived until 1816, when lancer regiments were formed as the result of practical experience of the effectiveness of the Polish lancers in the Peninsular and Waterloo campaigns.

There was a rather quaint cavalry drill, sometimes referred to as the 'Caracole', in which a regiment stood in mass formation, facing the enemy, but just out of firearms range. Each rank, in turn, rode forward, halted, discharged their pistols, and then trotted to the rear to reload. At Edgehill, 1642, when both sides were inexperienced and ill-armed, Prince Rupert (Lieutenant-General, in command of the Royalist cavalry, at the age of twenty-two), caused a panic among the Roundheads by ignoring this precedent. His men had very few pistols, so he ordered them to advance at the trot, in accordance with the accepted drill, but instead of halting, to break into a gallop and charge right in.

The guns—18-pounders known as Culverins; 6-pounders called Sakers; Minyons, 3½-pounders; and Faulconets, 1½-pounders—were in a primitive and clumsy stage of evolution, some of the larger ones being so heavy that as many as twenty-six farm horses were used to draw them. The lighter field pieces were generally divided up among the infantry regiments and placed under their colonel's orders. (The barrel of a gun is so named because it was originally built up of iron staves bound with hoops on the same principle as a wine barrel. As muskets, etc., developed from small cannon adapted for hand use, the same word was applied to all firearms, and eventually acquired its present meaning.)

The strength of an infantry battalion in the 'New Model Army' was about 1,200, but as the proportion of muskets increased and their fire became more effective, it was reduced to a more manageable size and by the year 1700 it was down to about 450. It was divided into half-companies or platoons, on the Swedish system introduced by Gustavus Adolphus, of which the odd numbers fired while the even numbers loaded and vice versa.

ARMOUR

Body armour was almost in its last days, but at the beginning of the Civil War there were a number of fully armoured horsemen on both sides, most of them probably wearing an ancient suit taken out of store for this emergency. Cuirasses or 'shells', consisting of front and back plates, and helmets of the barred and lobster-tailed type were more or less standard equipment for the remainder of the Horse. Pikemen wore a 'pot' or steel helmet (not so very different from a modern one), a shell and 'tassets' which were steel scales or hinged plates covering the thighs.

But it was gradually being decided that the amount of protection given by armour, now that bullets could pierce it, did not justify the slowness and fatigue entailed by its weight. Horse, however, continued to wear cuirasses for some years, as, being more mobile than infantry, they were usually fairly immune from the clumsy and inaccurate muskets, and needed protection more against sword-cuts, for which the cuirass was admirably suited. Gunners employed on field works, etc., also wore them until well into the eighteenth century. Late survivals of armour were the 'skull' or iron cap worn inside the tricorne hat up to about 1750, and the 'gorget' or throat-piece, worn by officers until 1830. This, however, diminished in size and became merely a small crescent-shaped ornament, which was worn when on duty, on the same principle as a modern policeman's wrist-band. But, although body armour was eventually completely discarded, the competition between missiles and other kinds of armour is never-ending, and continues now in more and more extravagant forms, such as super-tanks, battleships, concrete fortresses, etc. (It now appears that body armour would have been revived in 1945 had the invasion of Japan taken place, as the Americans had suits of laminated glass, which had been found to give efficient protection against bullets and splinters. Experiments were also made during the 1914–18 war, with specially processed metals, with no very serviceable results.)

FOUNDATION OF THE REGULAR ARMY

On Charles II's accession in 1660 the remains of the Parliamentary army, which had fought so many battles against Charles I, obviously had to be disbanded, and thereafter it became necessary to establish a small force, if only to act as a bodyguard on state occasions and to give the necessary prestige to the Sovereign. This army was at first not officially recognized by parliament and consisted of only five regiments, but it gradually grew into the regular army, and its descendants are serving to-day. The following are a few of the oldest regiments with the dates of their embodiment in the present army.

The Life Guards, 1660.

The Royal Horse Guards, 1661. This regiment had served in the Parliamentary army and was to be disbanded in 1660. The order was not carried out and the regiment was included in the royal establishment on 26th January 1661.

The Grenadier Guards, 1660. They were then known as 'The Royal Regiment of Guards', and had been with Charles during his exile.

The Coldstream Guards, 1660. This regiment had served in the Parliamentary army, and was known as Monck's regiment.

The Royal Scots (the 1st Foot), 1670. The regiment then had the title of 'Lord George Douglas's Regiment' and claimed descent from a Scottish legion employed by the Romans. Hence its nickname—'Pontius Pilate's Bodyguard'. It was serving the King of France and came over to England for a short time in 1662. Its continuous existence began under Charles I in 1633.

The Queen's Royal Regiment (*West Surrey*), (the 2nd Foot), 1662.

The Buffs (*The Royal East Kent Regiment*), (the 3rd Foot), 1665. This regiment was first raised by Queen Elizabeth, as 'The Holland Regiment' in 1572. In 1665, when Charles II declared war on Holland, they were serving with the Dutch and naturally refused to fight against England, and so were taken into the King's army.

The King's Own Royal Regiment (*Lancaster*), (the 4th Foot), 1680.

The Scots Guards, 1685. This regiment was originally formed about 1639.

A number of regiments were added between 1685 and 1689, more in 1701, and others at intervals up to 1800. One or two disbanded regiments were reformed in the nineteenth century. *The Irish Guards* were raised in 1900 and *The Welsh Guards* in 1915, and three cavalry and nine infantry regiments were taken over from the East India Company after the Mutiny, about 1860.

THE FIRST BATTLE HONOUR

The earliest battle honour is 'Tangier', and is borne by *The Royals*, *The Royal Scots*, *The Queen's*, *The Grenadier Guards*, and *The Coldstream Guards*. Tangier, as well as Bombay, was included in the dowry of Catherine of Braganza when she married Charles II. Bombay was rented to the East India Company for £10 a year! But the 'Royals' (1st Dragoons), nicknamed 'The Tangier Cuirassiers', and *The Queen's*—the 2nd Foot, were raised to garrison Tangier where, from 1662 to 1689, they had the regular army's first experience of savage warfare and the North African climate. They were joined later by the two Guards regiments and *The Royal Scots*, the main purpose of the garrison being to prevent piracy, which was rampant in the Mediterranean and the eastern Atlantic, by maintaining a base at Tangier for the Navy. The Pascal Lamb, which forms the badge of *The Queen's*, was the crest of Catherine of Braganza, and, apart from the cross in various forms, is the only sacred emblem worn as a regimental badge. In early times the regiment was known as 'The Tangerines', and also as 'Kirke's Lambs'—Kirke being the name of their Colonel.

HORSE AND DRAGOONS

Between 1681 and 1689 the seven regiments of Horse (later Dragoon Guards) and six more regiments of Dragoons which later became *The Royal Scots Greys*, the *3rd*, *4th*, and *7th Hussars*, the *5th Lancers*, and the *6th [Inniskilling] Dragoons*) were formed. Dragoons were originally mounted infantry, as distinct from Horse, which was heavy cavalry. They fought on foot and were paid less and had inferior mounts. In due course they became light cavalry, all except the 1st, 2nd, and 6th, which became heavy regiments. It is slightly confusing to trace how the Horse were made into dragoons, and the dragoons, in effect, became Horse at later dates. The name dragoon came from 'dragon', the nickname of a musket with which they were armed in the very early days, and illustrations of the seventeenth century show them blasting off these ponderous weapons just over the ears of their, apparently, very docile horses.

GRENADIERS

Grenadiers were introduced into the army in 1678, and soon every infantry regiment had a company of them. Apart from their special training in handling and throwing grenades, these companies were an early example of the principle of forming units of picked men for special work. The most efficient and the tallest men were selected, and the company usually marched at the head, and was the show-piece of the regiment. Sometimes the grenadier companies of several regiments were temporarily made into a special service battalion to carry out some important task. The grenades, with which they were armed in addition to the musket, sword, and bayonet, were round and about the size of a cricket ball and were filled with powder, with a fuse projecting on one side, which was lighted from a slow match wound round the left wrist. There was a very precise drill for the whole company to throw them in volleys. The word grenade was originally *grenado* from the Italian, which, in turn, probably came from *granato* = a pomegranate, as it resembled this fruit in size and shape, with the protruding fuse-tube corresponding to its hardened calyx. The 'British Grenadiers' of the eighteenth century, with their tall mitre-shaped caps, were among the most picturesque figures of any period of military history.

HORSE GRENADIERS

The system of grenadier companies was adopted in the cavalry at about the same time as in the infantry, and troops, known as *The Horse Grenadier Guards*, were added to *The Life Guards*.

FUSILIERS

The formation of the earliest fusilier regiment, *The Royal Fusiliers* (*City of London Regiment*), the 7th Foot, followed in 1685. They were then known as *The Ordnance Regiment*, or *The Royal Regiment of Fuzileers*. Their original purpose was to act as escort to the guns (and incidentally to prevent the civilian drivers, who had practically no discipline, from panicking). They wore grenadier caps, at first smaller than those of the grenadier companies, but later of the same pattern. All fusilier regiments, of which there are now seven: *The Royal Northumberland*, *Royal* (City of London Regiment), *Lancashire*, *Royal Scots*, *Royal Welch*, *Royal Inniskilling*, and *Royal Irish*, wear, in full dress, a cap similar to that of the Guards (which is the final form of the grenadier cap), but smaller and not of bearskin, but of seal or racoon. The name fusilier came from an improved type of musket, which was used only by special units and officers, and was known by its French name—the *fusil* or *fusee*. The escorts for the guns were the first troops to be armed with flint-lock muskets, owing to the fact that sparks, drifting from the fusecord or 'match' of the old matchlock musket, quite often caused the open powder barrels standing beside the guns to explode.

THE MUSKET AND BAYONET REPLACE THE PIKE

By the end of the seventeenth century, when muskets and musketeers had increased greatly in efficiency, the pikes, of which the proportion in each regiment had progressively diminished, were finally abolished. The usefulness of both weapons had been combined by the introduction of the bayonet in 1670 (named from Bayonne, as it was a French invention), which was screwed into the muzzle of the musket to convert it into a pike. This, however, had obvious disadvantages and after the disaster in the pass of Killiecrankie, during the Scottish Rebellion in 1688, when two English regiments were routed owing to being unable to fire after fixing bayonets, a new pattern was designed. This had a hollow 'cranked' hilt which fitted over the muzzle, carrying the blade on one side. The only survivals of the pike after this change, were the 'espontoons' or 'spontoons' (half-pikes) carried by officers, who also had fusils and swords, and the halberds of the non-commissioned officers. One other survival, in military language, is the word picket, still in constant use, which originally meant a party of pikemen.

MARLBOROUGH'S VICTORIES

The regular army, though still very small, was well trained and in good form when Queen Anne came to the throne in 1702. Soon after this John Churchill, later Duke of Marlborough, was commanding an expeditionary force on the continent and winning victories which contributed largely towards our present position in European affairs. These are commemorated by some of the most treasured battle honours on the Colours of the older regiments—names such as Blenheim (1704), Ramillies (1706), Oudenarde (1708), and Malplaquet (1709).

In addition to these best-known battles there were numerous sieges and other actions and the accounts of these campaigns and the previous war of 1692–97 abound with familiar names, such as Ostend, Mons, Namur, Béthune, Menin, Dunkirk, etc. The war (which, to put it briefly, was fought to prevent France becoming more powerful by inheriting the Spanish throne, contrary to an existing agreement) lasted from 1702 to 1711, but field armies appear to have been kept in the Netherlands both before and after those dates.

MANNER OF CONDUCTING WARS

In the seventeenth and eighteenth centuries things moved in a somewhat leisurely manner. The main fighting normally took place during the summer months and the custom was, when the weather had deteriorated badly, to go into 'winter quarters' just as Julius Caesar did, in the old school books, and to observe a sort of 'close season' until the following spring. There was no organized system of providing rations, and consequently armies had to occupy country where they could live on local produce. But they had to keep open lines of communication by which to receive supplies of ammunition, equipment, and reinforcements, and to evacuate wounded, and this necessitated strongly defended bases and traffic centres.

Holland and Belgium, often referred to as 'the cockpit of Europe', were conveniently situated for attacking France, then the most powerful European country, or for access to Germany and central Europe. They were rich agricultural countries with good communications by river and canal, which enabled supplies to be moved when mud and winter conditions made the primitive roads and cart-tracks impassable. They possessed fortified towns strategically situated for controlling the waterways and roads and, as the result, became the traditional battleground for wars in Western Europe, and have retained this unenviable distinction up to the present day.

SCALE OF OPERATIONS AND METHODS OF FIGHTING

The forces used were very considerable and the actions fought would not, even now, be regarded as small battles. As an instance, at Blenheim, the allied loss was 4,485 killed, 7,525 wounded, and 273 missing and prisoners, while that of the enemy (consisting of French, Spaniards, and Bavarians) was about 10,000 killed and wounded, and 13,000 prisoners, including Marshal Tallard, their Commander-in-Chief and, of course, great booty in Colours, guns, baggage and stores. Thirty squadrons of French cavalry were said to have been drowned in the Danube.

The establishment of a battalion in 1703 was twelve battalion-companies, each of 60 men, and a grenadier company of 70—about 800 in all—12 or 15 battalions seem to have been quite a normal task-force for a particular job during a battle, or as a reinforcement.

Some very sizable road convoys moved to and from Ostend, which is shown by an account of a French attack on one of 800 wagons, on 28th September 1708. The escort of British infantry, with one troop of cavalry, beat off three times their number of enemy, who were accompanied by field artillery.

STORMING PARTIES

At the siege of Lisle (Lille), 1708, there was a French garrison of 15,000 and 50 allied battalions were detailed for the siege and covering force. The two storming parties were made up of approximately 1,600 grenadiers (the grenadier companies of about 25 battalions), 2,000 'workmen' and 30 carpenters to remove the palisades. It is not clear whether the 'workmen' were civilian labourers or working parties of troops, but as their job evidently was to move up close behind the grenadiers, who acted as a covering force, and clear a way through the palisades for the main body of infantry to advance into the defences, it seems much more likely that disciplined troops would have been used than civilians.

Before the attack it is stated that the batteries fired 'volleys'. The enemy met the storming parties with case shot, musketry and the explosion of mines. As an instance of regimental casualties in this action the 23rd Regiment (now *The Royal Welch Fusiliers*) lost 4 officers and 118 other ranks killed, and 11 officers and 245 other ranks wounded.

MINING

The siege of Tournai, 1709, appears to have been the scene of a remarkable contest in mining, there being more mine galleries than trenches above ground. A warren of tunnels extended for miles and counter-mining went on continuously. Often enemy mines were found, after laborious digging, far outside the citadel, and the powder was removed. There were numerous fights with sword, pistol and bayonet, when the opposing tunnellers met underground, and sometimes, owing to the darkness, men fought against their own side. Frequently whole parties were asphyxiated by the gases from explosions, or drowned by inundations. The most destructive mine recorded in this siege, went up on 26th August 1709, and '400 officers and men were blown into the air and their limbs were scattered to a great distance', according to the words of the laconic report.

VILLARS' FORTIFICATIONS

The *ne plus ultra lines*—a boastful name given by their designer Marshal Villars, were a sort of Maginot Line of great length, built with all possible engineering and tactical skill, packed with troops and guns and provided with every obstacle and device yet thought of. But by a few clever moves involving bluff and counter-marching by night, Marlborough outflanked and by-passed

31

them, making them useless, much as the Germans did with the Maginot Line itself in 1940.

BATTLE DRILL

Much of the fighting during Marlborough's campaigns consisted of attacking entrenchments and towns, but when the enemy could be manœuvred into a battle in the open, it must have been a sight for the gods. In spite of Shakespeare's 'villainous saltpetre', it was a combat of stout hearts and, given reasonable generalship on both sides, there was little doubt that the best men won.

Usually the battle opened after a dignified and unhurried deployment into line from marching columns, bands playing, Colours flying, and every man in step and looking straight to his front. This movement was covered by the cavalry and field guns, and might take several hours to complete. Finally the opposing armies were drawn up in solid lines, facing each other across a gap of perhaps fifty or sixty yards. The dressing was done by roll of drum, the sergeants lining the men up with the shafts of their halberds, while the Colours and band took post in their correct positions and the officers, according to their rank, aligned themselves in or behind the firing line.

The drill for loading muskets was a very lengthy affair, and included the following words of command: Handle—Cartridge! Prime! Load! Draw—ramrods! Ram down—Cartridge! Return —Ramrods! Make—Ready! Present! Give—Fire! (The word of command Fire! now in use, originated from Give—Fire! which, in the days of matchlocks, meant apply the match to the touch-hole, and the words 'round' and 'ball cartridge', in present use, probably dated from about the fifteenth century.)

It was discipline indeed to carry out this drill with the required precision, and not to hurry it, while the enemy were also preparing to fire.

The normal procedure thereafter was to exchange volleys, making considerable pauses for the smoke to clear, until one side was getting the worst of it, and showed signs of becoming 'jittery' and confused. Their opponents then charged with the bayonet to complete their victory and drive the remnants off the field. It did not always work out as precisely as this, though, as the unexpected was always liable to intervene, e.g. the sudden opening of fire from a battery just moved into an advantageous position, or an unheralded cavalry charge.

THE BRITISH INFANTRY

There were never any troops to equal the British infantry for discipline and sheer doggedness and determination, and for will-ing self-sacrifice and endurance when called on by a good com-mander, and they earned several remarkable tributes in those early days, such as 'their wonderful bravery and constancy' re-ferred to in a letter by the King of Prussia in 1704.

They were undoubtedly the outstanding success of Marl-borough's wars and always acquitted themselves well, while the fortunes of the cavalry were more varied.

THE ARTILLERY

Artillery had improved considerably since the days of Henry VIII, when an expert wrote a book on gunnery, in which he gave a formula for 'causing any great piece of artillerie to make in his discharge an exceeding great noyse and marvellous rore'. Guns were now cleverly sited and concealed, and did great execu-tion at short ranges.

CAVALRY EXPLOITS

Among numerous feats of arms performed in these campaigns, two cavalry regiments particularly distinguished themselves and both were given the honour of being permitted to wear grenadier caps. The Grey Dragoons, as they were then called—later *The Royal Scots Greys*—broke up the French 'Regiment du Roi' at Ramillies and captured its Colours, and the 'Royal Irish Dra-goons'—later the *5th (Royal Irish) Lancers*—did notable service at Blenheim, where they cut up a French cavalry regiment and brought back their kettle-drums as trophies. At Ramillies the two regiments charged together and disintegrated three battalions of the Grenadiers of Picardie, and were then charged by French cavalry.

BLENHEIM

At Blenheim five infantry regiments—the 10th now *The Royal Lincolnshire Regiment*, the 15th, now *The East Yorkshire Regiment*, the 21st, now *The Royal Scots Fusiliers*, the 23rd, now *The Royal Welch Fusiliers*, and the 24th, now *The South Wales Borderers*—under Brigadier-General Rowe, attacked the village, which had been entrenched and fortified with stockades by the French. In order to arrive with every man's musket loaded and thus be able to produce the greatest possible volume of fire at the critical moment, they had to march in line, under fire from guns and muskets, without returning a shot, until the officers could touch the palisades with their sword-points. They lost heavily during the advance, but their discipline proved equal to this very severe demand and, after prolonged and sanguinary fighting, Blenheim was taken.

MARLBOROUGH'S NARROW ESCAPE

Marlborough narrowly missed an untimely and somewhat ignominious end at Ramillies, on Whit Sunday, 1706. He was almost cut off by some French cavalry, while doing some reconnaissance on his own, and had to make a dash for it. While in full gallop, with his pursuers close behind, he came suddenly upon a very wide, open ditch. His heavy black charger made a great effort to clear it, but stumbled and came down on the far side. Marlborough was dismounted and his horse bolted, leaving him to continue as best he could, heavily impeded by his long heavy coat, stiff large-topped boots, and full-bottomed wig.

Fortunately, the Frenchmen's mounts jibbed at the ditch, giving him a few moment's grace, and an allied infantry regiment happened to be moving towards him. He reached them, nearly winded, just in time, for the French were so close that, in their excitement after having recognized their quarry, some of them rode on to the bayonets under which he took refuge.

MARLBOROUGH'S DEATH

This famous commander died in 1722, and it is recorded that his funeral was the first occasion of using the drill movements 'Reverse—Arms', and 'Rest on your arms reversed', this solemn ritual evidently having been invented specially to show an unusual degree of respect. The custom of firing three volleys over the grave of a soldier is said to have originated from the early German mercenaries, who fired one for each of the Trinity.

He had been a leader, who understood his men and who, at least mentally, shared all their feelings and their hardships. It has often been said that he did more than any other General has ever done to improve the conditions of their lives and to remove abuses. Besides being a sympathetic and inspiring human being and a very great General, it can be said of him that he never lost a battle, or failed to take a fortress to which he had laid siege.

In spite of the loss of Queen Anne's favour, after all his achievements in her service, he did not lose the respect of his troops (to whom he was affectionately known as 'Corporal John'), even after she had stripped him of all his offices. One proof of this was an incident which occurred when he was travelling, now in retirement, near Ghent. Two whole regiments in garrison there—the 8th, now *The King's Regiment (Liverpool)* and the 18th, later *The Royal Irish Regiment*, marched out several miles, with the civil dignitaries of the town, to welcome him and the Duchess at a village on their route, where the garrison had ordered 'a handsome breakfast' to be prepared.

DETTINGEN, 1743

The army saw service again in the war of the Austrian Succession, in which the principal battles were at Dettingen, the last battle in which an English king commanded his army in person, and at Fontenoy.

The 22nd Foot, now *The Cheshire Regiment*, won their acorn and oak-leaf badge at Dettingen. Some French cavalry had managed to penetrate close up to an oak tree where George II was standing. They were about to attack him and his Staff, when the 22nd sent a party of men at the double, who formed a ring round the tree and, after some enthusiastic fighting, eventually drove off the enemy. When this tense episode had ended, the King, wishing to give some token of his gratitude, picked a leaf off the tree and handed it to their commander, saying that he would like the regiment to wear oak leaves as a memento of its prompt and efficient handling of the situation. The regiment still places oak-leaves on its Colours and headdresses on the anniversary each year.

During this battle the King saw the 21st Regiment, now *The Royal Scots Fusiliers*, fire volleys at a French cavalry regiment and then charge them with the bayonet, killing a very large number and chasing the survivors off the field. This was an unheard-of exploit for infantry and contrary to all the accepted rules, and he made a special point of complimenting all ranks on their daring accomplishment.

The 8th Horse, later the *7th Dragoon Guards*, also had a very busy time on that day, and one of their Standards was narrowly saved from capture by the magnificent bravery of Cornet Richardson, who was surrounded by the enemy and received more than thirty wounds, but still held on to the Colour and kept them at sword's length until he was eventually rescued. He recovered, and later the King made a personal presentation to him of the Standard he had saved. This was handed down to his descendants and is now in the Royal United Services Museum. There was nothing in the nature of the V.C. in those days, or he would have received one, but the honour conferred on him was a unique distinction of the highest degree. There is a pair of French kettle-drums in the Officers' Mess, which forms another link with Dettingen as they were captured there by the regiment.

FONTENOY, 11TH MAY 1745

This was an exceedingly tough battle which ended in a defeat for the British, owing to their commander not handling his reinforcements correctly at the critical moment.

The British and their allies advanced silently to their battle stations at 2 a.m. on a cold foggy morning, in preparation for a dawn attack on the French who were entrenched in the village of Fontenoy and the neighbouring woods and farms. The enemy cavalry and infantry were both most handsomely dealt with by the British (whose allies completely let them down) but our infantry were more than once marched through the most devastating cross-fires of case shot from concealed batteries which literally tore great gaps through the ranks.

Even this slaughter did not shake them, or prevent them from decisively defeating the French infantry and gunners, but it was after doing so, when they were almost exhausted, that the Irish Brigade (serving with the French) made a bayonet charge which proved to be the finishing touch.

This was an instance of masterly use of reinforcements by the French, but at this critical stage Cumberland, who had more troops available, lost his nerve and did nothing, with the result that confusion grew and spread and the whole force made a muddled retreat. This, however, was reorganized by the regiments themselves and did not become a rout. The laurel wreath in the badge of the 34th (*The Border Regiment*) commemorates the part they played in covering the retreat.

In this battle the French used breast-deep trench redoubts and had protected and camouflaged their guns.

The 42nd Highlanders, now *The Black Watch*, used a battle technique of their own country. Their procedure was to load, wait until the moment when the enemy were just going to fire a volley, and then the whole line would fall flat on the ground. If this was timed exactly the enemy fired at the empty space above them. They then stood up quickly, fired their volley, slung their muskets, and rushed in with claymore and target while their own smoke concealed the first part of their charge, and the French were still unloaded. Though very successful, this stratagem does not seem to have appealed to the English Generals, and the 'P.B.I.', with characteristic stubbornness, continued to stand and 'take it'.

Statistics can easily be overdone, but the numbers in this battle are of interest as they give an idea of its scale. Cumberland had 46 battalions, 90 troops of cavalry, and 90 guns many of which, however, were only 3-pounders. Marshal Saxe, one of the most renowned of French commanders, had 106 battalions, 172 squadrons of cavalry and over 200 guns. Casualties were estimated at 8,000 French and 21,000 British and allies. The 3rd Guards, now *The Scots Guards*, lost 437, which gives an impression of the fighting, as these battalions were probably not more than 500 to 600 strong at the beginning. The enemy Irish Brigade lost a third of its strength, including its commander, Colonel Dillon. In those days nearly all the seriously wounded died, either from ignorance of surgery and hygiene or from simple neglect. There was no proper medical service, and ounce lead balls did not make clean wounds like modern .303 high velocity bullets.

The French commander wrote in his dispatch, 'we have gained a victory, but may I never see such another'.

There is a well-known painting by Philippoteaux, depicting an incident at Fontenoy, which illustrates the survival of chivalry and the pedantry of warfare at that time. The French and English are drawn up in line of battle a short distance apart and an officer of the British Guards Brigade has advanced a few paces and is bowing and sweeping off his three-cornered hat, making a request, 'Que Messieurs les ennemis tirent les premiers'. This is reported in ancient documents as actually having happened.

HIGHLAND REGIMENTS

The next active service was in the Scottish rebellion of 1745. From that time highland regiments played an important part in all the wars in which the army was concerned. The oldest one was the 42nd (originally 43rd), now *The Black Watch*, which was formed in 1739 from several independent companies of highlanders. Several other highland regiments were raised about this time, and disbanded a few years later, as the custom then was to raise new regiments when there was a big job on, rather than to form service battalions of existing regiments as is done in the twentieth century.

REGIMENTS OF HORSE CONVERTED TO DRAGOON GUARDS

The eight regiments of Horse, excluding *The Royal Horse Guards*, were gradually made into dragoons, starting in 1746 with the first three, after which the others were re-numbered. This was done entirely for parsimonious reasons, as dragoons received less pay, rode cheaper horses, and generally cost less to maintain, but as some consolation, they were given the title of Dragoon Guards. The 2nd Horse became the 1st Dragoon

Guards, and the others eventually all came in one number higher than their original number as a regiment of horse.

LIGHT DRAGOON TROOPS

In 1756 an entirely new form of cavalry was introduced. One troop from each regiment was given a special course in clearing obstacles, fighting in rough and enclosed country, scouting, patrolling, etc., after which they became the Light Dragoon Troop. They remained a specialist troop after training, and a light dragoon helmet was designed for them, to be worn as a distinction. The strength of a troop was about seventy of all ranks—light, agile men not more than 5 ft. 8 in. tall, and mounted on horses about the size of polo ponies. They could thus do a number of things which the heavy troops had never learned, and were much speedier and able to act more quickly when an opportunity presented itself.

There were reports that in Marlborough's time regiments of horse carried out charges at the trot, but there is also evidence of their riding into the enemy at full gallop. So one is left in doubt as to whether the first statement is anachronistic and more in keeping with the days of Agincourt. Then the knights were so heavily armoured that only a horse of the 'Shire' type was strong enough to carry them and its own armour. They were unable to mount without assistance (sometimes in the form of a small sheerlegs crane) and did undoubtedly move no faster than at a trot.

CLOTHING SUPPLY

The supply of clothing for the men was always a severe headache for the Colonel, who had to provide it on a very inadequate allowance, and had the worries of a careful housewife in getting new garments made out of old. Marlborough had done his best, in his time, to reorganize the system, which was then a subject of almost unlimited corruption. In those days the Colonel had twopence a day (deducted from the soldier's pay of eightpence) to spend on clothing. Numerous officials were involved and took their 'rake-off', the contractors used 'utility' materials, and the Colonel had to make up deficiencies out of his private income.

'COMMANDOS', 1758

In 1758 a special brigade was formed from the light troops of nine cavalry regiments, under Colonel Eliott (later Lord Heathfield, the renowned defender of Gibraltar), of the Horse Grenadier Guards. Their purpose was to act in combination with the Navy in making raids on the coast of France, which they did with great success, destroying marine arsenals and warships in the harbours of St. Servan and Cherbourg, and also making surprise attacks on inland towns. They carried out many experiments at Portsmouth with various types of landing craft for men and horses. Apart from the horses it reads almost like 1944.

PLATE II

(1)

1520

Yeomen of the Guard

Halberdier

(2)

1644

Royalist Horse

Officer

(3)

1685

The 2nd Horse. Later the 1st Dragoon
Guards

*Cornet with the Colonel's standard and
troopers*

(4)

1660

The Royal Regiment of Guards.
Now the Grenadier Guards

Officer

PLATE II

Figs. 1, 2, 3 & 4

PLATE II (1) YEOMAN OF THE GUARD. HALBERDIER. 1520

The Yeomen of the Guard are illustrated at this date, though it is earlier than the period covered by the book, because they are the oldest permanent force still in existence, and as a link with mediaeval times, it seems appropriate to include them.

They were the personal bodyguard of the King, raised for this purpose by Henry VII. His son, Henry VIII, added to them a corps of nobles (the Gentlemen-at-Arms), whose uniform was so fantastically extravagant that, for a long period, they disbanded themselves, being unable to afford the upkeep.

The Yeomen at this time were active troops, consisting of cavalry, bowmen, and halberdiers, and they are seen in antique illustrations of the 'Field of the Cloth of Gold', the execution of Lady Jane Grey at the Tower of London and various other historical incidents.

Their uniform, which has changed surprisingly little up to the present day, was typical of the costume of the Tudor period, with puffed and slashed sleeves and breeches, low-crowned hat with narrow brim, stockings and buff leather shoes.

The sword and halberd seem to be rather an oddly assorted pair of weapons, as one could hardly bring the sword freely into play without laying down the halberd. But, no doubt, the latter frequently got broken in action or was grasped by the enemy in such a way as to put it out of action; the sword then came in for the final bout. In any case no soldier, however armed, was complete without a sword at this period.

Other weapons in use at this time were the 'hand gonne', or 'harquebuss', a cumbersome matchlock musket, fired from a rest, the bow, and the pike, with which the bulk of the infantry were armed.

Cannon were used chiefly for the moral effect produced by their noise and smoke, as they were still extremely inefficient. This applied almost equally to all fire-arms and Henry VIII, who was an expert archer, had much greater faith in the bow. A trained English bowman could shoot very accurately and, when required, he could have six arrows in flight at the same time. In this way a very effective 'barrage' could be laid in front of an advancing enemy.

Cavalry had regained their old position on the battlefield, after a period in which they had been of minor importance. About the time of Agincourt, 1415, armour had got so far out of control that the knights' chargers, heavy animals like modern farm horses, borne down by the terrific weight, could scarcely trot and became hopelessly bogged if they had to cross any soft ground. The knights themselves could not rise if they fell and when wounded, even slightly, would suffocate or die, like a sheep on its back, unless they were soon extricated. After this had been proved by sad experience, it became the usual practice for them to copy mounted infantry tactics and do the actual fighting on foot. In the sixteenth century, however, they again fought mounted, in full armour, though not so heavy as in earlier times, and used lances, swords, battle-axes and maces. They were identifiable by the crests on their helmets and the armorial bearings on their banners and saddle-cloths.

Apart from the Yeomen of the Guard, uniform, if any, was usually limited to the red cross of St. George on a white ground, worn on various parts of the clothing. Foot soldiers wore odd assortments of armour, some of the commonest pieces being the 'morion' or steel helmet; 'vambraces' (arm-plates) and the 'jack' (or jacket) lined with small steel plates. Silk quilted armour was also worn by the wealthy.

PLATE II (2) AND PLATE III (5) ROYALIST AND PARLIAMENTARIAN SOLDIERS. 1642–4

The Civil War began with no uniform at all, as there was no standing army, except a small force of Yeomen of the Guard. So the story begins with the two armies dressed according to the men's stations in civil life, each soldier bringing his own, or ancestral weapons and armour and the mounted men providing their own horses.

There was naturally a considerable degree of similarity between the opposing forces, as they had all lived side by side in the same country, but their antagonistic political and religious views produced marked differences. On the Royalist side dress was a subject to which a great amount of artistic study was given and there were more men who had the money to indulge their tastes than on the other side, though both armies did contain men of all grades of life. The average Parliamentarian took a grim and Puritanical view of life and regarded foppery as being immoral, and their shorn hair, which was another protest against frivolity, gave them the nickname of 'the Roundheads'.

A few of the most characteristic features of the period were—the 'sombrero' type of hat, often decked with ostrich-feathers, the short jacket or doublet, shaped away on the hips, leather jerkins—very like modern ones, and the very nonchalant loose, soft, riding boots, which came up to the thigh, or could hang round the ankles when this was more convenient. A large amount of lace was worn, chiefly by Royalists, in the shape of Vandyck collars, cuffs, etc., and buttonholes bound with lace (which later became a feature of uniform of the regular forces) were then in fashion.

The bottle-like receptacles hanging from the musketeer's shoulder-belt, each contained a measured charge of powder and the bullets were carried in a small leather bag attached to the lower end of the belt. Helmets and cuirasses were often painted black to save polishing and prevent rust. The 'lobster-tailed' helmet, with metal earpieces and bars to protect the face, was the pattern most favoured on both sides, but there were many other types in use.

The Civil War lasted seven years and during this time a considerable degree of military skill and of uniformity grew up on both sides. It became necessary to replace private clothing by bulk purchases, as individuals often had not the means or the opportunity to re-equip themselves and this gave the colonels the chance to get their regiments gradually into uniform, beginning with the coats. Each chose his own colour scheme—often that of his own coat of arms, and the result was regiments dressed in green, yellow, blue, white, buff, red, grey, etc.

The 'New Model Army' of the Roundheads went furthest of all towards being a regular force as we understand it, and was dressed all in red. Its organization, equipment and training contributed much experience towards the regular army, formed at the Restoration, and some of its regiments were re-embodied in the King's army, within a few minutes of their disbandment —e.g. Monck's Regiment, now *The Coldstream Guards*, and the Oxford Blues, now *The Royal Horse Guards*. This had the fortunate result of making the army, at its beginning, representative of all parties and from then on it has always preserved a tradition of remaining impartial and without bias towards any political party.

PLATE II (3) THE 2ND HORSE: LATER 1ST DRAGOON GUARDS. 1685

This regiment was raised in June 1685 as the 2nd Horse, and became the 1st Dragoon Guards in 1746.

The dress of this period, though still strongly reminiscent of the Restoration period, with a distinct Cavalier tradition, was becoming less free and easy and showing many signs of the discipline and increasing uniformity of the regular army.

The large-brimmed hat, with ostrich feathers for officers, was worn (turned up on one side) by infantry, cavalry, and artillery (except grenadiers, pikemen, and dragoons), and the peruke and large lace cravat continued to be worn by officers.

The coat was long and loose-waisted with short sleeves and very large cuffs, and officers had gold or silver lace sewn along all the seams. Sashes or 'scarves' were worn by all ranks of Horse regiments, those of the officers being generally of gold or silver net, and those of infantry officers of gold and crimson interwoven. In addition to the ordinary uniform there was a grey fatigue dress, which was used as service dress by the units stationed in Tangier about this period.

Soft buff leather boots had now given place to blackened ones with stiff tops. Cuirasses were worn by Horse regiments until about 1698, and were again issued in 1707, during the War of the Austrian Succession. Steel helmets were being given up, and in their place an iron 'skull' was worn inside the hat.

As in the Middle Ages only a curb rein was used, with a very fierce bit with long powerful levers linked together, and large spurs with vicious-looking rowels were worn. From these it appears that either the horses were wilder in those days, or the average of horsemanship was not up to modern standards. On the other hand, it may only have been due to the fact that the methods of life generally were still somewhat barbarous.

The saddle was a very uncomfortable-looking affair with crudely shaped framework and inadequate padding, but the holster caps and saddle cloth were elaborately ornamented and embroidered. Most regiments were mounted on black horses, but the officers of some rode chargers of a different colour, so that they could be distinguished easily.

In Horse regiments there was a Standard (described as a cornet, and carried by a Cornet) for the Colonel, the Lieutenant-Colonel, the Major, and one for each troop, some regiments having crimson ones and others Standards of the facing colour. They were made of double silk damask, with gold or silver (or mixed) fringes, tassels and embroidery—in the case of The Queen's Horse, gold and black. Even in those days, when the value of money was far higher than in later times, a Standard cost as much as £40. The Colour pike was similar in shape to a knight's tilting lance, with fluted surface, the lower end of the lance being supported in a leather socket on the stirrup.

PLATE II (4) THE ROYAL REGIMENT OF GUARDS: NOW THE GRENADIER GUARDS. 1660

This illustration shows a part of the regular army in the first year of its history. It was then a miniature personal army of the King, consisting of 'His Majesty's Own Troop of Guards', later the 1st *Life Guards*, 'The Duke of Albemarle's Troop of Guards' (the title was held by Monck), which became the 2nd *Life Guards*, 'the Royal Regiment of Guards', and 'Monck's Regiment', or *The Coldstream Guards*, named after a small town near the Scottish border, whence they marched to London to restore the monarchy. Monck's Regiment had been in existence earlier than the Royal Regt. of Guards, but the latter, by order of the King, became the senior in the new army. A not too restrained comment on this decision was the adoption by the Coldstreamers of the motto 'Nulli Secundus'.

The Household Cavalry and the Foot Guards still retain this tradition of being a separate small army and keep up many ancient customs. They have subtle differences from the other regiments in almost every detail, from their Colours down to the spacing of their buttons and their marching speed, and they have been able to preserve more historic atmosphere than any other part of the army.

The restoration of the Monarchy brought with it the return of colourful and elegant dress, after the long interval during which the grim sobriety of the Puritans had eclipsed much of its splendour. Charles II's reign was a period of super-sophistication which resulted in effeminate and extravagant fashions for men, who used perfumes extensively and even went so far as to wear 'patches' on their faces. As a counterpart to this women liked to imitate masculine dress as far as they could, when riding or out in the country. Even in military uniform there was a profusion of ribbons, trailing feathers and long curls, and the very large cuffs and hats were in keeping with this ensemble.

The peruke is said to have originated from the sycophantic flattery of the men of Charles's court, who copied his curls when he was a small boy. He returned the compliment when he grew up and copied their perukes.

The bows of ribbon on the shoulders of the officer were worn to denote rank. The Spanish rapier was another affectation of the period.

PLATE III

(5)

1642

CIVIL WAR PERIOD

Royalists
Musketeer
Cuirassier
Trooper

Parliamentarians
Trooper
Pikeman

(6)

1660–1695

RESTORATION PERIOD

Gunner	*Musketeer*	*Grenadier*	*Dragoon*	*Pikeman*
1695	1660	1680	1672	1660

(7)

1712–26

EARLY GEORGIAN PERIOD

A 'Royal' Regiment	A Line Regiment	The 3rd Foot. Now the Buffs	The Life Guards	The Honourable Artillery Company
Sergeant, 1712	*Private man,* 1712	*Grenadier,* 1726	*Trooper,* 1712	*Sergeant,* 1723

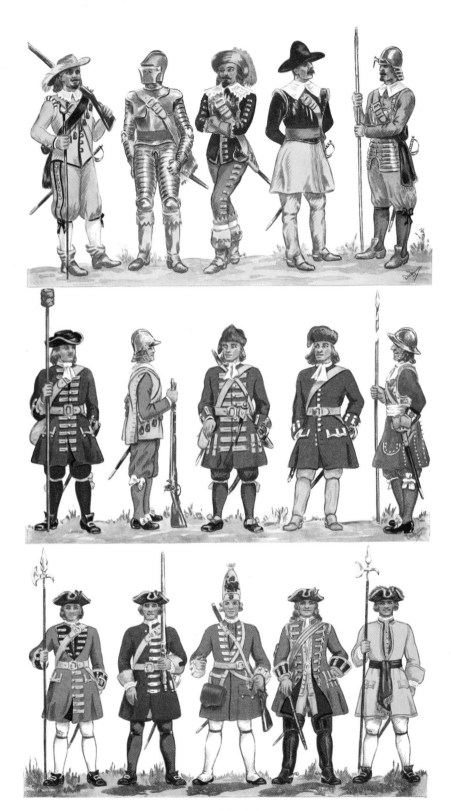

PLATE III

Figs. 5, 6 & 7

PLATE III (6) RESTORATION PERIOD. 1660–95

Being of the same period the notes on Plate III (5) are combined with those on Plate II (2) page 42.

Trains of artillery, which were disbanded after each campaign, covered the duties of engineers in addition to those of artillerymen and included in their ranks gunners, petardiers, matrosses, artificers and pioneers, as well as farriers, wheelwrights, smiths, armourers and all the usual tradesmen. They were normally dressed in red until the Royal Regiment of Artillery was permanently established on 26th May 1716, and from then had a blue uniform with scarlet facings. When artillerymen went on service they used to have special issues of 'harquebuss armour, carbine-proof', until well on in the eighteenth century.

Musketeers wore red jackets under buff leather coats, the sleeves of which had slits in front for the arms to come through, so that they could be thrown back to give more freedom of action.

Pikemen, whose numbers were diminishing, were the senior and most respected branch of the infantry and generally wore coats of the regimental facing colour. They still wore the cuirass, but tassets—the steel plates which covered the thighs, had been discarded after the Civil War. They and the musketeers continued to wear the 'pot' or steel helmet.

The words of command, 'Order', 'Port', and 'Trail—Arms', which are still used in rifle drill, were first invented for the pikes.

Grenadiers made their first appearance in 1678 and wore caps trimmed with fur, which, after many changes, ultimately developed into the bearskin caps now worn by the Guards. They had yellow loops across the fronts of their long coats. They were for many years the only infantrymen who had slings on their muskets and they carried swords, bayonets and hatchets for hacking down the enemy's wooden pallisades. The original type of bayonet, which screwed into the muzzle, was in use until 1690.

Up to 1689 there were seven regiments of Horse (later Dragoon Guards), and seven regiments of dragoons, which later became *The Royals*, *The Royal Scots Greys*, *The Inniskillings*, the *3rd*, *4th*, and *7th Hussars* and the *5th Lancers*. Some of the dragoons wore fur caps, while regiments of Horse, who were otherwise similarly dressed, wore the universal felt hat and feather.

Shoes of a brogue type (this was originally the Scottish word 'brog'), and stockings were still the normal leg-wear for dismounted troops. The stockings, though very thick and probably more or less waterproof, must have been very inadequate in the mud of Flanders, which our troops so often experienced.

Hair was worn long and was cut level with the top of the shoulders, but if a man could not grow it to a sufficient length, he had to have a wig or false switches attached to his natural hair.

There were a number of infantry regiments still wearing blue or grey coats near the end of the century.

PLATE III (7) EARLY GEORGIAN PERIOD. 1712–26

In the reign of George I, 1714–27, perukes went out and the hair was either done in the 'Ramillies tie'—a straight tail encased in leather binding, or 'clubbed'—combed into a tail doubled up and fastened with a leather strap. Lard or pomatum and liberal quantities of powder were rubbed or combed into it, leaving it extremely greasy and white in colour. The whole performance was a messy and irksome duty and one which occupied a considerable amount of time each day.

The third flap of the hat-brim was turned up in Queen Anne's reign, 1702–14, producing the 'Ramillies' and the larger 'Kevenhuller' tricorne hats. The brim was bent in so that points were formed in front and at each side (though some regiments wore them in other positions).

Spatterdashes or gaiters had changed the appearance of the men considerably. At first they were usually white, but later—about 1749, black ones were introduced for non-ceremonial occasions and some regiments wore brown canvas ones in fatigue dress.

When on working parties the men used to turn their coats inside out, giving a strange appearance, as a regiment, for instance, with yellow linings, would seem to be dressed all in yellow. There were also coarse fatigue jackets, described as 'surtouts'. Later the waistcoat was worn for fatigues, and only 'defaulters' on punishment drill were made to turn their coats inside out as a mark of disgrace.

The method of turning up the corners of the coat-skirts so as to form two triangles on each side, showing the long waistcoat in front and at the back, developed about 1730–40. (The French wore their coats in this manner in 1914.)

The fur trimming on the grenadiers' caps was replaced by a stiff embroidered linen front soon after its introduction, and it attained a high mitre-like shape about the beginning of the eighteenth century. The grenadier of the Buffs is shown wearing the crest of the Colonel, Sir Charles Wills, on his cap—a demi-gryfon rampant, sable, holding a battle-axe.

The Life Guards were dressed similarly to the regiments of Horse, except that they had lace loops, and carbine belts of regimental pattern. The carbine was either carried slung by its trigger-guard from a swivel attached to the carbine belt, or was carried in a leather bucket in front of the saddle, with a supporting strap attached to the holster cap, the barrel resting under the man's right arm.

The H.A.C. wore the old buff leather coat over a scarlet waistcoat. The gold lace on the seams, and the sash and halberd denoted the rank of sergeant. This corps was descended from 'the Guylde of St. George', appointed by Henry VIII in 1537 'to be overseers of the science of artillerie, that is to witt, long bowes, cross bowes and hand gonnes'.

Both scarlet and crimson coats were worn at this time and in some units the officers and sergeants had scarlet and lower ranks crimson. (This practice continued, with the substitution of red for crimson, until about 1830 in the cavalry, and 1872 in the infantry.)

In the position of 'Attention' (the word of command was 'Take—Care'), the feet were placed some distance apart, as illustrated.

PLATE IV

(8)

1688

Train of Artillery

Officer

General Officer

(9)

1742

The 4th or King's Own Royal Regiment
(Known as Barrell's Regt.)

(10)

1745

The 8th Horse. Later the 7th Dragoon Guards

Cornet with Standard

The 11th Dragoons. Later the 11th Hussars

Farrier

PLATE IV

Figs. 8, 9 & 10

PLATE IV (8) TRAIN OF ARTILLERY. 1688. (See also notes on Plate III [6])

The Royal Artillery wore red uniforms until 1716, with a few exceptions, one of which was the Train sent to Ireland in 1688 with the army which was to deal with a French force supporting the ex-king James II, which had landed at Kinsale. The personnel of this Train wore blue with orange linings—William III's colour.

There were several interesting features in the uniforms of this date. The baldric, or embroidered swordbelt, was a very decorative piece of equipment, which gave scope for some individuality in its design, and was worn until the beginning of the eighteenth century, after which it was replaced by a leather waistbelt worn over the waistcoat.

The sash, at this period, was very large and was designed to form a sort of hammock-stretcher, by inserting a pikestaff or pole through a hole at each end, to remove the officer from the field if he became a casualty.

The riding boots, known as 'Gambadoes', were shorter than the old type and the tops were strongly stiffened to prevent the legs being crushed in a cavalry charge. Enormous spur-protectors were worn.

The amount of gold lace on the uniforms depended mainly on the affluence of the wearers, as there were no 'Dress Regulations', and a General probably had more than a regimental officer. But, apart from this, there was little to indicate his rank. This probably accounts for the fact that in contemporary portraits, Generals, besides nearly always being depicted in armour, according to the traditional fashion of portrait painters, almost invariably carried their batons, whether in battle, or engaged in any other occupation.

In those times the equivalent of the modern Staff car, or the trailer caravan used by Generals in recent years, was a coach and four. A General would travel in this and use it as his office and billet and mount a horse when near the scene of action. The led horses had leopard skins spread over the saddles to keep them dry and clean.

The method of distributing orders and messages was, for short distances, by means of 'Runners', who were easily recognizable by brass-headed staves, similar to those of Drum-Majors, which they carried. For long distances Staff officers, trumpeters and cavalry troopers were used. Junior officers employed on this work became known as 'Gallopers'.

PLATE IV (9) THE 4TH OR KING'S OWN ROYAL REGIMENT. 1742. KNOWN
AS BARRELL'S REGIMENT

This illustration shows the type of uniform in which the infantry fought at Dettingen, Fontenoy, Minden, in the Scottish Rebellion of 1745 and in

51

Canada. Almost the only difference on Service would have beeen that the officers' coats had plain lapels without lace loops.

Infantry officers, when dismounted, including Lieut.-Colonels, carried the 'espontoon' or half-pike and a fusil, in addition to their swords. The sash was worn over the right shoulder by infantry and the left by cavalry and artillery.

'Royal' regiments had blue facings and blue breeches, but as an economy the men's 'second best' breeches used to be made out of their part-worn red waistcoats. Equipment consisted normally of a shoulder belt supporting the cartouche box and the waistbelt, from which the sword and bayonet were suspended, but in marching order various haversacks and a water-bottle were slung in accordance with the Commanding Officer's orders. The two ends on the shoulder belt, which appear like tassels, were a brush and a picker for cleaning the mechanism and the touch-hole of the musket.

The use of grenades had, for some rather obscure reason, been discontinued early in the century, but the grenadier companies remained as picked 'storm troops' until the Crimean War. They continued to wear their match cases for many years after this date.

Various types of forage caps were worn in the eighteenth century, the best-known of which was a sort of stocking cap with a tassel, something like the grenadier cap, without its stiff front.

At this period a firing line consisted of three ranks, one kneeling, and two standing; so 'column of route' (formed by turning the line to a flank) meant marching in threes, a system which was reintroduced shortly before the recent war.

The Colours went into action in the centre of the Line, and so were in the centre of the marching column. Prior to 1751, when new regulations were brought in, the 4th had an unusual pair of Colours, displaying a crown and crossed sceptres on each.

PLATE IV (10) 8TH HORSE: LATER 7TH DRAGOON GUARDS. 1745. 11TH DRAGOONS: LATER 11TH HUSSARS. 1745

The 8th Horse was raised in 1688, under the title of the 'Earl of Devonshire's Regiment of Horse'. It was later known as 'the Black Horse', but this was due to its facings (which were worn until 1914) rather than its horses (it was usual for regiments of heavy cavalry to be mounted on blacks). The 7th are now amalgamated with the 4th Dragoon Guards to form the *4th-7th Royal Dragoon Guards*, R.A.C.

The Standard is the one carried at Dettingen by Cornet Richardson and bears on one side the full Coat of Arms of General Ligonier, and on the other which is illustrated, his crest and motto 'Quo Fata Vocant'.

British cavalry were organized by troops, squadrons not being formed until the nineteenth century, and the number of troops varied up to as many as eight or nine, with about sixty to seventy men in each.

There was usually one Standard or Guidon to two troops (Guidon — guide homme). The size of these varied considerably, but they were generally about 2 ft. 6 in. square.

Cavalry Colours were regulated at the same time as the infantry ones, under the Royal Warrant of 1751. This ordered the King's Standard or Guidon to be crimson and to bear a central device of the crown over a rose and thistle united on one stem, and the royal motto. The white horse of Hanover was in the first and fourth corners and the number, or 'rank' as it was called, of the regiment in the second and third corners in gold or silver on a compartment of the facing colour. Fringes, cords, and tassels were to be of gold and crimson silk mixed.

The second or third Standards or Guidons were to be of the facing colour, with similar devices arranged differently, with the regimental 'rank' in the centre and the third one to have a figure 3 under the motto.

The Guidon had a slit dividing the fly into two tails with rounded corners. This became the regulation Colour for heavy and light dragoons; the Household Cavalry and the Dragoon Guards retaining the rectangular Standard.

Farriers generally had a different uniform from that of their regiment—in this case a blue coat instead of a red one. They wore a sort of grenadier cap with a fur front, and a buff leather apron, carried axes and were frequently mounted on greys. In *The Life Guards* the farriers still wear blue tunics in full dress, carry axes and have black helmet plumes instead of white.

CHAPTER II · 1759-93

'It is with a regiment as with a wife, you espouse her for life and are one flesh with her. You must never permit the least reproach to be spoken against her, as you love your own honour.

'Understand then (it is an order). The —— Foot is to be for you the ne plus ultra of martial perfection and you shall strive with all your might to keep it so.'

(Sergeant Lamb of the 9th.)

POLICY IN EUROPE

Though when dealing with foreigners the British often appear as one of the world's stupidest nations, one must admit that our much maligned statesmen did at least possess an eye to the future when arranging alliances and manipulating the scales of power in Europe.

We were not a large enough nation and not sufficiently militaristic to fight any of the great Powers single-handed on land, though we tackled them well enough at sea. Accordingly the policy has always been to form alliances against the strongest Power, so that it should not become a menace to our existence, and in practically all European wars, though our troops formed only part of an allied army (as they did in 1914 and again in 1939) ours was the winning side.

BRITISH MILITARY REPUTATION

In the wars of the first half of the eighteenth century, the army had revived and enhanced the ancient and outstanding reputation gained by its ancestors at Crecy, Agincourt and many other medieval battles, which had faded somewhat during the intervening centuries. It was always small in numbers, but in quality it was now recognized as being second to none and its Generals felt able to face heavy odds with equanimity when the need arose. Its strong points were toughness, discipline and, particularly, shooting. For centuries every fit man of military age had learned and practised shooting, and competitions, in the earlier days with the bow and later with the musket, used to occupy much the same position in village life as cricket matches do now. Everyone has read of the prodigies performed at these gatherings—splitting willow wands with arrows at incredible ranges, William Tell acts,

54

etc., etc., and this accomplishment of good shooting was maintained with the musket long after the last arrows were loosed in battle about 1627.

The English bowmen, whose storms of accurate and rapidly released arrows had so often been the downfall of superior and over-confident French armies, now had descendants who did them credit, in the efficient and smartly drilled line regiments, whose disciplined fire was known as the most deadly in Europe.

THE PRUSSIANS

Our intelligence system appears to have been fairly good even then and the army was kept up to date by observing the methods of its foreign contemporaries, and taking a tip from anything which was seen to be progressive. The French were by far the most important nation on the continent, but it is interesting to note that the Prussians were already a formidable and highly militarized power and were being built up into an imperialist state by Frederick the Great (who died in 1786). Quite a number of ideas originating from that source were incorporated in our system of training.

CONSTRUCTING THE EMPIRE

The treaty of Utrecht, which followed after Marlborough's battles, in 1713, did not by any means produce rewards proportionate to his series of brilliant successes, but it did provide one or two of the keystones of the present Empire—Nova Scotia, Hudson's Bay, Newfoundland, Gibraltar. Minorca was also included, but was lost later on.

The second half of the eighteenth century was our greatest period of empire building, and with the exceptions of Australia and New Zealand (annexed in 1788 and 1769), events conformed to ancient tradition and nearly every part of it was disputed with France. We came up against them in India, North America, and the West Indies, in addition to the usual battlegrounds in Europe and the Mediterranean. Our acquisitions of colonies were nearly always made for purposes of trade, but the army always had to secure them, with the support of the Royal Navy, which carried out the essential duties of clearing the seas and transporting and supplying the troops. But it was not often that we were left in peaceful possession and the continued existence of the Empire depended entirely on the ability of the two Services to keep open the sea routes and to protect it against the depredations of jealous powers. This position has changed very little up to the present time, except for the facts that there are now three Services instead of two and that the Dominions, now self-governing nations, take a great part in the general defence of the whole Empire.

BATTLE HONOURS OF THIS PERIOD

This struggle with France resulted in wars in many distant countries, and the battle honours on the Colours of regiments give some idea of the ubiquity of the army at this period: Guadaloupe, 1759; Quebec, 1759; Warburg, 1760; Martinique, 1762; North America, 1763–4; Havana, St. Lucia, 1778; then some Indian ones: Plassey, 1757; Pondicherry, Carnatic, Rohilcund, Mysore, etc.

WOLFE'S ORDERS

The taking of Quebec is probably one of the best-known stories which these 'Honours' bring to mind, and though it was the victory which won Canada, it also resulted in a serious loss to the army. At the height of the battle both General Wolfe and Montcalm, the French commander, were mortally wounded. The pity was that Wolfe's unusually promising career ended at the age of thirty-two, at a time when his services would have become increasingly valuable. He was a quite exceptional officer, in a class with Sir John Moore, though physically he was not robust, and his ideas ran well ahead of his time. His memory is perpetuated in the 17th (*The Royal Leicestershire Regiment*), whose band always plays 'Wolfe's Lament' just before the National Anthem, and the officers of this regiment, and of the 15th, 31st, and 47th (*The East Yorkshire Regiment, The East Surrey Regiment*, and *The Loyal Regiment*) have a black line in the lace on their full dress uniform as a sign of permanent mourning for him.

His orders to the 20th Regiment (*The Lancashire Fusiliers*), when he commanded it, form a most interesting document, and show his complete understanding not only of his profession, but also of the minds of his subordinates. Incidentally, the following quotation shows the treatment which was to be expected by any man who might misbehave in the presence of the enemy.

'A soldier that quits his rank, or offers to flag, is to be instantly put to death by the officer that commands that platoon, or by the officer or sergeant in rere of that platoon; a soldier does not deserve to live who won't fight for his King and country.' (From 'Instructions for the XX Regiment [in case the French land]', dated at Canterbury, 15th December 1755.)

MINDEN, IST AUGUST 1759

The Seven Years War, which began in 1756, was another of the series of wars in which we fought to maintain the balance of power in Europe. There were many battles, including Minden, Warburg, Kloster-Kampen, Kirch-Denkern, Vellinghausen, etc.

Minden is one of the high-spots in the annals of the British infantry, and is likely to be remembered as long as the army exists.

The six 'Minden regiments', the 12th, 20th, 23rd, 25th, 37th, and 51st (now *The Suffolk Regiment, Lancashire Fusiliers, Royal Welch Fusiliers, King's Own Scottish Borderers, Royal Hampshire Regiment* and *Yorkshire Light Infantry*) were literally on top of the world on that day.

They were intended to seize a minor objective on a part of the battle front, and their subsequent exploit was due to a misunderstanding of the orders, deliberate or otherwise, which might easily have resulted in their annihilation. Actually it developed into one of the most superb actions ever seen in war, which ended in the rout of the whole French army, over 50,000 strong.

These six regiments, supported and flanked by seven battalions of Hanoverians and Hessians, advanced towards the enemy's impressive battle array in two lines, the 12th, 23rd, and 37th leading. They were watched with some consternation as they marched forward, seemingly ignoring the village of Hahlen, which they were to have attacked, and going straight on towards the French main body. They passed through a cross-fire of thirty guns on one flank and thirty-six on the other, suffering terrible losses, but apparently unperturbed.

At length it became clear that their object was to emulate, on a really big scale, the achievement of the 21st (*The Royal Scots Fusiliers*) at Dettingen, as they were now facing the French cavalry, who were drawn up in battle order, 10,000 strong, and were the pride of their army—well mounted, equipped and trained, and dressed in dazzling uniforms.

This enormous body of horsemen exultantly charged down on the thin lines of infantry, but, to their extreme astonishment and chagrin, met with total failure and were knocked down in heaps by their steady well-disciplined volleys, fired at close range. Six separate times they reformed and charged again, but only once did a squadron get through the front line and it was then nearly exterminated by the second line. After this they gave it up as hopeless and, as they fell back in confusion, the British and German infantry followed them up. To quote from Carlyle's *Frederick the Great*, 'the whole 75 squadrons of them—between their two wings of infantry are seen boiling in complete disorder', a sight which could not have had an encouraging effect on the said wings of infantry.

The British now came under sustained musketry as well as artillery fire, but continued to advance. Then two brigades of French infantry endeavoured to attack and halt them, but they were given such an enthusiastic reception that they were soon obliged to withdraw in very poor condition.

After this a large body of Saxon troops came forward in another effort to stop this menacing advance, but were scattered in flight after causing very little delay.

It seemed that absolutely nothing could stop these amazing British infantry, loyally backed up by the Germans, who pressed on so relentlessly, through or over any troops who attempted to stand before them, and were superior to all the efforts of the enemy. Alone they ruined the morale of the whole French army, and panic spread from end to end as they came near their main line-of-battle, which, had it stood firm, could probably have shattered them.

Contades, its commander, said, 'I have seen what I never thought to be possible—a single line of infantry break through three lines of cavalry ranked in order of battle, and tumble them to ruin.'

The French would have been destroyed but for the cowardice of Sackville, the commander of the British cavalry, who repeatedly refused to go in and complete their discomfiture. As it was, they lost over 7,000, and the allied casualties were 2,822, of which the six regiments had over 50 per cent.

These regiments still celebrate Minden day in various ways, and all wear roses in their caps on the anniversary, in memory of their ancestors, who advanced through rose gardens to the battleground and are said to have decorated their tricorne hats and grenadier caps with the emblem of England. An interesting coincidence is that *The Yorkshire Light Infantry* kept Minden Day at Minden in 1946, being quartered there in the B.A.O.R.

WARBURG, 1760

This battle is notable for a memorable feat by the cavalry, under the Marquess of Granby, when they drove 20,000 French troops off the field in a mixed rabble of Horse, Foot and Gunners. Thus they wiped out the disgrace unjustly put on them by their previous commander, Lord Sackville, at Minden. The Warburg regiments are: *The Royal Horse Guards*, the 1st, 2nd, 3rd, 6th and

7th Dragoon Guards, the 1*st*, 2*nd* and *6th Dragoons*, and the *7th*, 10*th* and 11*th Hussars*. (The hussars were then dragoons.)

The various public-houses about the country named 'The Marquess of Granby' are connected with this victory, as the Marquess afterwards provided these taverns for some of the cavalry N.C.O's who were disabled at Warburg, to set them up in civil life. The expression 'Going for it bald-headed' had its origin at Warburg, where Granby finished leading the great charge with bald head gleaming in the sun—his wig and hat having gone with the wind.

EMSDORF, 1760

At Emsdorf the 15*th Hussars* (then light dragoons) earned a unique distinction which consisted of being allowed to wear the following inscription on their helmets, 'Five battalions of Foot defeated and taken by this regiment, with their Colours and nine pieces of cannon, at Emsdorf, 16th July 1760'.

MINORCA, 1756, 'HONOURS OF WAR'

The defence of Fort St. Philip, in Minorca, was a minor epic, which like many of the incidents which give most pride to the service, ended in a defeat by overwhelming numbers.

The 4th, 24th and 34th Regiments, now *The King's Own Royal Regiment (Lancaster)*, *The South Wales Borderers*, and *The Border Regiment*, were besieged in an antique and ruinous citadel by 16,000 French troops, and held out under great privations for seventy days. In the last assault alone, which was only partly successful, they inflicted 2,000 casualties on the enemy, their own strength by then being about 1,500.

The days of chivalry were not entirely dead and the terms of the surrender granted by the Duc de Richelieu, of which the following is an extract, were a rare tribute from an enemy.

'The noble and vigorous defence which the English have made having deserved all marks of esteem and veneration that every military person ought to show to such actions—and Marshal Richelieu being desirous also to show to General Blakeney the regard due to the brave defence he has made—grants to the garrison all the honours of war that they can enjoy under the circumstances of their going out for an embarkation: to wit, firelocks on their shoulders, drums beating, colours flying, twenty cartridges for each man, and also lighted matches.'

The matches would presumably be for the guns, as matchlock muskets went out of use in the preceding century.

A remarkable fact is that General Blakeney was eighty-four

years old at the time when he put up this excellent defence. There was, apparently, no age limit for superannuation, but he must have been a very tough octogenarian.

THE AMERICAN WAR OF INDEPENDENCE, 1775–82

There was one very serious and most regrettable event during the course of Empire-building—the American War of Independence. This war was due to Whitehall mentality being out of touch with conditions in America, and treating the colonists more like subjugated enemies than blood relations. (It has often been said that the Empire grew up in spite of the Government and people at home, rather than with their help, and that it was made and tended by the types of men and women who do not stay at home.) British renegade preachers and other agitators fomented the trouble, which might otherwise have subsided, and France, Spain, and Holland came in against us when we had become well involved. This war is unique in being the only one for which no battle honours were granted—perhaps because the government felt a certain amount of shame and remorse, as well as owing to its unsuccessful ending.

Our troops had nothing to be ashamed of and fought many successful battles, but they were up against something new in the guerrilla tactics of the Americans and were consequently at a great disadvantage, and on several occasions the position became hopeless, owing to lack of supplies and reinforcements.

(The first Boer War, 1881, is in many respects a parallel, our troops still in red coats and trained to fight in close order, being opposed by invisible guerrillas and skilled hunters.)

In spite of all this the men did well. They adapted themselves to the country, learned a great deal from friendly Indians, and worked like slaves hauling 'batteaux' up the rivers, carrying heavy loads, felling trees, making roads to take guns up mountains, and even moving warships overland in sections. They marched enormous distances, fording great rivers and creeks daily, without change of clothes or tents to sleep in. They fought well on every occasion in spite of much smallpox and other sickness, and often lived entirely on salted meat and weevil-riddled biscuits. The regimental officers were generally very good, things were well organized at regimental level, and discipline was above reproach.

There was, up to a certain point, every prospect of winning the war, but it was a period when the grinding of personal axes was an industry which flourished more blatantly than it does now. A crowning example of this was the appointment of Lord Germaine, formerly Lord Sackville, of infamous record at Minden, as Secretary for the Colonies. This resulted in self-interest becoming a leading factor in the appointment of some of the commanders, and contributed heavily towards the disastrous end of the war.

The story of General Burgoyne's surrender at Saratoga, 17th October 1777, after the men had cheerfully endured all the hardships and disappointments a soldier can experience, is a very sad one. Lord Mahon says in his *History of England*, that the surrender of this small number of men—about 3,500—had more far-reaching results than many a campaign in which hundreds of thousands took part. Before the final parade the regimental Colours were burnt, and with sorrow and humiliation several fine regiments went into a long and most unhappy captivity. It was not until almost exactly four years later that Lord Cornwallis surrendered at York Town in similar circumstances. The war ended in 1782, when George III conceded American Independence which their Congress had claimed from 4th July 1776. Amongst other things it had shown very clearly that the training for a war against a professional European army was not suitable for a campaign of this nature. The red-coated soldier, who could move or fire only when the word of command was given, was at a serious disadvantage. He found himself fighting against American irregulars, who could move about and take cover more or less as they pleased, wearing inconspicuous clothing, in addition to which they knew the country and could find a living wherever they went. Given a stand-up fight the British regulars would win every time, but this did not often come their way.

One gets the general impression that the main characteristics of the two nations were then very much the same as when General Eisenhower, in 1945, said that he would prefer using American troops where he had work requiring speed and dash, but that when it was a case of slogging through, inch by inch, he would rely on British troops.

ARMY LIFE IN THE EIGHTEENTH CENTURY

Life in the army in those days could hardly be described as attractive. The troops generally lived either under canvas, or billeted in houses or taverns, and the very few barracks then in existence would have made passable imitations of medieval prisons.

A private man's pay, after deductions for clothing, etc., amounted to only two or three shillings a week, and even this might be filched from him by an unscrupulous N.C.O., who had such power that he could intimidate him against complaining to an officer. (Hence the very strict orders now in force against N.C.O's borrowing money from private soldiers.) But, as some compensation for the very small pay, a few pence were enough to get drunk on, and the expenses of female society were proportionately low. These were the only recreations available, apart from some gambling in the barrack rooms, where cheating at cards was considered merely smart, but debts were discharged with a rigorous code of honour. Games and sports do not seem to have been organized in those days and there were very few entertainments of any sort.

The Tower musket weighed fifteen pounds, and was kept beautifully polished, with its butt and hand-guard stained and elbow-greased to a rich deep mahogany colour. Each man was more or less his own armourer and carried spare parts and made his own bullets. The powder charges were made up in paper cartridges and inside the 'cartouche box' or ammunition pouch was a wooden or metal 'magazine' with holes for them to fit into. A flint only lasted for about twenty shots, and rain made firing almost impossible by damping the powder in the priming pan. The weapon was only accurate up to about fifty yards, but nearly all firing was done in platoon volleys. (The Americans used rifles, which were more accurate and had a much longer range, but could not load them quickly, and many were discarded in favour of the old smoothbore.)

The bayonet was as important as the musket, and quite frequently orders were given that certain attacks were to be carried out with muskets unloaded, so that only the bayonet could be used. This was done either to aid surprise, especially at night, or to ensure the speediest possible result.

All training and fighting was done in what was practically a greatcoat, worn over the 'waistcoat', which was a sleeved underjacket. There was much polishing and pipeclaying to be done, and hairdressing was a most tedious and irksome task. Training consisted of a great deal of drill, platoon firing exercises, marching, and little else except guards and fatigues.

Punishments were very severe and for the more serious offences—'immorality, misbehaviour, or neglect of duty' consisted mainly of floggings—very cruel ones, too, amounting in some cases to as many as 1,500 lashes—not all at one session, obviously. But there was a drummer at Gibraltar in 1727, who had received 25,000 lashes in the fourteen years he had served in that station, and was 'hearty and well, and in no ways concerned'. Lesser crimes were punished by solitary confinement in a tiny dark cell, known as 'the black hole', which included a diet of bread and water (the present No. 1 punishment diet in military prisons).

The women in those days were a pretty rough lot ('married quarters' consisted of a space at the end of hut or barrack (*barraca,* Spanish = hut)) separated from the other men only by a curtain), and they, too, were punished for gross misbehaviour. Sometimes they were whipped and sometimes given an hour in the 'whirligig' —a revolving cage, which was kept turning by two men, and made the victim 'a little giddy and landsick'—not an edifying spectacle, evidently. This was done in public and a further alternative was a kind of pillory, in which the woman had to sit, chained by her neck and wrists, with a placard pinned on her stomach describing her offence.

Desertions were fairly common as the result of harsh treatment by N.C.O's, or boredom with the routine, the lack of amusements or variety, and the generally vile conditions regarding rations and quarters. An added cause for men becoming bored was that units did not have frequent changes of station as they do now. It was nothing unusual for a regiment to remain for thirty or forty years in one locality. So a man might do the whole of his service in one or two stations in the same country. As an instance of this, the 14th Dragoons, later *14th Hussars,* served in Ireland from 1747 until they embarked for the West Indies in 1795.

This system resulted in the acquisition of multifarious local interests—many officers and men going so far as to own farms and businesses—and the accumulation of kit and possessions which, though they may have added to the amenities of life, were good neither for mobility nor morale. No doubt these weaknesses were realized, but it was not until the Cardwell system of 1881 that a thoroughly organized programme of trooping seasons and regular tours of foreign stations was developed.

On the whole life in the ranks was definitely not a soft one—no cubicles or bedside lamps, or plain clothes off duty, in those days. The men were undoubtedly a tough lot, either fellows with soldiering in their blood, or men with shady records, or men who had entered the army against their own wishes. But the various types soon shook down together and were moulded by the system into good trustworthy soldiers, and acquired the old spirit which has always been, and still is the mainstay of the army. Of this the following quotation is an example. (Sergeant, addressing recruits): 'The ——th were ever the boldest Corps in the King's Army and the truest on parade. What is more, we fought at Fontenoy, Dettingen and Minden under the guiding eye of the

Most High God.' Each regiment was the best in the whole army, just as it is to-day.

DIVERSE CONDITIONS OF WARFARE

The numerous wars of the eighteenth century, which were carried on under such diverse conditions as regards enemy, climate, country, supplies, etc., were invaluable to the army in advancing its training and organization. There was fighting against French and Red Indians in the forests and mountains of North America, sometimes under Arctic conditions, the storming of fortresses like Quebec, 1759, the American War, seaborne enterprises in the West Indies, and actions against vastly superior numbers of natives in the tropical heat and dust of the Indian plains.

PLASSEY, 1757

An instance of this last was the battle of Plassey, where Clive had about three thousand men, consisting mainly of the 39th Foot, now *The Dorsetshire Regiment*, and some gunners and sepoys against Suraj-ud-Daulah's 60,000.

His amazing success was due to a combination of audacity and duplicity, for Clive, in addition to being an able commander, did not scorn to use the weapons of the East, and met double-dealing with intrigue. So when his ridiculously small force went into action he had hopes that its task would be less formidable than it appeared.

The Rajah's army going into battle was an extraordinary sight —elephants, camels, Standards, Horse and Foot, armed with shields, spears, matchlocks, scimitars, and every imaginable antique or modern weapon and piece of armour. Suraj himself was seated in a richly decorated howdah, accompanied by the usual retinue of sword- and fan-bearers, umbrella boys and other hangers-on. The guns were mounted on mobile wooden platforms, drawn by teams of oxen, over whose heads they fired, with gaudily caparisoned elephants pushing from behind—a burlesque forecast of modern self-propelled guns. They were shockingly handled and could only get off a shot about every half-hour.

Masses of men cumbered the ground in every direction but, except for some French gunners, who fought well, most of them were half-hearted and contented themselves with noise and futile movements. Rain came on during the battle and damped the natives' powder, as they had no protection for it, and though Clive's pact with Mir Jafar, an aspirant for the Rajah's throne, did not work owing to the latter's cowardice, yet suspicion of treachery was so rife among them that none trusted his neighbour.

Gradually the mass disintegrated as various commanders and their followings decided to make for home, and the remnants were finally scattered by the absurd little British force, which killed about 500 of them.

This battle restored British prestige in Bengal, which had sunk very low, and Suraj-ud-Daulah, who had been the perpetrator of the 'black hole' outrage in Calcutta, was captured.

The Dorsetshires, who were the first British regiment (apart from the Company's own forces) to serve in India, have on their badge the words 'Primus in Indis', and the battle honour 'Plassey' is on their Colours. They also own a silver-headed Drum-Major's staff, presented in memory of Plassey, by the Nawab of Arcot.

MARINES AND 'HORSE MARINES'

During these wars any regiment might be detailed to serve with the fleet, as Marines. *The Welch Regiment* took part in Admiral Rodney's 'victory of the saints', in the West Indies in 1782 and won the naval crown on the colours. This very unusual distinction was also granted to *The Queen's* and *The Worcesters* for similar service in 1794. Another regiment serving with the Navy gave rise to the old joke about the 'Horse Marines'. Some troops of the 17*th Lancers* (then dragoons) served in H.M.S. *Hermione* in 1795, an almost unique experience for a cavalry regiment.

GIBRALTAR, 1779–83

Gibraltar was besieged by the French and Spaniards from 1779 to 1783. It was there that General Elliot, later Lord Heathfield, and nicknamed 'the old cock of the rock', made such a fine defence, and with the aid of Lord Howe's skilful naval action to bring in provisions, ultimately exhausted the enemy. The regiments taking part in the defence, which have the motto 'Montis Insignia Calpe' on their colours, and the castle and key copied from the arms of Gibraltar, are *The Suffolk, Dorsetshire, Essex, Northamptonshire Regiments* and *The Highland Light Infantry*. The Gunners and the *Royal Sappers and Miners* (formed in 1772) also had special opportunities and made full use of them, and during the siege they excavated many of the now-existing gun emplacements.

Towards the end of the siege there was an incident of unusual interest. The enemy, who wanted to put an end to the operations, decided to bring artillery into close range, which they did by mounting a number of guns on wooden hulls or platforms and towing them close in under cover of darkness. *The Royal Artillery* quickly thought of an answer to this stratagem, and fired red-hot balls at the wooden batteries, which caused them to take fire and blow up. The procedure sounds not without risk to one's own side, as there must have been a good chance of premature explosions when loading the guns, or of the powder barrels going off, but it seems to have been eminently successful, as all of the ten floating batteries were destroyed.

'Gib' was first captured in 1704 by a force under Sir George Rooke, and subsequently three attempts were made by the Spaniards and French to re-take it, in 1704, 1727, and 1779. In the recent war batteries were constructed in Spain covering 'Gib' and the Straits, and all seemed ready, except the German help, which did not arrive.

LIGHT DRAGOON REGIMENTS

The experience gained from these widespread wars resulted in some important changes in training and equipment. In 1759, after the experiment with light dragoon troops, referred to in the last chapter, the 15th, 16th, 17th, and 18th *Light Dragoon Regiments* were raised. These regiments proved themselves of great value to the army in protecting it on the march, and so increasing its mobility, improving its intelligence system, and coming quickly on the scene at psychological moments when cavalry action was vital to success. As time went on more regiments were formed and light cavalry became a prominent feature of the service.

LIGHT INFANTRY

A similar process was carried out among the infantry, which began in the North American war in the 1750's, against the French, who were frequently aided by Indians. Fighting took place in dense and trackless forests and mountains, where slow-moving troops were at a heavy disadvantage against the hunting skill of the natives. Their cumbrous uniforms, equipment, and methods of fighting impeded their progress through the trees and scrub and over crags and gullies. General Wolfe, with the approval of Sir Henry Clinton, the Commander-in-Chief, decided to have a proportion of specially trained infantry, who could scout and skirmish, move about quickly and quietly, and use individual initiative without waiting for words of command. To put this into practice he formed 'the Light Infantry', a small corps of men hand-picked from their regiments and chosen for their efficiency, toughness, and high standard of intelligence. They were lightly equipped, their dress was modified, and they were given a special course of training which was originally based on the system of the American Rangers. 'The Royal Americans', or 60th Regiment, and 43rd Regiment (now *The King's Royal Rifle Corps* and *The Oxford and Bucks Light Infantry*), provided a number of the first entrants.

The system was so successful that a light company was formed in every infantry regiment, and they and the grenadiers became known as the 'Flank' companies. Later whole regiments were converted into light infantry, this being regarded as one of the highest compliments they could receive.

RIFLE REGIMENTS

A further development followed in 1797, when a battalion of the 60th was made into a Rifle Corps, with a dark green uniform, in imitation of the Austrian Jaegers, and armed with (muzzle-loading) rifles of foreign manufacture. They carried the impersonation so far as to become the only regiment in the army which wore moustaches, but actually many of the men were Germans. (On 29th May 1815, the whole eight battalions of the 60th became Rifles).

This was followed by the formation of The Rifle Corps in 1800 which became the 95th Regiment, and is now *The Rifle Brigade*, armed with the muzzle-loading Baker rifle, which was made in London.

The remainder of the infantry used the 'Brown Bess'—a smoothbore, flintlock, with an effective range of about a hundred yards. It fired a ball weighing $1\frac{1}{4}$ ounces, and its calibre was very large—·753 inch. The idea of rifling, to give the bullet a spin and so make it go straighter, had been thought of in the early sixteenth century. But the difficulty had been that, in order to make the bullet fit into the grooves it had to be driven down the barrel with a mallet and rod, a process which did not facilitate rapid loading. This was to some extent overcome by casting the bullet with a band on it to fit the rifling.

CAMOUFLAGE

Probably few people realized at the time that the green uniform of the Rifle regiments, being the first really serious attempt at camouflage, presaged the ultimate doom of red coats and all conspicuous apparel for active service purposes.

SIR JOHN MOORE'S LIGHT BRIGADE

Sir John Moore, who was a very enlightened and progressive soldier, had served in the 51st, now *The Yorkshire Light Infantry*, as an ensign and as a field officer, was a great believer in light infantry. Shortly before the Peninsular War he trained a special brigade at Shorncliffe, composed of the 43rd, the 52nd, of which he later became Colonel Commandant, and the 95th, (now the *1st* and *2nd Oxford and Bucks Light Infantry* and *The Rifle Brigade*). Napier wrote of them that 'he so fashioned them that afterwards, as the Light Division under Wellington, they were found to be soldiers unsurpassable, perhaps never equalled'. The Officers of the 43rd and 52nd still wear a black sword-knot of the old pattern as a mark of exceptional respect to the memory of Sir John Moore, who besides being one of the army's ablest Generals, was also one of the most likeable.

RIFLE AND LIGHT INFANTRY REGIMENTS AT THE PRESENT DAY

The functions of light infantry and Rifle regiments no longer differ from those of other regiments, as the training of all has progressed to the same level. But history is repeating itself in the formation of Commandos, which have a similar relationship in comparison with ordinary regiments to that of the light infantry in the early days. These regiments, however, still take the greatest pride in their well-earned titles, which marked them out as specialist troops, and put them in a class by themselves. They still retain many of their old customs, such as marching at the trail with a speed of 140 paces to the minute. (Ordinary infantry pace is 120, and the stately tread of the Guards, 116.) Except on ceremonial parades they halt and stand at ease, or come to attention and step off at the trail simply on the command 'Halt' or 'Quick— March', whereas other regiments would have three words of command for each of these movements. They carry their rifles at the 'shoulder', and Rifle regiments fix 'swords' instead of bayonets. (With the Baker rifle a sword bayonet was used, which had a half-basket hilt.)

Both Rifles and light infantry have bugle bands instead of drums and fifes, and use special 'horns' or calls of their own. Bugles were invented for light infantry, to do away with the encumbrance of drums, which were formerly the normal instrument for giving orders and signals to a regiment. To commemorate this fact, bugle strings of green are worn by all except 'Royal' regiments, which have variegated ones of red, yellow, and blue.

The horn, originating as some think from the bugle horn with a connection with the forest outlaws of Robin Hood's era, but more probably from the powder horn of the early light infantry, is incorporated in some form in the badge of each of these regiments. It was worn on the epaulettes of the officers of the light regiments and light companies of heavy regiments, and an order of 28th December 1814, enjoined the wearing of the horn and regimental number on the chako, in place of the usual brass plate.

Rifle regiments, like light cavalry—lancers and hussars—have no Colours, but all have a very large number of Battle Honours, which are inscribed on the badges of the 60th and the Rifle Brigade. The old peculiarities of dress of these regiments had many features in common with light dragoons, including the Maltese cross in the badge, and later with hussars.

The present Light Infantry Regiments are: *The Somersetshire, Duke of Cornwall's, Oxford. and Bucks., King's Own Yorkshire, King's Shropshire, Durham,* and *Highland,* and the Rifle Regiments are: *The Scottish, King's Royal, Royal Ulster,* and *The Rifle Brigade.*

THE ROYAL ENGINEERS

In 1787 a big advance was made in the formation of *The Royal Engineers* as an established branch of the service. For many years they had existed under unsatisfactory conditions, in connection with other branches and civilians, and this was their charter of freedom and the beginning of great developments. *The Royal Engineers* were a Staff Corps, composed of officers, and were not amalgamated with the Corps of *Royal Sappers and Miners* until 1856.

THE ROYAL HORSE ARTILLERY

The process of forming mobile light units was still incomplete, as there was no really mobile artillery, and the field-guns were drawn by teams of heavy farm horses, at walking speed, with civilian drivers in smocks, carrying carters' whips. But in 1793 'A' and 'B' Troops of *The Royal Horse Artillery* were formed, 'A' being the chestnut troop, which later became so well known. These troops had lighter guns and horses, and postillion drivers were mounted on the three near-side animals. Some of the gunners rode and some sat on the limbers, and the troop was able to keep up with cavalry over any reasonable country. The men were dressed like light dragoons, and this new branch of *The Royal Artillery* probably aroused quite as much interest as airborne troops did 150 years later. They were nicknamed 'The Galloper Guns' and 'The Flying Artillery'.

In view of the recent far-reaching developments in rockets, it is a notable fact that a R.H.A. rocket troop was in existence in 1805.

Rockets for military use were invented by a Colonel Congreve, who afterwards became Controller of the Royal Laboratory. A whole rocket weighed as much as 42 lb and carried a missile of about 18 lb., in the form of a 'carcass' (a thin perforated case filled with explosive), a shell, or case shot, to ranges of 2,000 to 3,500 yards.

They were not popular owing to an unpleasant tendency to take a boomerang course and return to explode among our own troops, but were used on various occasions, sometimes very successfully, until the Boer War of 1881. After this little was heard of them until the recent war—another instance of the revival and development, with the aid of modern science, of an obsolete weapon.

LORRY-BORNE INFANTRY, 1790–1800

A further effort to increase mobility was the introduction of a special horse-drawn vehicle for the rapid transit of infantry, which was known by the rather quaint names of 'expedition' or 'military fly'. Rowlandson did some illustrations of them showing men, in uniforms of about 1790, seated on long open carriages, drawn by four horses with postillion drivers. The men sat back to back as in an Irish jaunting car, about thirty on each vehicle, and there was a high black dashboard ornamented with the Royal coat of arms. There is evidence that this form of transport was used in England on various occasions, but overseas campaigns appear to have been run on less extravagant lines.

COMPARISON—1750–93 and 1914–45

There is a striking similarity between the processes of modernization in these two periods—in the first, light dragoons, light infantry, horse artillery, the Royal Engineers, and in the second— mechanized cavalry, lorry-borne infantry, commandos, airborne troops of all types, R.E.M.E., etc. In the eighteenth century it was the speeding-up of ancient methods of locomotion—horses and horse-drawn guns and vehicles, and the feet of the infantryman. In the twentieth century it is the same process, using recently acquired methods of transit—the petrol engine and its child, the aircraft.

In 1793 the army had certainly changed very considerably since the days of George II, 1727–60, when ponderous precision had been the watchword to the detriment of speed, and when it was more important for a man to carry out his drill correctly, than to get in the first shot before the enemy.

In the decisive stages of battles, between the main bodies of armies, the old close order system still prevailed, and firing was by volleys only, on the word of command. But in a world which was already approaching the machine age, life was beginning to move more quickly, and one phase of this manifested itself in the speeding-up of the preliminaries of battles—the reconnaissance, the advance and the deployment—by means of the changes in training and organization which have just been mentioned.

PLATE V

(11)

1742–56

The Royal Artillery	The 9th Marine Regiment (52nd Foot) Disbanded 1748	The 17th Foot. Now The Royal Leicestershire Regiment	The 2nd Dragoon Guards (The Queen's Bays)	The 43rd (late 42nd) Highland Regiment. Now The Black Watch
Matross (Gunner's Mate) 1742	*Marine, 1742*	*Grenadier, 1751*	*Light Dragoon,* 1756	*Corporal, 1742*

(12)

1758

'The Light Infantry'	A 'Royal' Regiment *Drummer*	The 42nd or Royal Highland Regiment of Foot	The 64th Regiment (previously 2/11th). Now 1st Bn. North Staffs. Regiment	The 77th Montgomery Highlanders (Raised 1757, disbanded 1763)
Private man (From the 43rd Regiment)		*Grenadier-Sergeant*	*Fifer*	*Piper*

(13)

1768–99

The Loyal Associated Ward and Volunteer Corps of the City of London	The 29th Foot. Now the Worcestershire Regiment	The 7th Foot or the Royal Fusiliers (previously the Royal English Fuziliers)	The 13th Dragoons. Later the 13th Hussars	The Royal Horse Guards
Matross. Honorable Artillery Company, 1799	*Sergeant-Major, 1793*	*Fuzileer, 1768*	*Light Dragoon,* 1775	*Trooper, 1793*

PLATE V

Figs. 11, 12 & 13

PLATE V (II) 1742-56

Uniforms became more elaborate during the middle part of the eighteenth century, and it was a period when military movements were carried out in the most precise and ponderous manner, with innumerable words of command.

Lace was of regimental patterns, with various designs and coloured stripes or 'worms' running through it, but there were a few regiments which did not wear any. 'Royal' regiments wore blue breeches and others red, and waistcoats were generally red, but cavalry regiments had waistcoats and breeches of their facing colour, or of buff.

The first official clothing book was compiled in 1742, and in it the details of the uniform of every regiment were described, with hand-coloured illustrations. They show that each regiment, in addition to its distinctive pattern of lace, had its own design for the lapels, loops and arrangement of the buttons. Such apparently small differences mean a lot as regards *esprit de corps*, and the regimental spirit even now continues its fight against complete standardization.

A Clothing Warrant was issued in 1751 and, from that time, commanding officers, though they still made their own arrangements for the tailoring of the men's clothes, had to conform to orders and their personal arms were no longer to appear on Colours, grenadier caps, etc. The devices used in their place consisted mainly of the Royal cypher and crown, the white horse with the motto 'Nec Aspera Terrent', from the arms of Hanover, the Garter star and regimental numbers. Some regiments had badges, but it was not until the introduction of the Cardwell system (1881) that every regiment had its own badge.

Buttons were made of various substances such as pewter, tin, white and yellow metals. Sword and bayonet hilts, scabbard mountings, etc., were normally of brass.

The black cockade was worn from very early in the century, until the cocked hat went out of use at the beginning of the nineteenth century. After this a miniature edition was worn on the chako. It survived on officers' cocked hats and the top-hats of private servants, until those hats almost disappeared with the advent of mechanization. Even now it is seen on ceremonial occasions. It was pre-Hanoverian, but probably came to be regarded as the Hanoverian emblem in contra-distinction to the white cockade worn by the Jacobites. The button-shaped twist of cord now worn under the officers' cap badges in some regiments—notably among the Rifles and Light Infantry and *The Royal Berkshire Regiment*, is a modified form of the cockade.

73

The light dragoon helmet illustrated was made of boiled leather, with brass mountings, and at first had a cloth flap in front, like the grenadier cap. The cavalry consisted of (1) the Household Cavalry, (2) regiments of Horse, (3) Dragoon Guards, and (4) Dragoons. Each regiment had its troop of light dragoons from 1756. Except for these and the horse grenadiers, the tricorne hat was worn and the main differences were: (1) looped buttonholes of regimental pattern, (2) lapels to bottom of coat, (3) waist-length lapels, (4) no lapels, but loops of narrow lace.

The shoulder knots worn by the cavalry originated from cords which were carried for collecting forage and developed into an ornamental appendage, from which the more elaborate aiguilette was evolved. The white 'boot stockings', reaching above the knees, were worn to protect the breeches.

The gaiters, on the Marine, were of striped 'ticken' (cotton ticking) and were worn for coolness in tropical climates. The Marines were placed under the Admiralty in 1747, and in 1748 all the existing regiments were disbanded.

1742 to 1768 was certainly the most picturesque period as far as infantry uniforms are concerned and from then on there was a gradual but continuous process of stripping off the trimmings.

THE BLACK WATCH (THE 42ND)

The origin of this famous regiment dates back to 1725, when a system of Highland police was formed by Marshal Wade, to prevent cattle-stealing. In 1729 this force was divided into six independent companies because the Government resolved to make it part of the armed forces of the kingdom. In order to distinguish the Watch thus formed from the regular troops, who, because of their uniforms, were called 'red soldiers', it was decided to give it the title, 'The Black Watch'. These independent companies existed until 1739, when the Government decided to raise four additional companies and form the whole into a regiment of the line.

PLATE V (12) INFANTRY REGIMENTS. 1758

The earliest light infantry companies were formed on active service in America about 1758, and their uniform was an adaptation of the ordinary dress, to suit their work. A comparison with the grenadier of the 17th, in Plate V (11), will show how this was done.

The old English cap, with turn-up ear flaps, replaced the tricorne hat (actually it was made from it). The lace and the sleeves were removed from the coat, and wings, like those of the grenadiers but longer, were added, the sleeves of the waistcoat coming through the holes. Two small leather breast pockets were made for bullets and flints, and the spatterdashes were replaced by short gaiters.

Equipment consisted of a pack worn in the Indian fashion, with the canteen or mess tin hanging below it, the cartouche box and powder horn.

Arms were a fusil and a tomahawk—no sword or bayonet, and sergeants were armed in the same way as the men.

The grenadier sergeant of the 42nd (which received its 'Royal' title on 22nd July 1758) is wearing the fur cap which was then peculiar to Highland regiments. The grenadiers, only, had the red over-stripe in the tartan. There are two types of kilt—the belted plaid, which is kilt and plaid all in one piece, and the simple kilt or *feilidh beag*. In addition to the usual infantry weapons, highlanders all carried a pistol and a dirk, and the claymore replaced the ordinary hanger. They frequently carried a target, or shield, as well and when using it the dirk was held underneath in the left hand, so that with it a backhand blow could be given.

Up to 1749 the bands of infantry regiments, in accordance with traditional official parsimony, were civilians hired at the expense of the officers, and were often foreigners whose discipline and habits were unsatisfactory. After that date, however, they were enlisted men.

The instruments used at this period were, the hautbois, similar to the modern oboe, drums, and in some regiments the French horn, the clarinet, and the bassoon. The fife was an instrument of great antiquity, which for a long period had not been used, but about 1750 it was reintroduced and eventually every battalion had its drum and fife band.

The Clothing Warrant of 1751 ordered drummers to wear coats of their regimental facing colour, trimmed with regimental lace, except those of 'Royal' regiments who wore the royal livery—a red coat with blue lining and facings, adorned with Royal lace. They wore grenadier caps, embroidered with regimental devices, and drums on the front and on the rear turn-up flap. A peculiarity of drummers' coats (both Horse and Foot) was the tubular strips of material hanging loose from the back of the shoulders, ending about level with the waist. They resemble the sleeves of cloaks worn in the fifteenth century, which had slits in front for the arms to come though and hung empty from the back of the upper arm. (These were discontinued in 1768.)

Bands were small in numbers—sometimes only six or eight men, with a drum-major in charge, who carried a staff and wore a sash as they still do.

Several regiments changed their numbers at this period. In 1741 the 54th to 60th inclusive were raised as new regiments. In 1748 the 43rd to 53rd were disbanded. In 1755 the 52nd to 62nd were raised, and in 1759 the 15th to 18th Light Dragoons (later the *15th* and *18th Hussars*, and the *16th* and *17th Lancers*). In 1756 the 50th and 51st were disbanded and others were renumbered to fill the gaps. In 1756 the regiments 61 to 80 (except 77 and 78) and 86, were formed from 2nd battalions of other regiments. All this may sound rather confusing and perhaps unnecessary, but these and other changes must be taken into account when tracing the pedigree of a regiment.

PLATE V (13). 1768–99

The Clothing Warrant of 1768 carried the process of standardization a step further, and began to prune and reduce the exotic growths of the middle of the century and also to make the uniforms less cumbersome.

The bearskin grenadier cap, which had been in use for some time, was officially authorized, spatterdashes were reduced to knee length and infantry cutlasses were abolished except for the grenadier companies. Breeches and waistcoats were changed to white or buff, and the latter were considerably shortened. (Light Infantry continued to wear red waistcoats.)

The greatest change, though, was in the coat, which was quite altered in shape. It was cut away from the chest to the outside of the knees, the lapels were reduced to a width of three inches, and the 'cape' or turnover collar was introduced. (It could be partly buttoned-up by reversing the lapels.) Small neat cuffs replaced the large slashed ones and linings were all white, except for some regiments with buff facings which continued to wear buff linings, waistcoats, breeches and equipment until 1819.

The 'Flank' companies—grenadiers and light infantry—wore wing epaulettes, which from 1774 were blue for the Guards and red for other regiments.

Infantry N.C.Os. wore small white epaulettes, two for a sergeant, one for a corporal, and the sergeant's sash, which, from 1768, had a stripe of facing colour, was worn round the waist and under the coat until 1796, when the button-up coat was introduced. Sergeants carried swords, and halberds, which in 1792 were replaced by half-pikes with small cross-bars below the spear-heads.

Light infantry wore short-tailed jackets, like the one shown on the Volunteer, and half-spatterdashes. They had small buttons only, a custom which the officers of *The Oxford. and Bucks. Light Infantry* still retain, together with the gorget buttons (so-called) and cords of Peninsula days.

Light dragoon regiments were dressed like dragoons except for their helmets (dragoons wore cocked hats) and their light short boots, until 1785, when they were given blue shell jackets—at first cut like a 'shell' or cuirass, the sleeves of the waistcoat coming through the holes.

The cut of the cavalry coat was altered like that of the infantry, in 1768, and there seems to have been some indecision about epaulettes in the Dragoon Guards and dragoons—1764–88 one fringed epaulette on the left shoulder, then two, then wings lined with metal scales, then in 1811, with the Service jacket, plain shoulder-straps of facing colour.

About 1775 the first neat and compact equipment made its appearance. It consisted of crossbelts, with an oval breast-plate, carrying the cartouche box and bayonet, and a pack supported on the shoulders by an independent breast harness. The water-bottle had a separate sling.

The Royal Fusiliers, being the *City of London Regiment*, and also *The Grenadier Guards, The H.A.C., The Buffs. The Royal Marines*, and *The Royal Northumberland Fusiliers*, claim the ancient privilege of marching through the City with bayonets fixed, drums beating and Colours flying. *The King's Own Scottish Borderers* have a similar prerogative in Edinburgh.

PLATE VI

1751

The 2nd Horse (until 1746 the 6th Horse). Later the 5th Dragoon Guards

Kettle drummer

PLATE VI

The uniform of cavalry bandsmen followed similar rules to those laid down for the infantry—coats of facing colour, except for 'Royal' regiments, etc.

The instruments used by the bands were drums—similar to the infantry ones, but carried on horseback, kettle drums, used in pairs (by regiments of Horse only), trumpets, and hautbois.

The drummers were in most cases mounted on greys (the 2nd Horse had a bay at this period), and the remainder of the regiment would, in most cases, have blacks, the officers of some regiments having chargers of a different colour from those of the men. Exceptions to the rule were the 2nd Royal North British Dragoons (*The Greys*), the 2nd Dragoon Guards (*The Queen's Bays*), and one or two dragoon regiments which had a mixture of colours.

Drummers of dragoons and of the light dragoon troops were dressed like infantry drummers, except for their riding boots, and wore grenadier caps, and carried their drums by slings over their right shoulders.

The drum banners of the regiments of Horse were treated with the same respect as the Colours, and the drummer, who was a fighting man, and went into battle with the regiment, was expected to lose his life in protecting them, if necessary.

CHAPTER III · 1793-1814

'Our white bones lie
'Neath the cloudless sky
Of the summer islands fair
And there's never a bay
In the Northland grey
But our British dead are there.'

The country now had to face one of the greatest crises in its history, comparable, having regard to population and the scale on which plans were carried out at that time, to the wars of 1914 and 1939, and equally vital to its survival.

EARLY BARRACKS

There had been peace from 1784 to 1793, and in this year the first systematic building of barracks began. Previously the men had usually either lived in camps, or been billeted in alehouses, a system which had obvious disadvantages. There was the usual protest that this meant the advent of a military tyranny, but nevertheless the building proceeded.

THE FRENCH REVOLUTION, 1789

In 1789 the French Revolution broke out with its accompanying massacres and wholesale guillotining of the aristocracy, and France fell into the hands of bloodthirsty tyrants, similar to the Nazis of 1939, who had risen to power so suddenly that their heads were turned and they thought nothing could stop them. Their reactions followed the usual course and they wanted to force their wonderful new system on the whole human race. Thus they and their followers became a willing horse for military adventurers, and when the right leaders appeared, as they always do, France began to make imperialistic invasions of many European countries, as well as some farther afield.

SCOPE OF THE NAPOLEONIC WARS

The ensuing wars lasted, with one break of about two years (1802 to 1803) until 1815. They were fought in France, Holland,

Belgium, Germany, Austria, Russia, Spain, Portugal, Italy, the West Indies, Egypt, South Africa, North and South America, and on most of the seas adjoining these countries.

NEGLECTED STATE OF THE ARMY

In the preceding few years of peace the army had suffered shocking neglect. In 1793, incredible though it may sound, it consisted of about 15,000 men at home and about twice as many overseas. Arthur Bryant says, very aptly, 'The English never prepared for war. Yet they never doubted that they would be victorious.' When volunteers were called for from the Brigade of Guards, to make some of their battalions up to strength to go overseas, every man on parade stepped forward; evidently the spirit was good in spite of all the material shortcomings. Recruiting was excessively bad owing to the grim conditions in the army, and the methods employed by the Government to fill the gaps were beneath contempt. They included releases of criminals, bribery to 'crimps', kidnapping, press gangs, and free commissions to men who raised a certain number of recruits (and no questions were asked as long as they were brought in). With such methods it was not surprising that discipline had to be harshly enforced and that service was unpopular. Early in the war patriotism does not seem to have been a strong influence.

THE NETHERLANDS EXPEDITION, 1793–5, AND OTHER EXPEDITIONS

There was a sort of 'Dunkirk' as the climax of the unfortunate Netherlands expedition, when we endeavoured to prevent the French from seizing Holland. This was due to lack of supplies, reinforcements and organization generally, and was a disaster of the first magnitude. Towards the end of this campaign, when the army was retreating across Gelderland, there was a blizzard of Arctic ferocity which raged for several days and produced a scene of indescribable desolation. Six thousand men and a great number of horses were frozen to death. (In this campaign the first military observation balloon was used by the French, but there appears to have been no repetition of their use until about the end of the nineteenth century.)

Thereafter we made diverse and spasmodic expeditions to the West Indies, where thousands of men died of yellow fever and other tropical diseases, and to South Africa, Malta, Minorca and other scattered objectives. The Cape of Good Hope was secured owing to its being the half-way house to India, and Malta was as important as it now is for its position controlling the narrowest part of the Mediterranean. But, unfortunately at this stage, there seemed to be little in the way of a general strategic plan, or of a real grasp of the true meaning of the war to the British Empire.

WELLINGTON AND NAPOLEON

During these preliminary phases the future leaders of the two main protagonists were normal unnoticed officers, serving with their regiments. Arthur Wellesley, later Duke of Wellington, was in the 33rd Foot, now *The Duke of Wellington's* (the only regiment named after a non-Royal personage), and was a Lieutenant-Colonel (purchase system), aged twenty-four, and Napoleon Buonaparte, a Corsican and therefore a foreigner, as Hitler was in Germany, was an artillery officer, also twenty-four years old. His first opportunity of drawing attention to himself occurred at the siege of Toulon (held by the British) in 1794, after which he 'never looked back'.

FRENCH LANDING IN PEMBROKESHIRE, 1794

There was a lot of trouble in Ireland, where the French made a landing, but were defeated soon afterwards, and a small French landing near Fishguard, in 1794, gained the unique distinction for *The Pembrokeshire Yeomanry*, of the only battle honour ever given for an action in the United Kingdom. It was said that a crowd of Welsh women in scarlet capes, looking on from a distance, played an important part in the battle, as the French mistook them for approaching British infantry and so surrendered without waiting for further rough handling.

THE EGYPTIAN CAMPAIGN, 1801

In 1801 took place the Egyptian campaign which began with General Abercrombie's landing at Abukir Bay, near Alexandria (the scene of Nelson's famous victory of the Nile in 1798), in face of a French army entrenched and fully prepared.

This operation, carried out in about 200 naval rowing-boats, had been rehearsed in Asia Minor, and though it did not go quite according to plan and there were some anxious moments, it was ultimately a complete success. It was scheduled to take place at dawn, but for unavoidable reasons the boats were not all at their rendezvous until 0900 hours.

The troops therefore landed in full daylight under fire from roundshot, grape and shells, which sank several boats. As they came in close musketry fire was added and French cavalry rode into the water and sabred a number of the tightly packed men in the boats. But, once ashore, a sharp short battle sent the enemy off in the direction of Alexandria, leaving the British free to land their stores and prepare for the next stage.

Twelve days later the French made a heavy counter-attack and in this action, known as the battle of Alexandria, the 28th Foot, now *The Gloucestershire Regiment,* won a notable distinction. They were occupying a partly constructed redoubt and the ruins of an ancient palace among the sand-dunes, close to the sea. They had been 'standing to' since 0300 hours on 21st March, as a French move was expected, and the attack came in that dim and chilly hour before dawn, which is so familiar to those who served in the two world wars.

After some firing away on the left, followed by a lengthy silence, the real show began. Shots and shouting on the right flank announced the withdrawal of the picquets, and soon afterwards came the sound of volleys and cannon fire. The 28th in the redoubt, which was not sufficiently finished to give them any cover, were attacked in front by a strong column of French grenadiers (later found to be a famous regiment called 'The Invincibles'). They stood in line, firing volleys at close range in the half-light, until through a break in the smoke someone suddenly noticed lines of French grenadiers approaching from the rear. The order was quickly given for the rear rank of the 28th to turn about, and each rank fought its own battle against superior numbers. For a long time the result was very much in doubt, but eventually the severely battered 'Invincibles' drew off, and the 28th, still cool and efficient, sent help to their neighbours, the 42nd (*The Black Watch*), who were surrounded.

It was a serious attempt by the enemy to get through this lightly held flank and would have meant disaster for the whole force if the 28th had not risen to the occasion as they did. There was more fighting in which they took part with the 42nd and the 58th (*The Northamptonshire Regiment*), and after a grand cavalry charge, supported by three infantry divisions, which failed to reach the British line, the enemy admitted their failure and withdrew. In memory of this exploit the 28th were given the 'back number', which was at first the number 28 worn at the back of the head-dress, but was replaced later on by a small sphinx badge.

The British loss on this day was 70 officers and 1,306 other ranks, against an estimated enemy loss of 3,000. The 'Invincibles' had 650 casualties, and the remaining 250 surrendered. Sir Ralph Abercrombie was nearly captured by French dragoons and later was hit in the thigh by a musket ball, from which he died. Sir John Moore was serving in this campaign.

A sidelight on the conditions of active service in those days is given in a book by Sergeant-Major Coates, of the 28th, published in 1836. He says that for over twelve weeks the regiment was on front line duty, and the night of the 3rd June was the first occasion, since they landed, on which they were allowed to sleep without wearing equipment. Considering the heat, the totally unsuitable dress and the load carried by each man, this was fairly tough soldiering.

There was no serious fighting after the battle of Alexandria, as the half-hearted French troops in Alexandria and Cairo surrendered tamely, and the British troops were withdrawn from Egypt.

THE FIRST WAR MEDAL

The earliest war medal was the General Service Medal (1793–1814) issued in 1848 to end a long-standing grievance, as previously there had been only a gold medal for senior officers. There were altogether twenty-nine clasps which could be awarded with the General Service Medal, one of the early ones being for the battle of Alexandria. In contrast to this delay of fifty-five years, the Waterloo medal was being worn in 1816. In addition to the ordinary medals, in some cases regiments had their own, which were awarded by the commanding officer. Regiments which took part in the Egyptian campaign of 1801 have on their colours the sphinx, with the word 'Egypt' above.[1]

THE DUKE OF YORK'S REFORMS

The Duke of York, who had been unlucky in commanding the ill-fated Holland expedition, afterwards became Commander-in-Chief at the Horse Guards, where he distinguished himself as a first-class administrator. Amongst many other reforms and improvements, he founded the Staff College and the Adjutant-General's and Military Secretary's departments, established a 'Corps of Waggoners'—the ancestors of *The R.A.S.C.*, and made serious efforts to curb the corrupt system of purchasing commissions and promotion and to get officers promoted on merit only.

NAPOLEON'S INVASION SCHEME

From 1803 to 1805 there was considerable excitement in England, as Napoleon had collected 100,000 men on the French coast near Calais and maintained them there with barges and all necessary equipment for an invasion. But, in spite of many efforts, the French could never succeed in luring the fleet into the Atlantic, so as to get control of the Channel, and—like the Germans in later times—they never got across. It was then that the Martello towers, which still stand in Kentish gardens, were built and the

[1] *The SERINGAPATAM MEDAL, 1799, and the India Medal, 1799–1826, though not dating as far back as the G.S. medal, were issued many years earlier.*

Hythe military canal, which became an anti-tank ditch in 1940, was constructed then to form a water obstacle against an invading force.

The battle of Trafalgar, 1805, completely destroyed Napoleon's ideas on the subject of invasion, as the French fleet was now beyond hope of obtaining control of the seas.

But the threat had cured the indecision of the government, the apathy and even downright disloyalty of some of the people, and from 1803 onwards England went seriously all out to win the war. The country was filled with a new spirit and in every town and village most of the men who were not in the regular forces could be seen enthusiastically training, in the varied and splendid uniforms of the 'Fencibles'. There was one village where *The Home Guard* in the recent war occupied a room used by the Fencibles for lectures, etc. A roll was found dated about 1804, in which the names were mostly the same as those of the 1940 men, being probably of the same families, about five generations back.

WARNING BEACONS

As in the time of the Armada there was a warning system of beacons, and on every prominent hill throughout the country watchers stood by ready to light the piles of brushwood. Their job must have had a certain similarity to that of *The Royal Observer Corps* in recent years and, like the bells which rang in September 1940 and brought *The Home Guard* to their battle stations, there was a false alarm of a French invasion. An accidental fire in Northumberland set the beacons flaming across the South of Scotland, and the Fencibles marched out to their coast positions, expecting an enemy fleet and landing force to appear across the North Sea.

DIVERSE EXPEDITIONS

Further operations were carried out in Italy, at the Cape, South America (whence the unfamiliar battle honour—'Monte Video' borne by *The Rifle Brigade*) and battalions of *The Royal Berkshire Regiment* and *The Rifle Brigade* won the battle honour 'Copenhagen' (1801) while serving as Marines under Nelson.

Some places in Italy, which have recently been much in the news, were visited by British troops in 1805, when a division was landed in the Naples area and there was fighting with the French, including the important battle of Maida. The XX Foot (now *The Lancashire Fusiliers*) disembarked at Castelamare, and proceeded to Torre del Nunciate (where they were reviewed by the King of Naples), Capua, Monte Leone, and other places familiar to members of the C.M.F. There were also Russian troops with this force, several of whom were frozen to death during a winter which seems to have been even worse than those during the recent war.

COMPULSORY SERVICE

Compulsory training for home service was adopted at this period as a temporary measure (its next application was in 1916), and the Militia was made into a reinforcement for the regular battalions and became what it was named at a much later date—a Special Reserve. The total strength of the army at home and abroad then numbered about 650,000, excluding Marines, but including the Volunteers.

BEGINNING OF THE PENINSULAR WAR, 1808

In 1808 began the largest and longest campaign of the period, and the only one in which British commanders had complete control and the main forces were British. This war went on until 1814, and according to Napier's history of it, the British won nineteen important battles and numerous smaller engagements, took four great fortresses, drove the French out of Spain, twice out of Portugal and penetrated into France. They inflicted 200,000 casualties and left 40,000 of their own dead in Spain.

ALLIES IN THE PENINSULA

A large number of Spaniards and Portuguese were fighting with us and though often a liability in a pitched battle, their hatred of the French made them useful as guerrillas and saboteurs. Enemy stragglers who were overtaken by them had a poor chance of survival.

FRENCH INFANTRY TACTICS

The French tactics throughout the Napoleonic Wars had this main characteristic. They always attacked with their infantry in massive columns on very narrow frontages, relying on weight of numbers to break through. This was the system devised by Carnot, French Minister of War in 1800, a soldier of considerable ability, whose task was to make armies as quickly as possible. He used picked men to go in front as skirmishers and formed the masses from the semi-trained and less soldierly men.

The British used to meet them in a thin line of two ranks, the front rank kneeling so that every man had a clear field of fire. Waiting till they had approached within short range (the old rule was, 'when you can see the whites of their eyes'), the officers gave the word of command, and they loosed off volleys into the solid mass. The front of the enemy column was suddenly transformed into a shambles of dead and wounded falling over one another, and those behind, while trying to deploy and unable to see or fire in the crowd, received further volleys, which threw them into worse confusion.

This was the moment for the British to make a bayonet charge and complete the demoralization. The whole mass would be forced back until it became a rabble in flight. The British knew exactly how far they were to pursue and would then reform ranks and await orders.

This scene was enacted time after time, but the French would not change their methods, even when their men were fully trained, presumably because they felt more confidence when formed in a solid body. This is somewhat hard to understand, as they would usually put up a remarkably stout fight, although their excitable temperament did make them liable to panic at times.

LAPSES OF DISCIPLINE

The discipline of the British in Spain caused some unfavourable comments, but actually it was admirable, with just one or two exceptions. These were almost invariably due to the capture of towns containing huge stores of wine, or their abandonment during the several harassing retreats which had to be carried out owing to the great superiority in numbers of the French. In every case the men were in a state of exhaustion following prolonged hardships and fighting. The worst of these incidents was at Badajos, where there was a three days' orgy.

BADAJOS

The taking of 'Badahoo', as the men called it, involved perhaps the greatest slaughter in the smallest space in any battle which has ever been fought, and it is an interesting example of the methods of siege warfare in those days.

The immensely strong fortress was built on the southern bank of the Guadiana, and the French had dammed the Rivillas stream to produce an inundation on the south-east side. The remaining sides were fortified with high bastioned walls of massive masonry, on which numerous guns were mounted. In front of these was a ditch which varied in depth up to thirty feet, and in addition, in some sectors there was a *fausse braie*, or false ditch, to form the first obstacle. There were also outlying forts which had to be dealt with before the main assault could be carried out.

The system, which had changed little during the previous two centuries, was first to decide on the weakest points, where attacks would have the best chance of success; then to sap in parallels, starting from outside the effective range of the defenders' weapons until eventually the trenches had approached near enough for the storming parties to assemble in them.

At the same time batteries were constructed in suitable positions, i.e. earthworks were built to protect the guns, gunners, and ammunition from artillery fire.

This work took weeks or months according to the weather, the type of soil and the amount of interference by the enemy. Troops had to be detailed to cover every approach to the fortress to prevent exit or entry and others to guard against relieving forces which might be sent by the enemy. When all was ready the artillery carried out a prolonged bombardment of the selected points.

Two previous attempts to take Badajos had had to be called off, owing to the strength of the place, casualties, and military requirements elsewhere. In the final siege it took ten days of continuous artillery fire to make breaches which would give a reasonable chance of success. The assault took place on the night of 6th April 1812.

Four divisions were to make simultaneous attacks on the breaches in different sectors of the perimeter, the 4th and light divisions working together at the point where most opposition was expected.

The main bodies of these divisions were to move forward two minutes after the storming parties, which contained a hundred men from each regiment, carrying scaling ladders and large haybags, with which to fill in parts of the ditch. These were preceded by the 'forlorn hope'—a party of volunteers, whose task was to probe the enemy's defence. If they could get in through a breach, the storming parties would follow immediately and then the main bodies. If they failed, the commander would then decide whether to involve other troops or not, and quite frequently the 'forlorn hope' met unexpectedly strong resistance and was wiped out. The name is a corruption of old German *verlorner Hauf* = lost party.

The attackers had to cover some open ground, from their trenches to the 'glacis' (ramp leading up to the outer side of the ditch), descend over the 'counterscarp' (outer wall of the ditch), cross a seventeen foot deep cut at the bottom, which was full of water, then climb the 'scarp' (inner wall of the ditch) and make their way over the broken masonry up to the gap in the walls. They would then, if not sooner, come face to face with the enemy.

They reached their assembly points in well-trained silence at about 2100 hours, and waited patiently for the order to move forward. The first sign of alarm was a 'fire ball' (the equivalent at that time of the Verey light) shot from the bastion of Santa Maria. It fell among some pioneers who quickly beat it out. Then there was silence until at last the final orders were passed along in a whisper.

Things went according to plan up to the point where the stormers were descending into the ditch. Then there was a powerful explosion—a mine fired by the French at the foot of one of the breaches—which caused five hundred casualties and lit up the whole area, showing everything to the enemy, who were seen crowding the walls in anticipation. The next moment a terrific racket broke loose, as the stormers were deluged with case-shot, musketry and grenades.

Men leapt into the ditch without waiting for their turn on the ladders, and landed on top of others, or in some places in several feet of water, and broke arms and legs. Ladders crowded with men collapsed or were shot down. Now and then the scene of confusion was illuminated by a blazing barrel of tar rolled down by the French (a forerunner of the *Flammen-werfer* or flame-thrower. This, however, was by no means an original idea as, in A.D. 668, Callinicus of Heliopolis invented 'Greek fire'—a highly inflammable substance reputed to be capable of burning even under water. Its composition is not definitely known, but it is said to have contained naphtha, pitch and sulphur, and to have been thrown by large catapults, either at ships or over the walls of fortresses.)

After a few minutes the muddle was sorted out, and officers had parties organized for storming the breach, which was no more than fifteen to twenty feet wide. Here they found a variety of obstacles prepared for them. There were loose planks studded with spikes, which slid down the slope as they trod on them, and above were heavy revolving beams full of swords and bayonets, which had been built solidly across the gap. Behind these was a mass of Frenchmen blazing at them as fast as they could fire the loaded muskets which were being passed up from behind, and guns firing case-shot. Periodically barrels of gunpowder with lighted fuses in them were rolled down the slope and exploded among the stormers, and by way of auxiliary missiles the French had collected on the parapet a supply of canon-balls, large stones, baulks of timber, old cart-wheels, etc., which they heaved over on to the mass of stormers waiting below.

The slaughter in such a confined space was terrible, and sometimes the whole of an attacking party was swept away by a discharge of case-shot. In one such instance Lieutenant Shaw of the

43rd (*1st Oxford and Bucks Light Infantry*), who was leading fifty men, found himself the only one left on his legs.

The men went fighting mad and repeated attempts were made for over two hours. After each failure a fresh party was collected and clambered up, with heavy losses, to the *chevaux de frises*, where they made superhuman efforts to get over or under the swords, or in the last resort at least to kill a Frenchman. This went on until the whole of the slope from the ditch was piled with dead and wounded, many of whom were roasted by the burning tar barrels.

But in this case bravery proved of no avail, and at midnight Wellington ordered a retirement. Even then the men twice ignored the bugles, and stood waiting to make another effort.

The 3rd and 5th Divisions, though, at the other breaches, had had better success, and soon afterwards when shouts and firing were heard inside the town, the remnants of the 4th and light divisions went forward again to join in the final victorious entry.

It was after this night of carnage, in which 300 officers and 5,000 men had fallen, that the troops, with hardly any officers left to restrain them, went wild and looted the wine cellars. After getting thoroughly drunk they temporarily lost all semblance of discipline and committed outrages which form one of the most discreditable incidents in the history of the army.

BATTLE HONOURS OF THE PENINSULA

Battle honours, to take as an example those of the *43rd* and *52nd Light Infantry*, which served in the famous Light Division, are: 'Vimiero', 'Corunna', 'Busaco', 'Fuentes d'Onoro', 'Ciudad Rodrigo', 'Badajos', 'Salamanca', 'Vittoria', 'Pyrenees', 'Nivelle', 'Nive', 'Orthes', 'Toulouse', 'Peninsula'. These make a longer list than the honours of any other war, but they were all well-earned ones.

TALAVERA

An interesting sidelight on the spirit of the British regiments is given in the French dispatch about this battle, which complained quite solemnly that 'the English were beaten but would not run'. As the result of their being so stupid the French were beaten in the end.

END OF PIGTAILS AND POWDER

Rolica, August 1808, was the last battle in which the army as a whole wore queues and powder in their hair. The 29th, now *The Worcestershire Regiment*, were the last in the Peninsula to cut their hair, and it is recorded that they fought at Vimiero, a short time afterwards, with it still done in the old style.

ARROYO DOS MOLINOS

A peculiar coincidence occurred in this battle, where the 34th Foot, now *The Border Regiment*, the only one to possess this battle honour, encountered the 34th French Regiment of the Line, capturing all its survivors together with some French Staff officers of high rank. The drums and the drum-major's staff of the French 34th are still in the possession of *The Border Regiment*.

SALAMANCA

There were many instances where regiments were almost wiped out in the fierce volleying contests and the storming of heavily defended fortresses, which took place so frequently. One of these was the 11th Foot, now *The Devonshire Regiment* which, after the battle of Salamanca, had only four officers and sixty-seven men left, and became known as 'the bloody eleventh'. There is a story that before the battle began they found themselves marching close to and parallel with a French regiment, but as neither had orders to attack, the officers of both sides saluted with their swords and the two regiments marched on, with bands playing, and without firing a shot, to their places in the opposing lines. A tune played by the band of the 11th on this occasion—'We've lived and loved together'—became the regimental march.

ALBUHERA

One of the fiercest battles of the whole war was fought at Albuhera, about twenty miles from Badajos, the siege of which was temporarily abandoned by Sir William Beresford in order to meet and deal with Marshal Soult's advancing army.

A memorable feature, which resulted in the introduction of lancer regiments, was the destruction caused by the Polish lancers, who nearly annihilated Colborne's brigade, and then followed up their successes by barbarously attacking hundreds of wounded as they lay on the ground.

Many regiments were decimated and all, including Spaniards, Portuguese and Germans, behaved with admirable stoicism. An example of unsurpassable devotion to duty was given by Lieutenant Latham of the Buffs, after the Brigade had lost 1,200 men in a space of about five minutes. 'At that moment Lieutenant Latham seized the Colour before the lancers could carry it off, and was immediately attacked but, fighting with his sword, although wounded in several places, he refused to give it up. A

French hussar, grasping the Colour staff, cut open Latham's head, severing one side of his face and nose. Several hussars now surrounding him, tried to take the Colour away, and one cut off his arm. He dropped his sword, but continued the struggle with the Colour pole, but must have been killed outright but that his assailants got in each other's way. At last thrown down, wounded in many places, he tore the silk from Colour staff, and lay on top of it, while lancers were trampling their horses on his prostrate body and spearing him.'[1]

Almost incredibly Latham eventually recovered, but was shockingly disfigured.

The 57th Foot, now *The Middlesex Regiment*, in Houghton's brigade earned their nickname 'the Die-Hards', from Colonel Inglis who, when severely wounded, insisted on remaining where he fell, in front of the Colours, urging his men in their critical situation to take careful aim and to die hard. The loss of the 57th was 20 officers and 420 men, out of 30 officers and 570 men, and it is said that No. 2 Company's rations for the following day were drawn by a drummer, who took them away in his hat. Many other regiments suffered almost as heavily.

The battle was very nearly lost, but was retrieved at the last moment by the historic advance of the Fusilier Brigade—1st and 2nd Battalions of the 7th, now *The Royal Fusiliers*, and the 1st and 2nd, 23rd, now *The Royal Welch Fusiliers*, who arrived during the battle, after a forced march from Badajos, and went straight into action.

SINGLE COMBAT

Light dragoons came very much into the limelight, and carried out scores of brilliant actions, and an officer of one of these regiments wrote in his memoirs that it was no uncommon thing for a French cavalry officer to ride out from his troop and challenge a British officer to single combat, in the style of Bruce and De Bohun, while the opposing troops looked on from a reasonable distance. He himself killed one who challenged him, but could not help admiring his chivalrous and youthful spirit, and regretted having to put an end to him.

SPORT AND HORSEMANSHIP

The first-class horsemanship of the cavalry was due to the fact that nearly all the officers were keen hunting men. Wellington had a pack of hounds sent out and there were regular meets during the winter while static warfare went on around the lines of

[1] From *"British Battles on Land and Sea"* by Field Marshall Sir Evelyn Wood, V.C.

Torres Vedras. Several times the hunt became involved with the enemy, and once Tom Crane, the Duke's huntsman, who became something of a celebrity, was captured with his pack, but they were returned quite safely within a few days.

Coursing was popular with all ranks and also led to some queer incidents, of which the following is one. Before the battle of Salamanca, Wellington rode along the line, which was already under artillery fire, and halted to discuss final details with his Staff and a Spanish General. They were in an exposed and un-comfortable position, with cannon-balls bounding along the ground at odd intervals, but were deep in conversation, when a hare dashed past, pursued by a couple of greyhounds.

Wellington, in the middle of a sentence, dug in his spurs and departed in a cloud of dust, leaving the Spanish General utterly dumbfounded. The hare was soon caught and, in a few minutes, he returned and carried on the powwow from where he left off. This little *entre-acte* gave considerable pleasure to the men, and provided a comic relief to the grimness of standing still under fire.

HORSES

The horses knew their jobs almost as well as the men, and there is an account in the history of the 14*th Hussars* (then 14th Light Dragoons) telling how, after the horses had been groomed daily for some weeks in the market square of a Spanish town, they were turned out to grass a mile or two away, and the parade in the square was discontinued. But afterwards at the correct time every day one would hear a clatter of hooves in the street as they came cantering into the square and lined up in their troops.

On another occasion an officer's charger was shot in the head and, thinking it was dead, he left it and obtained another. After the action was over, when the regiment was re-forming, this un-fortunate animal appeared, staggering painfully, found its own troop and placed itself in the correct position, and then collapsed and died.

One of the worst features of war used to be the enormous casualties suffered by the horses, and though the cavalryman hated parting with his old friend, every animal-lover must be thankful that mechanization has now almost released them from service and from the undeserved horrors they used to endure.

'THE EMPEROR'S CHAMBERMAID'

One of the exploits of the 14th Light Dragoons, who served through the whole six years of the Peninsular War, was the capture, after the French defeat at Vittoria, of Joseph Buonaparte's coach. This contained a now celebrated trophy—a silver receptacle, which is kept in the Officers' Mess, and on certain anniversaries is filled with champagne and passed round the dinner table.

THE ROYAL ARTILLERY

The Royal Horse Artillery proved extremely valuable with their new mobility and power to defend themselves. There was a memorable occasion when Norman Ramsay, a Captain in charge of a troop of guns at Fuentes d'Onoro, 1811, was cut off by a large body of French cavalry. He took them completely by surprise by charging with the guns, straight through the middle of them, and his audacity was rewarded by his making a getaway. Had any of his gun-team horses been disabled it might have been a different story. (Ramsay was killed at Waterloo.)

There were also one or two important developments in gunnery which were made use of during the Peninsular War. In 1802 Major Shrapnell, R.A., invented a novelty in shells, which burst in the air, scattering a large number of heavy bullets, and could be used up to a range of 1,200 yards.

Another innovation occurred at the storming of San Sebastian, 1814, when about fifty guns gave overhead covering fire to the storming parties, dropping shells or balls on the defenders of the fortress walls, while they assaulted the breaches. This was the first occasion on which artillery was considered sufficiently accurate to permit such an operation.

AN UNNECESSARY BATTLE

The final battle of the war, at Toulouse, one of the bloodiest of all, which cost the French over 10,000 casualties and the British nearly 5,000, would never have been fought if modern methods of communication had been available. Napoleon had abdicated on the 5th April 1814, and this battle took place on the 10th, no news having reached either of the commanders. Hostilities ended on the 13th.

THE RANK OF COLOUR-SERGEANT

This rank was first introduced as a reward for distinguished service, by a General Order of 6th July 1813. There was one to each company and the pay was 2s. 4d. a day. Lieut.-Colonel Steevens of the 20th Foot, now *The Lancashire Fusiliers*, at a place called Lesaca, in Spain, 'conferred Colour badges on ten of the most meritorious sergeants of the regiment'.

The badge of rank, worn on the right arm, consisted of a

crown above a Union Jack, the pike upright and the flag flying to the left. Below this two straight swords crossed, points uppermost. Underneath the whole a single chevron of double narrow gold or silver lace.

In 1868 it was changed to three chevrons under crossed Union Jacks, surmounted by a crown.

With the introduction of the double company system (long used in continental armies), early in the twentieth century, the Colour-Sergeants of each pair of the original companies became the Company Sergeant-Major and the Company Quartermaster-Sergeant.

LIFE ON ACTIVE SERVICE

The conditions of active service early in the nineteenth century were different in many respects from those of the 20th, yet not so different as one might imagine.

The soldier was more cut off from home, as everything went by sailing ship, letters were scarce and long delayed, and leave boats must have been very rare, if one ever heard of them at all.

The supply system was rudimentary and there were often acute shortages of clothing, horses' feed, rations and all the necessities of life. There were times when the men were in rags and had to march immense distances with soleless or toeless boots, and carrying an average weight of 75 lb. of equipment. Occasionally when transport broke down the stores and even the cash carried for the men's pay, had to be dumped or destroyed.

Camps were poorly equipped and often there was nothing but a worn-out coat to keep a man warm in the bitter snows of continental winters, and no light to see by in the long dark evenings. There were no mobile bath units, no newspapers, no cigarettes, in fact no comforts except the local *vino*. One of the few ameliorations was that a certain number of wives and other women accompanied regiments on service and did what they could to relieve the discomforts and shortcomings of camp life. They had a pretty tough time themselves, and like the men they were used to rough conditions. But the men of those days were at least as handy at bringing in something for the pot, or chopping down an old door to warm themselves, as the 'old soldiers' of 1914 or 1939, and no doubt they were just as good at seeing the funny side of things when there did not seem to be much at which to laugh.

Battles generally consisted of a few hours of concentrated butchery, making a hideous shambles on a small area of ground. The slaughter was appalling and must have looked far worse at such close quarters than it does in a modern battle covering many square miles. An important difference was that one could always see the enemy, even before it began, and there was nearly always some hand-to-hand scrapping. It must have been less cold-blooded and impersonal than it often is nowadays. The red coats, bands, Colours, etc., and the fact that the whole thing was done as a drill, gave it a ritual and uplifting ceremonial effect, which is quite absent from a jungle or desert battle of the present era.

The firing, of course, was very different, consisting mainly of volleys of musketry at ranges up to about 100 yards, shrapnel, shells, and roundshot which ricocheted and bounded off stones and hard ground. Artillery range was about 1,000 to 1,500 yards and sometimes fifty or sixty guns made a concentrated bombardment. This did not compare with the volume of fire and the variety of missiles from modern weapons, but a soldier could not take cover as he must now, and had to stand still in close order and do his drill correctly under fire, which certainly needed good nerves.

One could watch a battle quite safely at a distance of half a mile or so, and could probably see the whole array from a bit of rising ground. When not in contact with the enemy there were no aircraft or long-range guns, or guided missiles to worry about, and barrack routine and training went on unhindered. It was dull and often accompanied by many privations, but without much danger. Life was as someone described it in 1914, a period of extreme discomfort punctuated by spells of terrifying frightfulness.

The many very grim retreats in the Peninsula involved marches which dragged on for weeks, in appalling weather and over mountainous country, without tents or any shelter for the nights.

But as one consolation there was no digging of slit trenches, which is now such a menace to troops on service, in fact there were usually no trenches at all except in sieges. But the system was growing up of using trench redoubts or fortified houses as strong points in a battle, if there was time to prepare them. There was static warfare at times, and this had a fully developed technique, including all the possible uses of trenches, shelters, breastworks, road blocks, and obstacles.

The orders regarding truces and fraternizing with the enemy were not so strict in those days. Chivalrous acts were quite numerous, and there were spells of 'live and let live'. Sometimes the opposing armies occupied the two sides of a river, and by mutual understanding, sentries refrained from firing on men getting water, or bathing and washing their clothes. At least one instance is recorded of the officer in charge of the picquets inviting his opposite number on the French side to dine with him. They would spend a cheery evening together and a few hours later perhaps be fighting it out hammer and tongs.

As regards 'frightfulness', life was definitely less civilized and orderly than now (though perhaps one might doubt it), especially among the guerrillas who often ill-treated and murdered stragglers. Bands of thieves quickly gathered after a battle, to loot the dead and the wounded, who often had to lie out for days before they could be collected. The discipline of our own army which, of course, contained some bad characters, was very strict, and the general standard of behaviour was high in comparison with that of other nations. The French also were normally an honourable enemy, and prisoners and wounded who fell into their hands were usually well treated. On the other hand, the ill-disciplined troops of the Revolution had at times committed atrocities on a par with those of recent wars—burning, torturing and massacring civilians. Napoleon himself used Hunnish methods in dealing with unwilling officials in captured Italian towns.

War gratuities were given for the Peninsular War under the name of Prize Money. There were six periods for which various amounts were awarded, and for the whole six years of active service a General received about £1,360 and a private £3 10s. 1d.

PLATE VII

(14)

1759

The Royal Artillery
Officer
General Officer

(15)

1759

The Life Guards
Negro Trumpeter

(16)

1759

The 1st Guards. Now the Grenadier
Guards

Ensign with Company Colour of 23rd Coy.

(17)

1793–1805

The Royal Horse Artillery
Officer (Service dress) 1793
Lieutenant-General (Half dress) 1805

The Rifle Corps. Now the Rifle Brigade
Officer (Service dress) 1800

PLATE VII
Figs. 14, 15, 16 & 17

PLATE VII (14) THE ROYAL ARTILLERY, OFFICER, GENERAL OFFICER. 1759

There was still nothing in a General's uniform which differed greatly from that of a Guards officer, except the baton, and a rather more lavish use of gold lace, and there was nothing to distinguish between a Major-General, Lieutenant-General, etc. The illustration shows the style of hair-dressing at this period, and the ribbon tails (still worn by officers of *The Royal Welch Fusiliers*), which protected the coat from the grease.

The shoulder-knot had developed into the more elaborate aiguilette somewhere about 1750, and this was worn by all officers until 1768, when fringed epaulettes were first adopted.

The Royal Artillery uniform was particularly decorative as it was one of the several periods when they had a large amount of gold lace. At intervals this seems to have been given up, at any rate as regards the buttonholes.

The gun with the Union flag was known as the 'Colour gun' and denoted the presence of an artillery, and sometimes a General's, headquarters. Actually *The Royal Artillery* never had Colours or battle honours, and as they took part in every important action, the latter were covered by their two mottoes— Quo Fas et Gloria Ducunt', and 'Ubique', and their guns were guarded as jealously as the Colours of a regiment.

The pike-like instrument, carried by the gunners was the 'field staff', the curved metal ends being the linstock cocks, to which was attached the smouldering fuse or slow match, for firing the guns.

PLATE VII (15) THE LIFE GUARDS. NEGRO TRUMPETER. 1759

Trumpeters in the early days were something more than musicians. They were chosen for having an acceptable manner and the ability to carry messages, parley with the enemy and act as special orderlies to the Generals, who usually had several on their Staff. They were non-combatants and carried swords with broken-off blades. Their position in the army was obviously associated with that of the Heralds of the 'knightly years'.

Later on, many regiments had a certain number of negro trumpeters and drummers on their strength. This was probably done to illustrate the growth of the Empire, and they were looked upon as curiosities by the civilian public, most of whom had never been abroad. At the same period it was fashionable to keep a coloured servant in the large houses, and these are often shown in George Morland's and other contemporary pictures. Some of the negroes in *The Life Guards* were chosen specially for their immense height.

The uniform was very similar to the present-day state dress of the Household Cavalry bandsmen, except for the hat which, during the nineteenth century, was replaced by the 'jockey cap'. This was a reversion to an Old

English cap of similar style, but with turn-up flaps, which was worn in the seventeenth century. The early light infantry cap was of this type. See Plate V (12).

The Life Guards were formed originally from a body of gentlemen who went into exile with Charles Stuart (later Charles II), and returned with him in 1660. In the seventeenth century their non-commissioned officers ranked equal to officers of other corps and were designated as Brigadiers and Sub-Brigadiers. (This non-commissioned rank is still used in some of the continental armies and in the Italian *Carabinieri*.)

PLATE VII (16) THE 1ST GUARDS, NOW THE GRENADIER GUARDS. ENSIGN WITH COMPANY COLOUR OF 23RD COY. 1759

In the seventeenth and early eighteenth centuries there was a profusion of Colours, and regiments had one each for the Colonel, the Majors, and all the Captains, in addition to the King's Colour. Many of them were painted or embroidered with fantastic designs, such as dolphins, cannon, flags, rising suns, etc., and the Colonel's crest or coat of arms usually held a prominent place, until 1751, when the use of private arms or badges was forbidden.

'Regulations for the Colours of the marching regiments' were issued in 1747, and confirmed by the Royal Warrant of 1751. Only two were now to be carried by a Foot regiment—the King's Colour, which was to be the 'great Union' (then only embodying the flags of England and Scotland, as the union with Ireland did not take place until 1801), and the 2nd or regimental Colour. This was of the facing colour, with a small Union in the upper canton, but in the case of regiments with white or red facings it was the flag of St. George with the small Union. Regiments with black facings had the St. George's cross and the small Union, with the other three cantons black. Except for the 3rd, 5th, 6th, 8th and 27th Regiments, which had badges placed in the centre, there was a central wreath of roses and thistles encircling the regimental 'rank' in Roman figures. The regiments with badges had their 'rank' only, in the upper part.

The Foot Guards still followed the old rules (as they do now) and the King's Colour remained crimson. They also kept their company Colours, with the company badges given to them by Charles II.

The method of saluting a General was for the Ensign to take off his hat and at the same time to flourish the Colour and spread it on the ground.

Saluting with the hand came in for other ranks at the beginning of the eighteenth century, and the reason was reputed to be the parsimonious concern of the authorities because the men's hats became dirty and worn from taking them off frequently. This does not appear to agree with the theory circulated officially in recent years, that saluting originated from the ancient custom of raising the visor to be recognized, when in armour, but it may be reconcilable if one supposes that a reversion to this method coincided conveniently with the desire to save money. (At the present time temporary soldiers who complain about saluting, do not seem to realize that even a junior officer has to return on an average the salutes of thirty men, and that consequently they only do one-thirtieth of the saluting he does.)

There was a very elaborate drill for the Ensigns bearing the Colours on ceremonial parades, which included various lengthy movements and flourishes, and it is recorded that the 1*st Guards* had a system of signals given with the Colour, for the regiment to carry out certain movements and formations. This may have originated the idea of semaphore signalling.

The Trooping of the Colours was a most meticulous ceremonial, used for bringing them on parade with full ritual and solemnity, in such a way that each man should realize that he was in the presence of these revered symbols and should do nothing to lower their unsullied record.

The gorget was the last survival of armour—originally a large neck plate, but now reduced to a crescent-shaped badge of office, worn only when on duty. It was at one time of different metals denoting ranks, but later of gilt or silver in accordance with the regimental lace. Officers generally had two scarlet uniforms, one fully laced and one with much less lace for 'half dress' or active service, and blue undress coats were also worn, as far back as the seventeenth century. White spatterdashes were worn on full ceremonial occasions.

The background shows the types of tents, and the wagons or tumbrils then in use, and a 'sutleress', who was the N.A.A.F.I. girl of that period, and kept a sort of very primitive canteen in the lines. Until late in the nineteenth century there were always a certain number of wives and other females who accompanied regiments on active service, and many of them performed actions worthy of D.C.Ms.

Tents very similar to those illustrated are still in use, and the bell tent, in slightly different form, appears to have been used before Agincourt and on the Field of the Cloth of Gold. It reappeared as an army issue about the time of the Napoleonic wars. The expression 'bells of arms', which used to appear frequently in orders, referred to bell-shaped structures in which the muskets, and later rifles, were kept when the men were not on parade.

PLATE VII (17) THE ROYAL HORSE ARTILLERY. 1793. LIEUT-GENERAL 1805
    THE RIFLE CORPS. 1800

This was the first uniform of *The Royal Horse Artillery*, and was similar to a light dragoon's dress, except for the jacket, which was like the light infantry one of this date, and that worn by the French Chasseurs. A short time later it was superseded by the light dragoon shell jacket, with corded front of regimental pattern. The 'turban' or 'puggaree' on the helmet was at first red, but was later changed to black.

A General's uniform differed from that of other officers in having chain pattern lace, gold interwoven sash, and a curved Mameluke sabre. The aiguilette had been retained when other officers ceased to wear it in 1768, and the buttons were now arranged, nine in each row evenly spaced for Generals, in threes for Lieutenant-Generals, and ten in each row spaced in pairs for Major-Generals.

The large cocked hat, at first worn square with the shoulders, gradually assumed an oblique position with the right corner forward (owing to its interfering with the firing of a musket), and finally it was worn fore and aft. This position was at first an affectation of officers returning from active service, but it was soon adopted by all. This hat went through several variations in size and shape, the points at one time being turned up and later drooping.

The Rifle Corps was formed in 1800, and the officers' uniform, except for being dark green, was very much like that of a light dragoon, with helmet and sabre of light cavalry pattern. The full dress of officers of Rifle regiments has remained like that of hussars, up to the present time, with cord loops across the front of the tunic, pouch belt, and a busby of regimental pattern. They wore pelisses during the period when Hussars did so.

Hessian boots came into general use, at this period, for officers of mounted and dismounted units, when in service dress, or half-dress, much in the same way as field boots did in 1915.

PLATE VIII

1804

The 14th Light Dragoons. Later the 14th Hussars
Officer (Service dress)

The 14th or the Bedfordshire Regiment. Now the West Yorkshire Regiment
Grenadier Officer

The King's Dragoon Guards
Officer

PLATE VIII

This was a period when uniforms, though still very decorative, were acquiring a new kind of smartness, due to the quickening pace of life and the increasing mobility required in war, which had resulted in garments being made less voluminous and more compact so as to lessen the restriction they imposed on movement. The need for concealment had not yet become pressing, as far as European wars were concerned, as ordinary musket range was still only about a hundred yards, and it was more important to be able to distinguish one's own side quickly, and for Staff officers and orderlies to be able to pick out officers without unnecessary delay.

The light dragoons' blue uniform was first authorized in 1785 and had not changed much, except that a large bearskin crest had been added to the helmet and the old frontplate of grenadier type had been removed. The 14th received the title of 'Duchess of York's Own' in 1798, and adopted orange facings and Guidons.

The large cocked hat shown was introduced in 1792, and was the universal head-dress of the army until 1800, with the usual exceptions (which did not apply to officers in full dress)—light dragoons, Horse Artillery, grenadiers, Rifle regiments, and light infantry. The latter wore close-fitting leather caps. By an order of 4th May 1796, grenadiers, fuzileers, *The Royal Artillery* and *The Corps of Royal Sappers and Miners* wore plain white feathers, light infantry, dark green, and the remainder white with a scarlet base.

In 1798 Dragoon Guards ceased to wear lapels, and laced buttonholes, as shown, were worn until 1811. The tails of their coats were short and reached only to the saddle. Two epaulettes were worn by them from 1788 and these were lined with steel plates. Cavalry officers, at this time, wore the pouch on the right hip. (Later it was worn high on the back.) The *2nd Dragoon Guards* wore brown overalls (not officially sanctioned until 1811) and white stable jackets, as early as 1795.

In 1796 the old infantry officer's coat, which had a cut-away front and hung open from the neck to the knees (see the Sergeant-Major in Plate V, 13) was replaced by one with lapels which hooked together down to the waist, or alternatively buttoned across as an ordinary double-breasted coat Other ranks at the same time were issued with a single-breasted coat without lapels, but having laced buttonholes, which fastened down to the waist. In 1804 officers would have had both the coatee illustrated, and the short service jacket.

The sash was now worn outside the coat, instead of over the waistcoat, and infantry officers tied theirs on the left, and cavalry on the right.

Officers of the majority of regiments had gold or silver lace buttonholes on lapels, collar and cuffs, but the 14th was at that time one of the 'laceless' regiments, and wore buff silk buttonholes.

Epaulettes had been worn since 1768. In the infantry, officers of the flank companies wore two, and battalion officers one. It was not until 1791 that field officers were distinguished by having two epaulettes, and at the same time grenades and horns were ordered to be worn on those of the grenadier and light company officers, who did not wear wings until about 1802. Wing epaulettes, though in order, were not often worn at this time.

In 1786 espontoons were discarded by officers and they ceased to carry fusils in 1792.

From 1796 the gorget for all regiments was of gilt metal. It was suspended by ribbons of the facing colour.

The grenadier cap in 1804 had a black metal front with silver or white devices, and the red cloth cap still showed through an opening in the back part of the bearskin, which had the hairs pointing upwards.

CHAPTER IV · 1815

NAPOLEON'S SURRENDER AND INTERNMENT

After Napoleon's grand fiasco in 1813, when he led half a million men to Moscow and came back with the miserable remnant of ragged frost-bitten wretches, who were all that had escaped from the combination of Cossacks, Russian winter, wolves and starvation, the French began to tire of his exploits and, in 1814, he surrendered and was interned on the island of Elba. This prison was much too near France to hold him and, by March 1815, he had escaped and was organizing fresh trouble. (At this time a detachment of the 20th Light Dragoons (later 20*th Hussars*) was serving with the Russian army during the Moscow campaign.)

NAPOLEON'S RETURN

Napoleon very quickly collected an army of his old fanatical followers. These were mostly veterans, but were hastily organized and equipped, and took the offensive against the British and Prussians, who had assembled forces in Belgium for dealing with such an emergency. There followed the Waterloo campaign, one of the shortest in history, ending with one of the world's most decisive battles. A very short account will give an impression of the methods of fighting employed at that period.

THE OPPOSING ARMIES

The strength of the armies is interesting, showing that the fighting was on a very considerable scale, though of course not comparable with the armies of 1914 or 1939.

These are the approximate figures (which, however, vary a lot in different accounts of the campaign): Napoleon 124,000 men and 350 guns; Wellington 106,000 with 200 guns. (Of these only about 36,000 were British, most of them raw reinforcements from the Militia. The others were Dutch and Belgians, of a not too reliable quality, and some regiments of the King's German Legion from Nassau and Brunswick.) Blücher's army consisted of 113,000 infantry, 12,000 cavalry and 312 guns. The first impression is that the French were outnumbered by nearly two to one but, in addition to the quality of Wellington's troops, one has to remember that the Prussians were not present until almost the end of the main battle. Consequently, the brunt fell on the 36,000 British.

QUATRE BRAS AND LIGNY

Wellington's and Blücher's armies had separate lines of communication leading from opposite directions, the former through Ostend and Brussels and the latter from the Rhine to Liége. This and the need for billeting the troops had resulted in their being spread out over a front of about 100 miles. Napoleon calculated that either force, if attacked, would be sure to fall back on its lines of communication, which would result in a gap forming between them. His strategy was to deal in this way with the Prussians first and then the British—a plan in which he nearly succeeded.

The nodal point in the roads connecting the two armies was the cross-roads known as Quatre Bras. Accordingly on the 15th June he sent a force rapidly along the Charleroi-Brussels road to attack the Prussians, who were concentrating at Ligny, and another to Quatre Bras to hold off the British while the Prussians were being dealt with. Wellington sent up reinforcements to Quatre Bras where they encountered Kellerman's cavalry corps and two corps under Ney. Blücher was confronted by 68,000 men with 210 guns, himself having 87,000 men and 224 guns present. Though a tough and reliable old man, he was by no means a quick-witted General, and he committed one or two serious blunders which resulted in his army being driven off in disorder.

At Quatre Bras Ney, at first, had twice as many men as Wellington, but he was deceived into thinking that reserves were hidden in the woods—a normal practice of Wellington's Generals—and so was over-cautious in getting into action, wasting time while British reinforcements were rapidly arriving. At the same time D'Erlon, one of Ney's corps commanders, received an order intended for the Marshal himself, for his corps to move off and join in the attack on the Prussians. He marched off without informing Ney, but was later recalled by him, with the fortunate result that his corps spent vital hours marching and countermarching and took no part in either action. Wellington was able to beat off the French and retire, under cover of a cavalry rearguard action, towards the site he had chosen for his stand against the main French army, but his troops had suffered severe casualties.

WATERLOO. SUNDAY, 18TH JUNE 1815

The battleground conformed in every respect with Wellington's well-tested ideas, which had often been put into practice in Spain. The main position lay along a low ridge, sufficiently steep to slow down enemy cavalry and with a sunken road running across the front which would form a useful natural obstacle. A reverse slope gave cover for reserves, which could be moved unseen by the enemy. The ground on both flanks was unsuitable for cavalry, and there were three features which could be made into strong points well in advance of the main position to act as breakwaters against the enemy's attacks. These were, from left to right, Papelotte village, and two farms known as La Haye Sainte, and Hougoumont. Before the battle Wellington had sent a detached force of 17,000 men to Hal, ten miles away, to protect his lines of communication, and had with him about 63,000 men and 156 guns. Napoleon had 70,000 men present, all of one nation, which was a distinct advantage, and 224 guns which were of superior calibre and range to the British artillery.

Wellington had asked Blücher to send him two divisions, to enable him to give battle on reasonable terms and the reply had been that not only would Blücher send two divisions, but would come himself (in spite of wounds received at Ligny) with his whole army. He made one condition, which was that if the French would not attack on the 18th, then the allies should attack them on the 19th.

It was a model battle in traditional style. The British main body was formed in line on the ridge, with cavalry and reserves concealed on the rear slope, and a line of guns in front of the infantry. The gunners' rôle was to fire until the enemy were almost up to the guns, then to double back and lie down under the bayonets of the infantry. As soon as the enemy retired, as no doubt they would, they were to rush back to the guns and blast them in the rear to hasten them on their way.

At close range they double-loaded the guns with case-shot, which scattered heavy bullets from the muzzle like the shots from a sporting gun. (The earliest forms of scattering shot were 'Langridge'—a collection of nails, stones and scrap iron, later made up into 'case' or 'cannister' shot, used from about 1480 onwards, and 'grape'—nets filled with bullets, so named because it resembled bunches of grapes, which was invented about the same time. Chain and bar shot—cannon balls linked together—came in at about the same period, but were mainly used by the navy to cut the rigging of ships.)

During the night there had been torrential thunder storms, which had reduced much of the ground to a quagmire, and had beaten down the fields of standing corn into sodden matted jungles. Both armies had spent a miserable night in the open, but the British had had their rations and had been able to light fires to warm themselves, while the French had had to exist mainly on wine and had not been allowed fires. In the morning they had to wait several hours for the ground to dry to some extent before beginning their attack, otherwise they would have been bogged on the way.

The French were drawn up on a slight ridge about a mile from the British, so that the opposing armies were in full view of each other and could see the whole array being drawn up and final dispositions being made, long before the battle began. When the French advanced, however, they disappeared in the 'dead ground' below the two ridges and could not be seen until they arrived within about 150 yards.

The battle began at 11-30 with a general bombardment and a strong attack on Hougoumont, the first of many during the day. Byng's Brigade of Guards was sent to reinforce the defenders and held the farm so stubbornly that there were a thousand casualties there in the first hour. Twice the buildings were set on fire, but the French were never able to establish a footing. During the bombardment the British infantry on the ridge lay down in their ranks, and there they had to stay and 'take it', while cannon-balls and shells ploughed through them and shrapnel burst overhead.

In the next stage eighty guns concentrated on the centre of the line, and at 2 p.m. massive columns of French infantry advanced. These nearly reached the sunken road and La Haye Sainte was furiously attacked and appeared to be in danger. The 5th Division charged them with the bayonet, and the Union Brigade (*The Royals, The Scots Greys* and *The Inniskillings*) went forward and completed their disorganization, riding amongst them and cutting them down right up to the French guns on the other side of the valley. It was at this stage of the battle that the celebrated incident took place when, as *The Greys* passed through the skirmishers of a highland regiment, the excitement became too much for their fellow-Scots, some of whom seized their stirrup-leathers, holding muskets and bayonets in their free hands, and let themselves be carried forward, in a semi-airborne state, in the charge. (A similar thing happened at St. Quentin in 1914, when *The Greys* were again assisted in a charge by some highlanders.) Further on they were joined by Lord Somerset's heavy cavalry brigade which had just slashed its way through Kellerman's cuirassiers, and both men and horses reached a pitch of elation which caused them to lose formation and dash on recklessly. Thus they were caught at a disadvantage by more French cuirassiers and Jaquinot's Polish lancers, and lost very heavily before they could reorganize and return to their position behind the ridge. General Picton, commander of the 5th Division and General Ponsonby, Union Brigade, were killed in this sortie.

At four o'clock the French guns bombarded the right of the line, and as great masses of cavalry were seen advancing, our infantry formed squares. It must have been a magnificent and sinister sight as this vast number of horsemen came forward, clad in all the colours of heraldry, with glinting steel and fluttering standards, trumpet-calls regulating their speed from the walk to the trot, gallop, and finally the charge. Our men watched them moving off until they disappeared in the valley, eventually arriving with their horses blown by the steepness of the ridge and the heavy going. The gunners let drive almost in a volley and blew gaps in their ranks, leaving trails of mutilated men and horses strewn on the slope.

They came on regardless, plunged through the sunken road and advanced resolutely into the smoke in front of the line of guns. The gunners doubled back to the cover of the bayonets. Then with rhythmic shattering crashes, volleys burst from the front of the squares, men and horses fell in scores and dismounted men ran to secure the terrified and riderless animals which careered wildly about the battlefield. With fierce determination the survivors reached the squares, only to find that neither men nor horses could penetrate the steady immovable lines of bayonets. The squares became like small islands, nearly submerged in a sea of milling horsemen, each invisible to the next, so that no one could tell how things were going with his neighbours. The French rode round and round making valiant efforts to find weak spots until, in the end, the strain became too much for human endurance, and when the British cavalry galloped on to the scene, they had become a confused mass, unable to resist, and were driven headlong down the hill.

Time after time they reformed and repeated their efforts, but the squares were dogged and rock-like, the results were no better and there seemed to be no end to their hopeless task.

In the final stages of these attacks, which continued for two hours, Marshal Ney led 77 squadrons, consisting of 12,000 horsemen—probably the largest mass of cavalry which ever took part in one charge. About two-thirds of them were killed or wounded.

Prussian troops now began to appear in the distance on the French right, and Napoleon's anxiety increased with the realization that his last chance of world conquest was strictly limited in time.

Another great infantry attack surged right up to the line. La Haye Sainte was taken and the position at Hougoumont was critical. But the British line stood firm, though the dead and wounded lay thick on the ground and the closing of many gaps had shortened the front of each battalion. Their volleys were still as effective and the bayonets still as menacing. Eventually the mass of Frenchmen fell into confusion and retired, hastened by heavy fire from the guns, and leaving the ridge still more thickly littered with bodies.

To Napoleon the strain was becoming intolerable. The Prussians were getting nearer and he constantly had to detach more troops to protect his right, while on the ridge in front the British line, which according to his reckoning ought to have been shattered, stood silently and menacingly awaiting his next move.

It was now or never. He made his last effort, by sending forward the Imperial Guards, his most trusted veterans, who had never yet failed him. He had kept them in reserve until the last and felt confident that by now the British must be nearly exhausted and that they would turn the scale. They came up the slope in grand style, preceded by skirmishers, with drums beating, Colours flying and their tall bearskin caps correctly aligned, as if on parade. There were two heavy columns of the 'Moyenne Guard' (not the 'old Guard', as has frequently been stated), one of them led by Marshal Ney. This determined assault was, without doubt, the critical point of the whole battle.

It looked like 'touch and go' when Colonel Sir John Colborne, commanding the *52nd Light Infantry* in Adam's Brigade, decided on his own initiative to abandon defensive tactics. He led the 52nd forward in a thin two-deep line against the seemingly victorious mass of French Guards, who had already forced back a part of the British line, and left-inclined his right wing so as to bring fire on to their left flank as well as their front. The 52nd then charged with the bayonet and routed the whole column, which was then pursued by the brigade. Thus Colborne was actually the originator of the forward movement which ended the battle, and he, with the 52nd, probably played a decisive part in history. (Almost a hundred years later, on 11th November 1914, at Nonneboschen Wood, the 52nd performed a similar feat, when at the crisis of the first battle of Ypres, about 350 of them decisively defeated 800 Prussian Guards.)

The other column of the Imperial Guard was dealt with in equally successful manner by Maitland's Brigade of Guards. On reaching the crest they were astounded at seeing nothing before them except a few mounted officers (of whom Wellington was one), apparently engaged in casual conversation and partly hidden by smoke. Suddenly there was a shout of 'Up, Guards!' and the line rose as one man, fired a volley, and were into them with the bayonet before they had recovered from their surprise. And so Napoleon's finest troops, and his last hope, followed the well-marked route—down the slope, in complete disorder and in full view of the whole French army. (To commemorate their distinguished part in this decisive defeat of the French Grenadiers of the Guard, the 1st Foot Guards were given their present title of *The Grenadier Guards*.)

The Prussians had by now made contact with Wellington, and the knowledge of this, coming simultaneously with the rout of the Imperial Guard, broke the nerve of the French troops. With the exception of one or two battalions of the Guard who stood firm until they were almost exterminated, the whole army panicked and quickly degenerated into a flying rabble, into which the British cavalry dashed like terriers chasing rats.

Then at about 8 o'clock, when the sun was setting on this grim shambles, came the welcome order: 'The whole line will advance,' and the tattered, smoke-blackened, and bloodstained regiments moved off with a cheerful step, knowing that they had done as good a job as any in the annals of the British Army.

The ridge was an amazing sight when they left it, covered from end to end with the sinister debris of battle and to give only one instance, where a battalion of *The East Lancashire Regiment* had stood, there remained a clearly defined square, marked out by the bodies of casualties. Wellington once remarked, when viewing such a scene, 'There is only one thing worse than a great victory, and that is a great defeat'.

The pursuit of the French was left to the Prussians, who hunted and slaughtered them all through the night, in their pitiless German way, and they must have suffered all the horrors of utter defeat.

The night on the battlefield was also pretty grim, and an officer wrote home that his regiment bivouacked among scenes of desolation, with the groans of the wounded breaking into their sleep. There was only a very sketchy medical service, quite inadequate for this sort of thing, and the only anaesthetic was alcohol, if obtainable, so it is not hard to imagine the condition of the wounded. All water within three miles, he said, was contaminated with blood to the colour of wine and, had he not been able to procure a little straw to sleep on, which showed that he was actively alive, he would certainly have been robbed by the bands of human vultures who were looting the dead and wounded alike.

Napoleon made one unavailing effort in the early morning, far from the battlefield, to rally some of his demoralized troops, and then made for Paris, where he tried to organize resistance to the advancing allies. This was cut short by his being forced to abdicate by the Chamber of Deputies, and he then made an attempt to escape to America, which was frustrated. Finally he surrendered on 9th July to the Captain of H.M.S. *Bellerophon*, and in October was removed to St. Helena, where he was detained until his death.

Wellington's army had 15,000 casualties, mostly British, many regiments losing 50 per cent of officers and men, the Prussians lost about 7,000 and the French about half their total strength, though, in the confusion of their débâcle, their casualties were never properly recorded.

This was the dramatic climax of a war which had lasted twenty years. The menace to Europe was at last removed and a long spell of peace followed. How many men lost their lives as the result of Napoleon's entry into world affairs, will probably never be known, but like the Kaiser and Hitler, he must have slain his millions.

(*Note:* Carrier pigeons are said to have been used at Waterloo, not by the army, but for speculative reasons by a well-known financier, who was thus able to receive private information of the result about two days before the official report arrived by horse and sailing ship. He was then able to spread a false account and manipulate the stock market to his advantage.

Another incidental point, which is interesting, is that officers and men who took part in the battle, were allowed to count two years' additional service.)

PLATE IX

(18)

1800–15

The
Royal Horse
Artillery

Driver, 1815

The Bank
Volunteers

Private, 1804

The
21st or Royal
North British
Fuzileers.
Now the
Royal Scots
Fusiliers

Fuzileer, 1805

The 11th
Light
Dragoons.
Now the 11th
Hussars

Trooper, 1800

The 3rd
Dragoon
Guards

Trooper, 1805

(19)

The Corps of
Royal Sappers
and Miners

Sapper, 1805

The Royal
Marines

Marine, 1805

The 1st
Foot Guards.
Now the
Grenadier
Guards

*Grenadier (full
dress)*, 1815

The 83rd
Regiment.
Now the Royal
Ulster Rifles

Corporal, 1815

The 93rd
Regiment.
Now the
Argyll and
Sutherland
Highlanders

Grenadier, 1815

(20)

The 2nd
(or Royal
North British)
Dragoons.
Now the Royal
Scots Greys

Trooper, 1811

The 10th
Hussars

Trooper, 1815

The 2nd
Life Guards

Trooper, 1815

The 9th
Light Dragoons.
Later the 9th
Lancers

Trooper, 1815

The King's
Dragoon
Guards

Trooper, 1815

PLATE IX

Figs. 18, 19 & 20

PLATE IX (18, 19, 20) THE NAPOLEONIC WARS. 1800–15

Cavalry and Horse Artillery

The wars of this period produced a good many changes in dress, most of which were designed to increase efficiency and aid mobility. Service dress became quite different from full dress, the latter being worn only for ceremonial parades at home until about 1816. After that date service dress was abolished in the belief that the last great war had been fought!

Wellington was not a stickler for parade uniforms on service and said he did not care what his men wore, as long as they could fight efficiently. He himself was usually as much as possible in undress, wearing a blue frock-coat and an exceptionally small cocked hat, minus feathers. But as far as the regiments were concerned it was a point of honour and of regimental discipline to keep the men smartly dressed, even under the most difficult conditions.

Cavalry dress had many alterations in 1811, when they were put into service dress. The cocked hat and the fur-crested light dragoon helmet (said to be almost the only purely English head-dress at that time) disappeared, and were replaced by the helmets, etc., shown in Plate IX (20). The one worn by the Life Guard is a development of the early light dragoon helmet, Plate V (13), with a Romanesque tendency, and that of the K.D.G. is similar to the pattern worn by the French cuirassiers until 1914. The light dragoon's shako anticipated the universal pattern, which was to come in after Waterloo. The grenadier cap of *The Greys* originated from Ramillies (1706). After that battle they wore French grenadier caps which they had captured there, until, some time later, they were granted the privilege of wearing British grenadier caps permanently.

A short-skirted jacket with a front laced as shown, and with plain pointed cuffs, gave a more workmanlike appearance. Light dragoons wore one with wide lapels, not unlike the plastrons of lancers, which came in about half a century later.

The striped girdle was more decorative than useful, as the leather sword belt, 2¾ inches wide, had to be worn under or over it until about 1827, when the girdle was discontinued by the heavy cavalry.

In 1811 overalls (which had been worn for several years) were officially sanctioned. They were worn over breeches and knee-boots, until 1822 when these were abolished, and had buttons or hooks all the way up the sides. This explains why, in modern full dress, a pair of cavalry trousers has the rather unexpected name of overalls, but there is still some justification for it, as they are worn over the half-boots which were named after the 'Iron Duke'. At this period overalls were of various colours—grey, blue-grey, dark brown and wine colour, and the stripes on them were varied by several orders, being sometimes of facing colour, and sometimes yellow or white, regardless of the facings.

Another change in 1811 was the conversion of four light dragoon regiments to Hussars, in imitation of Hungarian light cavalry. This involved the introduction of the busby, the pelisse, the barrelled sash and the wearing of moustaches. The 10th had been the first regiment to begin this change, having one troop of hussars some time before this, but they were not new in continental armies and the Duke of Cumberland, in about 1745, had imported one or two German hussars to use as orderlies. Our own light dragoons (from 1756 on) were sometimes referred to as hussars.

One other innovation about 1811 was the *sabretache*, a leather wallet suspended from the sword belt, which was worn by all ranks of cavalry until 1834, when troopers of heavy cavalry and of lancer regiments ceased to wear them. At this time heavy cavalry carried straight swords and light regiments had curved scimitars. The old swivel carbine belt, with ammunition pouch worn at the back, was still in use, and on service a folded blanket under the saddle now replaced the 'housing' or 'shabracque'.

The Royal Horse Artillery did not change their style of helmet and shell jacket, but continued to be dressed as light dragoons were before 1811, with their own pattern of cording on the front of the jacket.

Infantry, R.A., R.E., Royal Marines (18, 19)

In February 1800, the infantry, below the rank of Field Officer, took to the 'stovepipe' felt shako, which was light and comfortable and did not get in the way when firing, or catch in the bushes, or get blown off, like the huge cocked hat it replaced.

It was in turn superseded, in 1812, by the Waterloo shako, which had a leather plate in front, rather reminiscent of the style of the old grenadier cap before 1768. This was one of the most soldierly looking head-dresses the army has ever worn. The cords and hackles were green for light infantry, white for grenadiers, and battalion companies had white cords and red and white hackles.

The button-up jacket dating from 1796, but with short skirt from about 1802, retained regimental differences in the spacing of buttons and the shape of the lace buttonholes, which were either flat, pointed, or diamond-shaped at the ends.

Only the grenadier companies of the Guards wore bearskin caps, as in the Line regiments, and these appear not to have been worn on foreign service. The Flank companies of all regiments wore grenades or horns on their wing epaulettes, a custom which is still continued by light infantry and fusilier regiments.

Highlanders wore the ordinary short jacket and an ostrich-feather bonnet with short tails, the number of which varied according to the regiment. This had gradually developed from a tartan Balmoral, which in the early eighteenth century was decorated with a small bearskin tuft, and later with feathers of various kinds. Lowland Scottish regiments at this period were usually dressed like English Line regiments.

In 1808 hair powder and queues or clubs were abolished, and the order was acted on with such delighted alacrity that when a countermanding order came the next day it was too late for it to have any effect. Short hair and small side whiskers were now the order.

In 1811 trousers and short grey spats were officially sanctioned for active service—not very suitable for mud and wet, but much more comfortable than tight knee-breeches and gaiters. The latter were, however, kept for full-dress parades at home until 1821. In the West Indies and at other tropical stations the differences in dress were: no waistcoats, scanty linings, white cotton 'trowzer-breeches' (very like jodhpurs), and white cap covers.

N.C.O.s' chevrons, for all arms, though they had been worn for several years in some units, were not officially sanctioned until July 1802. A Sergeant-Major had four, a Sergeant three, and a Corporal two.

The Royal Marine is shown in the uniform worn at Trafalgar (21st October 1805), with a varnished naval hat, laced like a bishop's.

The Foot Artillery and *The Royal Sappers and Miners* were dressed and equipped like infantry, and their jackets, from 1813, were the reverse of one another as regards the red and blue. The yellow braid and diamond-shaped, or 'bastion', loops were a distinctive feature of both. The Sappers wore blue coats (of a similar cut) for a few years until 1813, when they asked to revert to red so as not to be picked out by the enemy when working with infantry. A sapper would have had a plain square buckle in place of the breast-plate, which was worn by officers and sergeants.

Numerous additional regiments of Volunteers or Fencibles were raised for home defence during the Napoleonic wars, and they seem to have more or less selected their own uniforms. The Bank Volunteer is wearing an out-of-date type of jacket, similar to that worn by light infantry before 1796, and a light dragoon helmet of about 1795 pattern, with a turned-up brim like a bowler (which was worn by light companies for a few years), but he has not the wing epaulettes which one would expect to see with it.

PLATE X

1811–12

The 8th Light Dragoons. Later 8th Hussars

Officer, 1811

The 45th or The Nottinghamshire Regiment. Now The Sherwood Foresters

Officer, 1812

The 3rd Foot Guards. Now the Scots Guards

Sergeant (full dress), 1812

The 60th or Royal American Regiment. Now The King's Royal Rifle Corps

Rifleman, 1812

The 20th or East Devonshire Regiment. Now the Lancashire Fusiliers

Fifer, 1812

PLATE X

PLATE X. 1811–12

The uniforms shown, with the exception of that of the Guards Sergeant, are 'service dress'. In full dress the coat with long tails was worn by all, including light dragoons, with white breeches. Infantry officers wore white stockings and buckled shoes, and other ranks wore black gaiters.

Several regiments of light dragoons serving in tropical climates at this period had a lightweight shell jacket of French grey material. The 8th were in India from 1802 to 1822, where they had a great deal of active service against the Mahrattas, the Nepalese, etc., and earned the battle honours of 'Leswaree' and 'Hindustan'. A peculiar tapering shako, with a peak which could be turned up, was worn in service dress by cavalry regiments, from 1809 to 1812. The spiral fringe is the edge of a 'wing' which, when unwound, hung down like the tail of an Indian's puggaree, and reached below the waist. On the inner side it was red, blue, etc., according to the regiment. In 1811 the light dragoons' uniform was completely changed, and the new one is illustrated in Plate IX (20).

The 45th Foot was one of three regiments which served throughout the Peninsular War, from 1808 to 1814, and on account of their doggedness and excellent work at Talavera they became known as 'The old stubborns'. The light infantry jacket was now worn as service dress by all infantry and with the short skirts the pockets, originally placed horizontally on the hips, were moved to a slanting position at the back. Later, on the coatee, and the tunic (which still survives) they were placed vertically on the skirts. The front of the jacket was similar to that of the coat shown in Plate VIII, but it was now usually worn with the lapels turned back only about three buttons from the top. Officers' shakos were decorated with gold and crimson plaited cords and tassels.

In 1810 officers were ordered to wear the following badges of rank: Field Officers—two fringed epaulettes, with a crown and a star to denote a Colonel, a crown for a Lieutenant-Colonel, and a star for a Major. Captains and Subalterns wore one epaulette on the right shoulder, with no badge of rank. Officers of Flank companies—two wing epaulettes, each bearing a horn or a grenade, for the light and grenadier companies respectively. (From 1809 to 1829 ordinary fringed epaulettes were worn on top of the wings by field officers of light infantry and fusiliers.) An adjutant wore one epaulette on the right shoulder and a plain shoulder-strap on the left.

The Guards, when in full dress, wore full-length white spatterdashes, and white stocks. Otherwise their dress was similar to that of Line regiments. The 3rd Guards served in the Peninsula and at Waterloo.

The 60th had a large number of battalions, several of which were 'Rifle Corps' or had Rifle companies. The Baker rifle was much shorter than the

'Brown Bess' smooth-bore, and was about the length of the S.M.L.E. rifle of the twentieth century. Sword bayonets were carried by Rifle Corps, and their green jackets, black equipment, and moustaches gave them quite a different appearance from the rest of the army. (The only other Rifle regiment was the 95th, now *The Rifle Brigade*.) The motto of the 60th, 'Celer et Audax' (Swift and Daring), describes their rôle at this period, as specially trained mobile skirmishing troops. Sergeants of Rifles and light infantry were armed with rifles and bayonets and did not carry halberds, or swords, and officers were armed with swords and small pistols.

Bandsmen wore coats of facing colour (with the exceptions mentioned in the notes on Plate V (12), until 1812, but the lacing had been standardized and more nearly resembled that on a private's coat, the numerous chevrons on the sleeves being worn or not, as the Commanding Officer decided. They wore wing epaulettes, and their full-dress head-gear was the grenadier cap. A short sword, with a blade about 24 inches long, was their special weapon. The fife case was carried on the right hip, attached to the cross-belt. The 20th, though not a fusilier regiment until 1881, were given the nickname of 'the Young Fuzileers' in the Peninsula, when they were brigaded with the *7th* and *23rd Fusiliers*.

CHAPTER V · 1816-54

During the Napoleonic wars our army had been in contact, friendly or otherwise, with most of the armies of Europe, and some innovations resulted from the study of their methods.

HUSSARS

On 18th April 1811, the 7th, 10th, 15th, and 18th Light Dragoon Regiments were converted into regiments of hussars, in imitation of Hungarian light cavalry. The word comes from *usz* = twenty, the Hungarian system being that one out of twenty men had to serve and be provided for by the other nineteen civilians. The change, however, does not seem to have affected much except dress and for many years the title, 'Hussars', appeared only in brackets after the original names of the regiments.

LANCERS

In 1816 some other light dragoon regiments were made into lancers, as the lance had been found an effective weapon when used against us by the Poles, in Spain and at Waterloo. They adopted Polish lancer caps and the loose trousers worn by the Poles. These appear to have had an oriental origin, as they resembled Mahommedan 'pyjamas', slightly modified. The lance had not been used by us since the Civil War, and the first regiment to use it again in action was the 16*th Lancers*, at Aliwal, in the Sikh War, 1846. From this date all the remaining light dragoon regiments were, at different times, made into lancers or hussars.

WAR-TIME SOLDIERS AND EMERGENCY COMMISSIONS, 1815.

One important fact has to be remembered regarding the regular army, which is that though regiments have remained in existence from as far back as 1660, the usual practice was to neglect them in peace-time and not keep them up to strength, with the result that, when they had to take the field, they were often composed largely of half-trained recruits hastily rounded-up when a crisis impended. Waterloo was no exception to this rule, as most of the Peninsular veterans had, in the short interval, been either disbanded or sent overseas. It appears, too, that the officer shortage must have been equally acute and that something similar to the granting of 'Emergency' commissions occurred, as the following incident shows. At Waterloo an officer, described as 'an amateur to the battlefield', picked up a piece of a buff regimental Colour, and seeing Colonel Tidy of the 14th Foot, now *The West Yorkshire Regiment*, innocently inquired if he had lost it. The Colonel, one of the old school, who took life rather seriously, was just able to reply, with temperature rising to boiling point, 'Lost a Colour? NO, sir! The 14th NEVER lose their Colours', and rode off at speed to avoid complete loss of his self-control. As a further instance of temporary commissions, at one time during the bad days of recruiting a commission was given free to any man who brought in a hundred recruits.

RECRUITING POSTERS

As regards recruiting, those who marvel at the salesmanship of modern recruiting advertisements—'No fares to work', etc., might like to compare this. From a poster for *The King's Dragoon Guards*, at the time of the Napoleonic wars:

> '*Any young man who is desirous to make a Figure in Life, and wishes to quit a dull and laborious Retirement in the Country, has now an Opportunity of entering at once into that glorious State of Ease and Independence which he cannot fail to enjoy in The King's Dragoon Guards. The Superior Comforts and Advantages of a Dragoon in this regiment need only be made known to be generally coveted.*'

It goes on to say:

> '*As recruits are now flocking in from all quarters, no Time is to be lost,*' and '*N.B.—This regiment is supposed to be mounted on the most beautiful, fine, active black Geldings this country has ever produced,*' and finally, '*The bringer of a good recruit will receive a reward of three guineas.*'

This poster was by no means outstandingly verbose, some even spoke of 'Heroes' required. The last sentence was perhaps a little naïve, but can anyone say that we were 'masters of understatement' in those days?

After Waterloo the usual parsimonious reaction set in and everything connected with the army was 'cut to the bone', its total strength being reduced to 101,000 at home and overseas.

PRIVATE THOMAS ATKINS, BIRTH OF

The celebrated Thomas Atkins was 'born' about this time, and is reputed to have served in the 23rd (*The Royal Welch Fusiliers*). There is no actual proof that he ever existed, but it appears that he was either a man well-known to General Sir Harry Calvert, who had served in the 23rd—possibly his batman; or he was invented by him. When Calvert was Adjutant-General at the War Office in 1815, he drew up a specimen of a new Army Book, which was the forerunner of A.B.64, and filled in the blanks with particulars of Private Thomas Atkins, No. 6 Company, 1st Battalion, 23rd Regiment of Foot, born at Odiham, Hants. This was circulated to all units, and T.A. therefore became a sort of 'unknown soldier' (though very much alive) for about a hundred years.

BAD CONDITIONS AFTER THE WARS

Conditions at this time were definitely bad. Barracks were overcrowded and insanitary, cooking was bad, pay was bad, and there was no recreation except beer. The men were only supplied with two meals a day, at 7.30 and 12.30, and the canteens were usually run by racketeers, who sold bad 'swipes' at outrageous prices. Many commanding officers (in direct opposition to Sir John Moore's teaching) thought the only effective method of maintaining discipline was to use the utmost severity in dealing out floggings.

'GOING TO THE HALBERDS'

Some of the old nicknames of regiments, e.g. 'The Steelbacks' (*The Northamptonshire Regiment*) and the 'Bendovers' (*The Manchester Regiment*), besides demonstrating the soldiers' sense of humour, are evidence of the prevalence of the punishment of 'going to the halberds'. According to some reports the method of administering it was not without its grim humour. Three of the sergeants' halberds were used to erect a tripod, with a fourth one fixed horizontally, to which the victim was tied, and the following procedure, reminiscent of the old woman in the nursery tale, who tried to drive her pig over a stile, was said to have been used. A drummer beat the offender. The Drum-Major stood behind him and the Adjutant behind the Drum-Major. Both were armed with canes—the former to beat the drummer, and the latter to take a cut at the Drum-Major, if the punishment was not being given satisfactorily. But the infliction of this punishment was sometimes a horrific performance. A cat-of-nine-tails was used and enormous numbers of lashes could be given, which literally flayed the man's back. It was not unusual for young soldiers on parade to faint or vomit at the sight.

UNPOPULARITY WITH CIVILIANS

There was great economic distress in the country and until 1829, when a proper police system was established, the troops were always called out to deal with any civil disturbances, and were therefore not popular among civilians. It is not surprising, therefore, that the best type of man did not join the army voluntarily. Those who did were, more often than not, 'down and outs', or men with bad records. Nevertheless the great majority in time became good soldiers and very seldom did the country any discredit abroad.

JUNGLE AND BUSH WARFARE

Owing to the depressed conditions of everything at home, resulting from the wars, there was a considerable amount of emigration to Canada, South Africa, and New Zealand (which had been annexed by Captain Cook in 1769.) The resulting complications between settlers of different races and natives led to some small military expeditions which provided experience of new types of fighting.

The New Zealand War, in 1845, required a new technique as the Maoris possessed considerable cunning. They would construct a 'pa', or tree-trunk stockade, which could only be dealt with by using artillery fire to breach it, and during the bombardment, they would hide in holes in the ground. When the 'pa' was considered ready for assault, they merely fled into the jungle where, miles away, they would have another 'pa' secretly prepared and ready for occupation, which meant that the laborious process of transporting guns and supplies through trackless forest had to begin all over again. They were armed with American rifles and gave quite a lot of trouble before the problem was settled.

The Cape War of 1850–2 must have had quite a modern aspect, as fighting took place, against the Kaffirs, in hill and forest country which was subject to tropical rains. Uniforms wore out in a very short time and the training given at home was found to be quite unsuitable. The result was that the men were dressed in suits of nondescript colour and had to learn bush warfare. The Brunswick percussion rifle, used in this campaign by the *The King's Royal Rifle Corps*, still had the old difficulty about loading. The barrel had two grooves and the ball had a 'belt' which was supposed to fit easily into them. In practice it took so long to load that each man was issued with a few rounds of smooth-bore ammunition for emergencies.

THE 'BIRKENHEAD'

Although the Kaffir War was not very memorable, there was an incident arising out of it which will not be forgotten.

In February 1852, a steam troopship, named the *Birkenhead*, with reinforcements for South Africa, struck a rock at Danger Point, a few miles from Simonstown, during the night. Instead of keeping her head up against the rock, the captain put her in reverse, with the result that the hole was enlarged and water rushed in at alarming speed, drowning many in troop decks and cabins.

There were families on board and the number of boats was quite inadequate to take the men as well, so the troops were paraded on deck, and those detailed to work the pumps, organize the families, etc., carried out their duties without the smallest hitch, while the remainder stood in their ranks.

The real test came after the boats had gone, and when only the after half of the ship remained, sinking rapidly. The captain then gave the order, 'Every man for himself', but the men, being properly trained soldiers, waited to be dismissed by their officers. Instead, two of them—Lieutenant Girardot, of the 43*rd Light Infantry*, and Captain Wright, of the 91st, now *The Argyll and Sutherland Highlanders*, at once addressed them, pointing out that the already overloaded boats would capsize if they swam out and tried to board them, and asking them to stay where they were.

Not a man moved until the ship sank under them, and out of 638 on board, 454 were drowned, but all the women and children were saved.

Only a very small number of men survived by clinging to the masts after the ship sank, and then swimming several miles through shark-infested water.

Napier wrote of these men: '... the records of the world furnish no parallel to this self-devotion', and the King of Prussia considered their discipline so admirable, that he ordered an account of the incident to be read out to every regiment in his army.

INDIA

These campaigns were, however, of a very minor nature compared with the far more important events which were taking place in India. In that country there was still a number of large Native States over which we held no actual control, and there was always the menace of the Afghans and frontier Pathans, whose natural occupation was fighting and who used to descend periodically from their desert hills into the plains to raid and to loot the less warlike and better-provided inhabitants. There was nearly always a small war going on in some part of India and there is not space here to mention them all.

BHARTPUR, 1824

The Indians were long experienced (with the aid of various Europeans) in constructing walled towns and massive fortresses, such as those still existing at Attock, Agra, Gwalior, and many others. There was one of these at Bhartpur in Rajputana, which Lord Lake had unsuccessfully tried to take in 1805. It was afterwards used as a challenge to British prestige and, after fresh insults arising from a usurpation of the throne of the Jat state, preceded by the usual intrigues and mysterious deaths, it was decided that action must be taken.

Siege artillery had to be brought from Agra and the usual procedure of sapping and bombardment was carried out but, so massive were the walls and bastions that this was insufficient, and mines were laid, to be exploded when the troops were in position for the final assault. First, two small mines went up, which brought the Jats crowding to the walls to meet the attack. Then came the show-piece, a mine containing 10,000 lb. of powder, which blew hundreds of them into the air. It was even more effective than *The Royal Engineers* anticipated, as the debris came down over the stormers' trenches and killed or wounded about twenty men.

Two storming parties, composed of the 59th Regiment (now *2nd Battalion East Lancashire Regiment*) and native troops, entered the fortress and eventually converged, both driving large numbers of Jats before them, on each side of a sixty-foot-deep nullah. Several hundred of the Jats fell backwards into it, forming a great pile at the bottom. Some wore cotton quilted armour, which in the very close fighting had caught sparks from the firing and had begun to smoulder, and as they lay injured in the nullah it burst into flames and set fire to the clothes of others, so that many, unable to move, were roasted in this pit of sorrow.

During the siege 'sharpshooters' were used to watch for any Jat who showed himself, and some time before the assault the women and children were evacuated through the British lines at the suggestion of Lord Combermere, the British C.-in-C.

The siege cost the British 569 casualties, but the effect in prestige was very satisfactory, as the natives had firmly believed that the place was absolutely impregnable.

AFGHANISTAN, 1842

The Afghan war of 1839–42, after a number of successful actions, produced one of our worst exhibitions of mismanagement, and resulted in the massacre of 4,500 troops and 12,000 camp followers—a column withdrawing from Kabul, which was attacked in the Khurd–Kabul Pass, at Jagdalak, and finally at Gandamak. The numbers of camp followers give some idea of the inefficient methods which must have been employed, and it seems that the column marched trustingly through narrow passes without taking the normal precaution of securing the heights on either side. The only British regiment in the column was the 44th Foot (now the 1*st Battalion Essex Regiment*), which was totally annihilated. There were practically no witnesses of what happened, as only one man, Dr. Bryden, escaped, but it is easy to imagine the panic of the followers spreading to the sepoys, the shooting-up, the knifing and looting and the customary mutilation of the bodies. It was the worst disaster we ever experienced in the East—until Singapore.

DEFENCE OF JELLALABAD, 1842

The British soldier has always risen to the occasion when such catastrophes have occurred, and in this case the contrast was provided and our self-respect was restored by the 13th Foot or *The Somerset Light Infantry*. They were holding Jellalabad, a frontier fort of the usual kind, built of mud bricks with a walled camp and village round it, when Dr. Bryden, after enduring great hardships, tottered in on a half-dead horse. His news left no doubt that they would soon be attacked by the victorious Afghans, and they had not long to wait before they were assailed on all sides by thousands of these fanatical warriors, who were now full of confidence and expecting to perpetrate another massacre. The 13th held on against repeated assaults, regardless of the fact that while the battle, which lasted about three weeks, was in progress, over a hundred earthquake shocks nearly demolished the fort. In the end the Afghans wore themselves out and, at the psychological moment, the 13th came out of the ruins and routed them with great slaughter. The regiment received special thanks from the Government of India, and was granted the title 'Prince Albert's', and the mural crown above the horn in the badge with the word 'Jellalabad'. As they marched down into the Punjab, on change of station, all the garrisons turned out in their honour. (This regiment has two other unique distinctions. It is the only non-'Royal' regiment to wear blue facings, and its sergeants wear their sashes over the left shoulder as officers used to, in memory of the battle of Culloden, where all the officers became casualties and the remaining sergeants brought the regiment out of action.)

After the disaster to the Kabul column, an avenging expedition had to be sent again to Kabul, where punishment was inflicted and the war was ended more or less satisfactorily.

MEANEE, 1843

The Scinde war produced a battle at Meanee, which gives the reverse side of the picture from the Afghan disaster. The British, with 3,000 men, composed of the 22nd Foot, now *The Cheshire Regiment*, some Bombay infantry, and the 9th Bengal Cavalry, attacked a force of 30,000 Baluchis, which had entrenched in a nullah. There was fierce and prolonged volleying and a lot of very obstinate hand-to-hand fighting, but the enemy could not manœuvre in the confined space at their disposal and in spite of their most manful efforts with sword and shield and *banduq*, supported by artillery, they lost 7,000 men and were eventually hopelessly defeated. They were good fighters, who afterwards took their place among the recruiting classes for the Indian Army (as did the Jats), and had they not made the blunder of concentrating in the nullah, the British, with odds of ten to one against, would have stood a poor chance of success. This campaign resulted in the annexation of Scinde. The sardonic pun 'Peccavi' (I have sinned) has been attributed to Napier himself, but this is unlikely for he was a soldier from the age of eleven and 'had little Latin and less Greek'. It is possible that Outram was the originator as it well expresses his feelings about the Scinde campaign.

THE SIKHS

In 1845 a really serious war began against the Sikhs of the Punjab, one of the most warlike and efficient peoples in India, who have since become so well-known in the Indian Army. They are not a race, but followers of a military religion and every Sikh's name ends in Singh, which means lion. They were brought up to believe that soldiering is the most honourable calling in life, and as they were men of fine athletic physique and had inspired considerable awe among the classes of natives then enlisted as sipahis by John Company, they were definitely a formidable enemy. They had an army of 60,000 at the beginning of the war, trained by French and Italian officers and organized on the same lines as the Company's regiments, uniformed in red and blue and well equipped, with a large and efficient corps of artillery. Their weakest point was their leaders, who were not very clever, were slow in making decisions, and sometimes not sufficiently resolute. The Sikhs began the war by marching into British territory with the idea of looting Delhi.

FEROZESHAH, 1845

The first battles were at Mudki and at Ferozeshah, where the enemy under Lal Singh proved themselves almost the equal of the British troops and very nearly too much for the sipahis and strenuous fighting went on for hours, with many casualties but no appreciable result. The 3rd Light Dragoons, later the *3rd Hussars*, made a very successful charge, right through the Sikh batteries, which was the outstanding incident of the day, but still did not decide the issue. Night came on with both sides severely battered, but neither giving way, and after fighting on by starlight for an hour or two, the two armies bivouacked a short distance apart. Next morning General Gough surprised the Sikhs by an attack on their camp at first light, drove them out and took their guns, stores and baggage.

The British were by now exhausted and had scarcely any ammunition left, when another large Sikh army appeared, and during the afternoon made repeated efforts to retake the village of Ferozeshah. Their commander, Tej Singh, however, had not the determination of Lal Singh, and when he saw the 3rd Light Dragoons preparing to charge, he gave up hope and his whole army followed his example, broke into chaos and decamped, leaving 73 guns and all their stores. He evidently had not realized that the British had been forty hours without food or water, in terrific heat and clouds of dust and in action most of the time. Both men and horses were in such a state that it was out of the question to attempt a pursuit.

During these forty hours much had hung in the balance, but the final result was a most important achievement. The two Sikh forces had numbered about 60,000, while the British were only about 18,000 strong. Had Tej Singh arrived on the scene earlier or, when he did arrive, if he had been more persistent against the worn-out troops who were practically down to their last round and whose guns could not fire at all, the result might have been different. This is one of many instances where a totally unexpected factor, or a piece of extraordinary luck, has intervened in battle to upset all normal calculations and decide the fate of armies.

AN OFFICER'S EXPERIENCE

While these two battles were being fought, Captain Biddulph, an officer of the 45th Bengal Native Infantry, had a view of events from the enemy's side. He was on his way by road from Amballa to Ferozepur, with the country, as far as he knew, in a state of peace, when at Mudki his party suddenly encountered the Sikh invading army which carried him off as a prisoner.

He was taken before Lal Singh, who asked if he would accept a commission with the Sikhs, and on his refusing he was stripped of his uniform and chained under a gun, where he remained for three days and nights, during which the battle of Mudki was fought. His gun does not appear to have actually opened fire, but the gunners stood to with lighted port-fires, ready to let drive. The Sikhs, all this time, were anxious to dispatch him, but the gunners, who were Mohammedans, for some reason protected him.

The day after Mudki he noticed a considerable deterioration in the arrogant manner of the Sikhs, and he was sent for and released. To protect him on his way, the C.R.A. sent two of his Mohammedan gunners to escort him to the British lines, where he duly arrived, clad only in a 'long red garment'.

The story ends satisfactorily as the benefactors were suitably rewarded by the Sirkar, and the son of one of them remained a friend of later generations of the family until shortly before 1914, and always visited any of them who were serving in his district.

ALIWAL, 1846

More battles followed at Sobraon, and at Aliwal where the *16th Lancers* carried off the honours of the day. There is a story that they repeatedly charged the Sikh infantry and guns without being able to make any serious impression, and that after this rather disturbing lack of success someone in the 16th had the idea of changing the lances over to the left hands, which small stratagem so upset the enemy that the last charge completely broke them up.

Some idea of the fighting spirit of the Sikhs is given by the fact that when their infantry were charged by cavalry, instead of adopting the usual defensive tactics, they would quite often rush forward to meet them with the bayonet. But besides being brave, they were cunning, and thought out special tactics of their own, one of which was to form triangles to receive cavalry, the apex facing the enemy, so as to give the smallest possible target to charge at, while the men on both sides could concentrate their fire. If the cavalry broke in, which was not easy, there was still the solid base of the triangle with which to deal. If things became too hot they would lie flat and let the horses pass over them (as the Arabs did later in the Sudan), rising immediately afterwards to shoot the cavalrymen in the back.

SOBRAON, 1846

At Sobraon the Sikhs made the mistake of constructing an entrenched position with the Sutlej river close behind them. They were eventually forced back by a bayonet charge, and the *3rd Light Dragoons*, after riding in single file, led by Sir Joseph Thackwell, through gaps blown in the defences by *The Sappers*, and then forming up just behind 30,000 Sikhs, drove the whole mass down to the river. Here they crowded, in their haste, on to a bridge of small boats, which capsized under the weight of bodies. Ten thousand were killed, mostly in the river, by grapeshot fired by *The Horse Artillery*, and they lost all their guns. The British losses were 317 killed, and 2,053 wounded. The 10th Foot, now *The Royal Lincolnshire Regiment*, took a leading part in the infantry fighting, and earned a most remarkable eulogy from their Brigadier.

Even after this the Sikhs were not finished and they raised a fresh army which fought at Ramnagar, where the 14th Light Dragoons, later *14th Hussars*, distinguished themselves, at Chilianwalah, where the 24th Foot, now *The South Wales Borderers*, were almost exterminated, and at Gujrat in 1849. The latter was their final defeat and the British pursued them right through the Punjab and re-took Rawal Pindi, Attock and Peshawur. After this they gave in, but a sort of mutual respect had grown up as the result of these tough battles, which made it easy to become reconciled, and a few years later they were giving most valuable assistance in suppressing the mutiny of the Bengal Army.

The Punjab now came under British rule and an incidental result of the war was that the Sikhs handed over, by way of indemnity, the Koh-i-Noor diamond, now in the Imperial crown, which they had previously looted from Shah Suja, the Amir of Afghanistan. At this time there were only about 40,000 British troops in India, and 200,000 sepoys, and fighting in that country was by no means finished.

NEGLECT OF THE ARMY AT HOME

The army in India was kept efficient by constant active service, but matters were different at home. Since the Napoleonic wars Parliament had settled down to its traditional peace-time antimilitarist views and grudged every halfpenny spent in providing for the services. People at home took no great interest in Indian and Colonial wars and concerned themselves mainly with money-making, under the pleasant delusion that they would never again be intimately involved in warlike affairs.

The Duke of Wellington was Commander-in-Chief, and though he had been one of our ablest Generals in the field, he does not seem to have distinguished himself in this appointment. Instead of modernizing and improving conditions in the army, everything was allowed to deteriorate and even the very necessary reforms made by the Duke of York lapsed into decay.

PERCUSSION CAPS AND RIFLES

There was no progress in training or equipment, except for one item which, though small, was very important. In 1839, twenty-four years after it had been invented and had been turned down by the War Office, the percussion cap was adopted for general issue. It was a small metal cap containing fulminate of mercury, which was placed over a nipple beside the touch-hole of the musket and exploded on being struck by the hammer, thus igniting the charge in the barrel. It was the same idea as the cap now sunk in the base of the metal cartridge case, and the various types of detonators now in use. It reduced misfires, which used to average as much as 40 per cent with the flintlock, down to a comparatively negligible proportion. The very small pouches worn on the slings of the cartouche boxes, carried by soldiers about the period of the Crimean War, contained these caps, and many units had a small pocket made in the front of the coatee for the same purpose.

About 1854 the army began to be rearmed with the Minié rifle, which was another muzzle-loader, but was accurate up to about 300 yards, whereas the old smooth-bore 'Brown Bess', which it replaced, was unreliable at anything over 80 or 90 yards. The Minié was in use at the same time as the Enfield rifle, which ultimately superseded it.

PLATE XI

(21)
1815
The Royal Artillery (Foot)
Officer
Gunner

(22)
1820
The 14th Light Dragoons
Later The 14th Hussars
Officer and Dragoon

(23)
1828
Officers:
The 42nd, or Royal Highland Regiment
Officer of the Light Company

The 52nd, or The Oxfordshire Regiment (Light Infantry)
The 88th Regiment, or The Connaught Rangers
(frock coat, and full dress)

The Royal Horse Artillery
The 15th Hussars

(24)
1837
Officers:
The 17th Lancers
The 8th Hussars

PLATE XI

Figs. 21, 22, 23 & 24

The officers of the Royal Artillery excepting Horse Brigades wore this coat only for a short period, in 1815. It was of the same style as the infantry officer's short coat, with lapels which either turned inwards or hooked together down the centre. In many illustrations of this period officers are seen with the lapels turned back only down to the third or fourth button, as on the highland officer.

Gunners were dressed more or less like infantrymen, except for the colour of the coat and the all-white plume. Attached to one of the crossbelts were a hammer and a pair of prickers, for cleaning the touch-hole of a gun. The red cord carried a powder flask for priming, and was similar to that worn by some of the Rifle battalions at this period, and by the cavalry in the previous century.

The 42nd officer is shown wearing the green hackle of the light company (the regimental one was and is scarlet), and the two wing epaulettes of an officer of a flank company. The jacket worn by highlanders was a short-tailed one, similar to the universal one, as doublets were not worn until 1855. Highland officers wore the sash over the left shoulder and the highland broadsword or claymore suspended from the usual shoulder-belt.

The tails of the ostrich-feather bonnet were short at this period, but varied somewhat according to the taste of the Commanding Officer. Sporrans were short and square and hose-tops were still not turned over.

The regiment marching in the background shows the field officers wearing cocked hats, the grenadier company, and some of the centre companies They are wearing 'service dress' trousers, and the breeches and hessian boots or gaiters, on the R.A. officer and the gunner, were the normal dress for home service. Grenadier caps were usually exchanged for shakos when a regiment went overseas.

Note.—The Royal Artillery and *The Royal Engineers* wore the same head-dress plume as grenadiers, and their present grenade badges appear to be connected with the same tradition. This may have originated from their dealing with the larger explosive missiles which, in early times, were round, like grenades, and consequently being given the same distinction as grenadiers regarding the plume. As previously stated, in the eighteenth century the right to wear grenadier caps was a very unusual privilege, and the R.A. do not appear to have worn them. Later on they became more associated with mounted troops, and followed their style of uniform rather than that of infantry.

PLATE XI (22) THE 14TH LIGHT DRAGOONS, LATER THE 14TH HUSSARS. 1820

In 1811 the light dragoon uniform of 1784, with its shell jacket and helmet, was discontinued, and a more conventional style was adopted.

The jacket had broad lapels (which were abolished in 1829) and miniature tails, and the bell-shaped shako was the one which became the universal pattern in 1816.

With the striped girdle, officers and sergeants ceased to wear their sashes. Officers' overalls were similar to those of the lancers—full and loose, but tapering in towards the ankles, and the silver lace stripes on them were only worn in full dress. At other times these were of the regimental facing colour, as shown on the dragoon (changed to white worsted lace in 1827).

Light cavalry used the curved sabre until 1840, when they were issued with straight swords like those of the heavy regiments. The first book of Dress Regulations for officers was issued in 1822.

In 1834 Guidons were abolished for all light dragoon, hussar and lancer regiments and in 1836 the uniforms of cavalry bands, some of them very fantastic, were abolished, and bandsmen had to be dressed the same as troopers. The reason stated was 'the inconvenience', on active service, caused by heavy losses among the trumpeters, owing to their conspicuous dress.

The 14th served right through the Peninsular War, and on one occasion their Prussian Eagle badge caused a party of them to be fired on by some Spaniards, who took them for Germans serving with the French.

PLATE XI (23) ARTILLERY AND INFANTRY—OFFICERS. 1828

From 1815 until the Crimean War, there was peace in Europe and many of the changes in uniforms were made with appearance as the main consideration, rather than the needs of active service. Training was also very limited and the army became, generally speaking, less ready for a sudden outbreak of war.

The 1816 shako, which had been copied from various allied forces, during the occupation of Paris after Waterloo, was the universal head-dress, except for the Household Cavalry, grenadier companies on home service, fusiliers, the Royal North British Dragoons (*The Greys*), who wore bearskin caps, and and the heavy cavalry, who wore helmets. Mounted troops and Rifles officers had worn cap-lines from the introduction of this shako, and from 1828 to 1830 all ranks of dismounted units wore them, plaited across the front in a great festoon and looped on to a button of the coatee. Light infantry and Rifles had green ones and in other regiments officers had gold, and other ranks white or yellow, cap-lines. The plumes were white for R.A., R.E., fusiliers and grenadier companies (the last two on bearskin caps) and white with a red base for centre companies. Hussars and lancers wore black 'hangover' horsehair plumes, and light dragoons white with the inner part red. Those of the cavalry officers were made of cocktail feathers and the sheen on the black ones often makes them appear green in illustrations of the period. Rifle regiments wore the same plumes as hussars, and light infantry generally wore green plumes of the ordinary shape. Both of these and the light companies of heavy infantry wore the horn badge, instead of the usual brass star front-plate. (Officers of Rifles and light infantry never wore the Waterloo shako, but kept the 'stove-pipe' pattern of 1800 until 1816.)

In 1820 service dress short coats were abolished (except for light cavalry and Rifles) and those worn closely resembled the coatee of 1796, the main difference being that the officers' lapels were wider. Hussars and the R.H.A. wore the shell jacket, the latter without the pelisse. Officers of Dragoon Guards again wore lace loops across the front of the coatee and an aiguilette, from 1820 to 1827.

Officers of light infantry and Rifles wore whistles and chains and curved sabres. Barrelled sashes with cords and tassels were worn by the R.H.A., hussars, and officers of Rifles. Officers of fusiliers, light infantry and grenadier companies had plain sashes with cords and tassels.

Trousers were bluish-grey for wear from October to April, and white for the summer. In full dress officers wore gold or silver lace stripes on the grey ones. Those of the cavalry were more varied, several regiments wearing scarlet or crimson overalls and some having lace Austrian knots on the fronts of the thighs. The cavalry also wore white trousers in the summer.

The frock coat had developed from the officers' blue greatcoat with a cape, worn at the beginning of the century, and had become so popular that, for some years, it was worn on practically all parades except ceremonial ones. At this time it was entirely plain, without epaulettes, and single-breasted, with a lining of scarlet shalloon. A sash and black leather sword belt (both round the waist) were worn with it.

In undress the shako was worn without the plume, etc., and with a cover of 'prepared linen'. Grenadier officers merely removed the plumes from their caps.

This practice of removing the head-dress ornaments and wearing cap covers, for undress or active service, originated in the Waterloo era and continued up to the South African War of 1899, when khaki covers were worn over white helmets, and even later when cavalry used to remove their plumes for manœuvres at home. Guards officers still wear khaki covers on their forage caps when in service dress, and white cap covers are worn in summer by all officers, with blue undress.

In the Sikh War, the first Afghan War, the Mutiny and other campaigns in hot countries, the old illustrations show the light dragoons with white covers over their shakos, and infantry with white covers and neck-flaps over forage caps or shakos.

PLATE XI (24) THE 17TH LANCERS OFFICER, 1837. THE 8TH HUSSARS OFFICER, 1837

These two regiments served together for so long, and were on such friendly terms, that they became known as the 25s—their numbers added together. They both have among their battle honours 'Alma', 'Balaclava', 'Inkerman', 'Sevastopol', and 'Central India', and both were in the famous Light Brigade.

They are shown during the period when William IV put them into red uniforms. The *16th Lancers* was the only regiment of light cavalry which did not revert to blue in 1840, and they wore scarlet up to 1914.

The tails of the lancers' coatees, at this date, were 7 inches long, and the lancer cap had a very large top, measuring 10 inches square. The height of the cap was 9 inches, and the officers' cocktail feathers were 16 inches long.

PLATE XII

(25)

1829–34

The 17th, or The Leicestershire Regt.
Bandsman. 1829

The Grenadier Guards
Bass Drummer. 1829

The 18th, or The Royal Irish Regiment
Officer (Grenadier Coy.) Frock coat. 1834

(26)

1830

The 35th, or The Sussex Regiment.
Now Royal
Officer

(27)

1840

The Royal Artillery
The Drum Major

(28)

1834–46

The 2nd Life Guards
Officer. 1834

The 6th Dragoon Guards
Officer. 1846

PLATE XII

Figs. 25, 26, 27 & 28

PLATE XII (25) 1829–34

The ancient custom, in non-'Royal' regiments, of bandsmen wearing coats of facing colour, was abolished in 1812, and about 1828 they were dressed in white coatees. There were various fanciful adornments, such as the pink trousers, tassels and plume of the 17th. Grenadier caps were still worn in some bands, and in others the ordinary shako. (The shako shown officially became out of date in 1828.)

A Sergeant-Drummer, or Drum-Major, carried a staff and wore an embroidered shoulder belt with regimental devices and a pair of drumsticks attached, similar to those worn at the present time, except that the drumsticks appear to have been full size, whereas they are now miniature replicas. He carried a sword suspended from a crossbelt, and wore a sash and usually an aiguilette, and had four chevrons on his right upper arm.

Coloured bandsmen, one or two of whom had been employed in nearly every regimental band, were then dying out, and those in *The Grenadier Guards* were some of the last survivors. The 'jewel'-studded turban and plume were evidently a copy of some maharajah's aigrette and ruby-bedecked head-dress.

The officers' undress uniform had one or two recent innovations. In 1829 the crossbelt was ordered to be worn in place of the black leather waistbelt, and in 1834 epaulettes (without fringes) were added to the frock coat, and a new cap was introduced.

1829–34 PLATES XII (26) AND XIII (29)

The 35th Foot was raised in 1701. It took part in the capture of Malta in 1800, and its King's Colour was the first British flag to be flown over the citadel, in memory of which the cross of the Knights of Malta forms the centre part of the badge. The feather at the top of the badge perpetuates the tall white feather worn in the head-dress until 1810, which was granted to commemorate the regiment's masterful dealing with the 'Regiment Royal-Roussillon', at the taking of Quebec in 1759. The orange facings, worn until 1832, when the 35th became a 'Royal' regiment, were conferred by William III, in 1701 and gave rise to the old nickname—'The Orange Lilies'.

There were many changes in dress at this period, mainly with the intention of reducing the fanciful superfluity of gold and silver lace, which had flourished since Waterloo, and had become a menace to the private incomes of the officers. (Their pay was not intended for them to live on.) Also dress had been overdone and the army was acquiring rather too much of the comic-opera style.

To begin at the top. The shako was reduced in height and all the lace and the cockade were removed from it in 1828. This made it look more bell-shaped as the reduction was made at the bottom. At the same time the feather was made all white for those who had worn red and white ones. (See Notes, 1828.)

In 1830 cap-lines were abolished for infantry, and the feather was shortened from 12 inches to 8 inches. Light infantry wore a green 'ball tuft' instead, from 1830, and in 1834 white ball tufts replaced white feathers.

All companies of Guards wore bearskin caps from 1832 and in about 1838 the tassels and front plates were removed from all grenadier caps, with the exceptions of the fusiliers' grenades and *The Greys'* thistle, and Hanover horse (at the back).

In 1829 a new plain-fronted officer's coatee (with short tails for high-landers) was introduced. It was tight-fitting with slash cuffs and a high stiff collar, and was always worn fully buttoned-up. The other ranks' coatee now also had slash cuffs and the Waterloo shoulder-straps were replaced by epaulettes. Other ranks' regimental lace was superseded in 1836 by plain white tape (which had been worn for many years by sergeants of the line). The Guards sergeants wore plain-fronted coatees from 1830 and those of line regiments from 1836.

Apart from the removal of other ranks' tail pockets in 1848, there were only very minor changes in the 1829 coatees until 1855, when they disappeared.

Good-conduct stripes were introduced in 1836 and were worn on the right arm—just above the cuff, for infantry, and just below the elbow for cavalry.

From 1830 all officers of regular units wore gold lace, and all wore two epaulettes. Badges of rank remained as in 1810, but the length of bullion fringe varied slightly for different ranks. Other ranks of infantry wore white fringed epaulettes (except Rifles, who had no fringe, and black epaulettes).

The gorget was abolished in 1830.

There were no notable alterations in equipment, except that from 1832 field officers wore a white waistbelt with sword slings and a brass scabbard, and adjutants the shoulderbelt with slings and a steel scabbard.

The mess-tin (illustrated on the gunner) appears to be identical with the one used for 'drumming-up' in 1914–18. ('Drumming-up', meaning to make tea, was the old name for 'Rouse' or 'Reveille', before bugles were in use, when drums were the normal method of broadcasting orders. 'Gunfire' once had a similar meaning, as the watch-setting gun, fired daily in garrison stations, also became a signal for brewing tea. So it seems clear that the soldiers' propensity for this beverage is no new thing.)

Sergeants' halberds were discontinued in 1830, and they carried swords and muskets. (Sergeants of light infantry had carried only muskets and bayonets since about 1758.)

There was a change in the colour of the trousers in 1828, when the sky-blue tint was replaced by 'Oxford mixture'—a blackish blue, for winter wear, and in 1833 the scarlet welt on the outer seams made its first appearance. In contrast to the coatee the trousers were loose and baggy.

PLATE XII (27) THE ROYAL ARTILLERY. THE DRUM-MAJOR. 1840

This uniform would appear to be a survival of the old rule, abolished in 1812, by which bandsmen of all 'Royal' regiments wore red coats. 'Royal' regiments with blue uniforms had scarlet facings—the converse of blue facings on scarlet.

Soon after this date, in 1851, *The Royal Artillery* band changed to blue coatees, and their last full dress uniform was similar to that of *The Royal Field Artillery* in 1914, except for a busby with a scarlet plume.

The grenadier cap worn by this Drum-Major was enormous at this period when they were at their greatest height, and the very large feather on it was almost the size of those worn at the Restoration period. The large moustaches, and whiskers which were in fashion at this time, seem to match the extravagance of the whole turnout.

(The light blue trousers, illustrated, went out of general use in 1828.)

PLATE XII (28) OFFICERS OF THE 2ND LIFE GUARDS 1834, AND 6TH DRAGOON GUARDS. 1846

The Household Cavalry wore this impressive bearskin cap, 14 inches high, until 1842, when they gave it up for the German silver helmet with pendant plume (made of hair-like pieces of whalebone), which still remains as part of their full dress. In 1834 the *2nd Life Guards* (as well as the 1st), had black lambskin saddle rugs, but they were later changed to white, and the devices on the shabracque (saddle cloth) were completely altered.

The Dragoon Guards had another change of head-gear in 1846, and it may be interesting to note the vicissitudes of their helmets, which at first seem rather complicated, from the cocked hat to the latest one, which dated from 1852.

In 1809 a tapering shako, with brass plate and turned-up peak, and a small red and white plume, was adopted for active service. This only lasted until 1812, when a leather helmet with horsehair mane, like that of the French cuirassiers (worn by them up to 1914), took its place. In 1822 the mane and 'shaving brush' were replaced by a bearskin crest. In 1834 another new helmet was issued and was described as of gilt and burnished metal, with ornamental scrolls on the sides, and an oakleaf-ornamented brass crest terminating in front in a lion's head and forepaws. A large removable bearskin crest was worn instead in full dress. This was an enormous and imposing head-dress, and probably very heavy. In 1846 the mane and brush were revived, on a brass helmet, and in 1852 the helmet assumed its final form with pendant horsehair plume. (There are excellent specimens of these head-dresses in the Royal United Services Institute in Whitehall.)

One of the many interesting antiquities, preserved by the Household Cavalry, is their retention of the old rank designations of N.C.O.s of regiments of Horse. These are: Corporal-Major (Sergeant-Major), Quartermaster-Corporal-Major (Quartermaster-Sergeant), Squadron-Corporal-Major (Squadron-Sergeant-Major), Corporal-of-Horse (Sergeant), and Corporal. In full dress N.C.O.s wear aiguilettes on the left shoulder instead of chevrons. (Officers wear them on the right.) This is probably a relic of the time when they were a corps of gentlemen, and their N.C.O.s ranked equal to officers of other regiments.

CHAPTER VI · 1854-6

THE CRIMEAN WAR

With the background of peace-time apathy and inefficiency, explained in the last chapter, and with no large-scale training and few officers or men who had ever seen active service, the army was once more sent into a European war.

Russia, since the defeat of Napoleon, had become the most powerful European country and, having designs on the Balkans and the Mediterranean, proceeded to attack Turkey. France saw an opportunity of recovering prestige lost in the Moscow retreat and declared war on Russia. Britain, anxious regarding the Mediterranean and Russia's expanding power, which might before long affect India, decided to join France and Turkey. This was the first time Britain had fought with France instead of against her, and it accords with the traditional policy of maintaining the balance of power by forming an alliance against the strongest power.

Our troops were first landed in Bulgaria, under the command of Lord Raglan, a veteran of the Napoleonic days, who in his advancing years could not modernize his ideas sufficiently to prevent his constantly referring to the enemy as the French! But as the Turks had already repulsed the Russians in that area, the troops were moved on to the Crimea, the object being to seize the naval base at Sebastopol and destroy the Black Sea fleet.

THE BATTLE OF THE ALMA, 1854

The first battle, at the Alma river, was fought with the same tactics as those used in the Peninsula and at Waterloo. The Russians came out of Sebastopol to fight, in order to break up the siege preparations and drive off the investing force. They were drawn up along a ridge and the British, French, and Turks advanced to the attack across open grassland, with infantry divisions in line, with Colours flying and bands and pipes playing, preceded by the light companies and riflemen in skirmishing order. The cavalry were on the right flank, guns in the intervals between brigades, and the whole line was several miles long. Frequent halts were made to correct the dressing and the intervals, and the C.-in-C. and his Staff rode in the centre.

This correct formation, however, did not last, as when nearing the Russian position they had to pass through some vineyards and enclosed land, skirt round a burning village, and then cross the Alma river. This was a fast-flowing treacherous stream, with deep and shallow water alternating, in which some men were drowned, and units became mixed. On the far side some Russian redoubts had to be dealt with and, being under heavy fire, the troops hurried forward to attack them, without waiting to re-form ranks. Many casualties resulted, but the Russians withdrew their guns prematurely and the redoubts were taken.

But the much-reduced regiments in the front line could not advance against the masses of Russians waiting to receive them, as the supporting units had lost direction and could not be found. Soon afterwards a bugle sounded the 'retire' and the call was re-peated all down the line. The officers of the 23rd, now *The Royal Welch Fusiliers*, had many casualties as they stood in a group dis-cussing this unaccountable incident. (It was then considered un-dignified to lie down or take cover on such an occasion.) The call was repeated, again passing right along the line, and all the troops began to retire, except the 7th, now *The Royal Fusiliers*, under Colonel Lacey Yea, who refused to move. This regiment shortly afterwards held off a Russian force of twice its own numbers, which came forward to retake the redoubts. Finally, after much confused fighting, an attack in force was organized, and the Russian masses were dispersed with the bayonet.

Half of the French troops never came into action, being too far to the right. The Russians neglected to defend a track leading round behind their left flank, along which a couple of British guns were brought into action against their rear, with great moral effect.

These vicissitudes were typical of most of the battles in history, and there have been few, if any, that went exactly according to plan.

The enemy, whose individual training must have been of a low standard, manœuvred their men in solid masses, as the French did in the Peninsular War, and thus we had the same ad-vantage of being able to use every weapon, while only a small proportion of them could fire at one time. Their movements were generally cumbersome and it took them a long time to decide on any offensive action. However, when properly led they were useful soldiers; though not as a rule very quick-witted. Their musket was much inferior to the Minié rifle, and our 18-pounder guns were far in advance of anything they had. In this battle the Russians lost about 9,000 men to the Allies' 4,000 or 5,000, and they went back into Sebastopol in complete disorder. The brunt of the fighting on our side fell on the 7th (*The Royal Fusiliers*), the 19th (*The Green Howards*), the 23rd (*The Royal Welch Fusiliers*), and the 95th (*The Sherwood Foresters*), each of which lost about 200 men.

SEBASTOPOL—TRENCH WARFARE

If the Allies had attacked Sebastopol immediately, while the enemy was confused and the defences incomplete, they might have finished the whole war in a few weeks, but wrangling among the various nationalities prevented any plan of action being formed in time to be of use.

PRIVATIONS AND MORALE

So the war dragged on for another eighteen months, involving two large-scale battles, a lengthy siege and constant minor engagements. These were accompanied by all the hardships which could be caused by severe winters, lack of every kind of supply, medical service and shelter from the weather, which resulted in an enormous amount of sickness. In spite of all these privations the spirit of the men was always excellent. All reports agree in saying that no man would think of 'going sick', however ill he might be, as long as he could walk to the trenches, because he realized that his doing so might make another man's duties just too much for him. The one exception with regard to morale was at the final assault on Sebastopol, at the end of the war, when the force was so reduced by casualties and sickness that the storming party for the Redan had to be formed mainly of very young, unseasoned reinforcements. It was a powerful redoubt, filled with guns and men, all ready for battle. Some of these young soldiers could not stand up to the storm of fire which met them, and in the end the attack failed, while a simultaneous assault on the Malakhof and the Little Redan redoubts by the French, succeeded and opened the way into the town.

THE SIEGE OF SEBASTOPOL

The siege of Sebastopol involved a long period of static warfare, during which the troops had spells in the trenches and then short rests in tents or huts in the rear, in much the same way as in France from 1915 to 1918, but under conditions which were 100 per cent worse in nearly every way. In France resting troops quite often found themselves on night expeditions to dig in the front line, but in the Crimea there were endless fatigues in bringing up supplies from Balaclava seven miles away, to the camps near the siege lines. Transport was a minus quantity and human pack animals had to be relied on to a great extent. The roads were appalling, but conditions were somewhat improved later by the laying of a light tramway on which the trucks were hauled by any horses available, including officers' chargers. But deficiencies still had to be made good by the men.

SNIPERS

One result of the trench warfare was that individuals developed a much higher standard of marksmanship with the new rifles than had previously been possible, and it was the custom to detail good shots to pick off enemy gunners, trench sentries, etc., at ranges up to about 300 yards.

This was an early stage of the art of sniping, which is now such an expert job, involving the use of telescopic sights, very specialized training and super camouflage. The following quotation is from the diary of Thomas Ainslie, a Militia company commander at Quebec in 1775, about eighty years before the Crimea:

'8th December, skulking riflemen watching to fire on those who appear on the ramparts. The indignation of our Militia is raised against these fellows who call themselves soldiers—they are worse than savages, they will ever be held in contempt with men of courage. Lie in wait to shoot a sentry, a deed worthy of Yanky men of war.'

BALACLAVA, 1854

The battle of Balaclava, when the Russians tried to destroy the British base, provided some of the most memorable incidents in history. The famous 'thin red line' of 93rd Highlanders, now *The Argyll and Sutherland Highlanders*, commanded by Sir Colin Campbell, kept at bay great masses of Russian cavalry during a very critical period. For a time their 550 men, standing two-deep across the valley, were all that was between Balaclava and a Russian force of 25,000 infantry and 3,000 cavalry, and Sir Colin said to them, 'Remember, men, there is no retreat from here. You must die where you stand.' This is the only infantry regiment possessing the battle honour 'Balaclava'.

The story of the famous charge of the Light Cavalry Brigade is too well known to need repetition in detail. A very efficient, well-trained and well-equipped brigade was squandered owing to the obtuseness and mental inactivity of its commander, and lost 247 men out of 673, and nearly all its horses, in a misdirected effort which produced small material results. The men, however, gave a classic and never-to-be-forgotten demonstration of discipline and devotion to duty, in attempting an impossible task, which had not really been intended. They charged the whole length of a valley under artillery and rifle fire from both flanks and from the front, right into batteries of guns and strong bodies of Russian cavalry, where they did considerable execution, after which the survivors had to cut their way back in small parties, still under fire. The regiments in the brigade were the 4*th*, 8*th* and 11*th Hussars*, the 13*th Light Dragoons* and the 17*th Lancers*.

This tragedy, however, did have a most remarkable moral effect, and henceforward the enemy had such respect for our cavalry that they constantly avoided action.

On the same day the Heavy Brigade, consisting of *The Royals*, *Greys*, *Inniskillings* and the 4*th* and 5*th Dragoon Guards*, under General Scarlett, carried out a charge which, though rather eclipsed by the dramatizing of the other, was a great deal more successful. In this case the brigade commander made his decision rapidly and correctly and seized an opportunity of attacking a large body of enemy cavalry whilst it was halted in massed formation.

Scarlett's brigade charged in three lines, led by himself, his A.D.C., his trumpeter and an orderly, and these four struck the enemy column first and alone. The General received five wounds and his A.D.C. fourteen. The brigade, about 800 strong, then crashed into the mass of 3,000 enemy cavalry, which they quickly transformed into a confused and panic-stricken crowd, killing a great number and driving the rest off the field.

INKERMAN, 1854

The battle of Inkerman was another Russian attempt to break out and raise the siege, and has often been described as 'the soldier's battle'. The British picquets were not too wide awake and were more or less surprised by a dawn attack on their camp in fog and rain. The Russians had been specially reinforced for this effort and it was a determined attempt to put an end to the siege and drive the Allies into the sea. The Russian troops detailed for the attack numbered 55,000 with over 200 guns, while the British and French available were no more than between 15,000 and 16,000 strong. Of this small number nearly 5,000 French never came into action.

The battle was an outstanding example of the value of discipline and fighting spirit. There was no time for the usual circulation of orders and battalion parades, brigade assemblies, etc., but wherever a party of men could be collected, someone took command and marched them off at once towards the sound of the firing. Cooks, batmen and all the 'odds and sods' of every description were included in these scratch platoons, and each man realized that it was a crisis of the first magnitude. (The conditions were in many ways similar to those existing in General Gough's 5th Army at the time of the great German push in 1918.)

General Pennefather, a quick-witted fighting Irishman, was the moving spirit of the defence. He at once took command of all troop. arriving in the enemy's vicinity, and organized a skeleton line, which was gradually thickened as far as possible, and carried out audacious attacks with small parties against large columns of Russians. The fog actually gave him some help in this; it was as if he was moving his men up behind a smoke screen and the Russians could never see how small the attacks were, until they had been struck by them and in most cases thrown into confusion.

When the end came, after several hours of intense fighting in mental and physical mist, the Russians had lost 12,000 men, compared to the Allied loss of 2,300, and the majority of them made their way back to Sebastopol in nerve-shattered crowds, moving at the double, many without arms or equipment, which had been thrown away to increase their speed.

At the crisis of the battle Marshal Canrobert, with a large force of French, many of whom had taken no part, lost his nerve and could not be dissuaded from withdrawing from the fight and leaving the exhausted and tremendously outnumbered British to finish the job alone. This they did in great style, with bayonet charges by hundreds or even scores of men against columns of thousands of Russians. Some of the regiments which particularly distinguished themselves in using the steel were: the 77th (*Middlesex*), the 49th (*Royal Berkshire*), the 41st (*Welsh*), the 30th (*East Lancashire*), the 20th (*Lancashire Fusiliers*) the 95th (*Sherwood Foresters*), the 21st (*Royal Scots Fusiliers*), the 63rd (*Manchester*), the 55th (*Border*) and *The Brigade of Guards.*

THE FALL OF SEBASTOPOL

Sebastopol was taken on 8th September 1855. This being made possible by the French success at the Malakhof and Little Redan redoubts.

It had been a very attractive and well laid out town, with handsome buildings and waterfronts, but it was in a poor state when the Russians moved out.

The final bombardment had lasted three days and had been followed by fighting in which the Allies had 7,000 or 8,000 casualties, and the Russians probably many more, so various parts of the town were littered with dead and wounded. Huge fires were raging, and at intervals magazines blew up with explosions like earthquakes and smoke darkened the whole town. All the Russian warships had been sunk and only the tops of their masts showed dismally in the harbour.

There was widespread evidence among the battered fortifications of the skill and efficiency of Todleben, the Russian C.R.E., and the excellence of his defensive works and underground shelters was greatly admired by officers who inspected them.

Apart from one or two naval actions in the Baltic, all the fighting had been in the Crimea, and the fact that the fall of one naval base ended the war shows the great difference between the wars of those days and the total variety of this century. In most cases only professional armies were then employed and were reinforced up to a point, beyond which it was not considered worth while. If they were beaten terms were made and, except in cases of invasion of a European country with intent to annex it, it was very rare for a whole nation to become involved.

THE VICTORIA CROSS, PHOTOGRAPHY, WAR CORRESPONDENTS, ETC.

This was the first campaign in which war correspondents were allowed (very much on sufferance) to accompany the army, and one effect was that their reports of the appalling conditions regarding supplies, produced violent agitation at home and forced the Government to pay serious attention. William Russell, *The Times* correspondent, said in one of his dispatches, 'I, myself, saw men dying on the beach, on the line of march, and in bivouac, without any medical assistance, and this within hail of a fleet of 500 sail, and within sight of Headquarters'. The army at one time reached a state when those who were still fit to carry on were literally in rags and one report said that 'there was nothing left by which officers could be distinguished, except their swords'. Afterwards conditions improved a great deal and about that time Florence Nightingale, 'the lady with the lamp', went to the Crimea and laid the foundations, against much obstruction, of the army nursing system, which later (after a lapse of some years) developed into *Queen Alexandra's Imperial Military Nursing Service*.

Other notable events of the Crimean War were the inauguration of the Victoria Cross, the use of Lancaster rifled cannon, which had a range of 5,000 yards, and the first photographic war records. One of the earliest V.C's was won by Sergeant Luke O'Connor, of the 23rd (*Royal Welch Fusiliers*), who was given a commission and later became a General. In spite of being badly wounded, he carried the Queen's Colour of the 23rd during most of the day at the Alma, no subaltern being left available for this duty.

A feature of this war was that the fleet, which lay outside

Balaclava, took part in actions within range of its guns, and some of the defences of the base were manned by *Marines* with naval guns. A great storm, in November 1854, sank many ships and flattened all the tents of the Light Division, which added considerably to the general discomfort.

An unusual event, after the signing of peace, was that the whole Allied army was reviewed by the enemy Commander-in-Chief, General Luders. Many of the British regiments remained in camp, now living in huts, until 1856, carrying out normal barrack-square training and field days.

MODERNIZATION AND TROOP TRAINS

After the war ended, having exposed to the world our peace-time inefficiency, which had made it almost impossible to reinforce or maintain the army overseas until the latter part of the campaign, an overhaul was carried out. The War Office was reorganized and government-owned small arms and clothing factories were established for the first time. (Previously arms were purchased from private firms and commanding officers had to obtain the men's clothing.) Permanent training camps were built at Aldershot and Shorncliffe (conveniently sited for expeditions to the Continent, or to repel invaders on the South coast), at Colchester and the Curragh; a musketry school was opened at Hythe, a gunnery school at Sheerness and the medical service was reconstituted. Many of the regiments returning from the Crimea were posted to Aldershot and arrived there by train, which was now becoming a normal method of transport. As early as 1840 the 20th Foot (now *The Lancashire Fusiliers*) had had this novel experience on a journey from Manchester to Liverpool. Uniforms and equipment were also modernized and made more serviceable and of better quality. Another change was that the 'flank' companies—light infantry and grenadiers—were abolished, as all companies were to be trained up to their standard.

VOLUNTEERS

The Volunteers, who had reached a strength of 463,000 in 1804, had dwindled away after 1815, and were reorganized in 1859, when it was thought that France was again becoming too ambitious. This began with the formation of small independent units in towns and villages, which were next grouped into larger administrative units. Their connection with the regular army was only very sketchy until the formation of Regimental Districts in 1881, when all Militia and Volunteer battalions became component parts of regular regiments. The Yeomanry, or Volunteer cavalry, who served under slightly different conditions, began their existence about 1804, and retained their independence. Most of them wore marvellous uniforms, which seem to have been designed by themselves and were more or less unfettered by regulation. Neither of these forces, up to 1914, could be sent overseas, unless they volunteered to go. The training they were able to carry out varied according to whether a whole unit lived in one large town or was scattered over a county, with perhaps a company in each town, having some of its sections, or even a few odd men in each of the neighbouring villages. In the case of the second type of unit, it was only embodied during the annual camps of a few days' duration and so could not be sufficiently trained until after it was called up for war service.

THE ARMY HOSPITAL CORPS

This was another development which resulted from the glaring deficiencies which had caused so many unnecessary deaths in the Crimea. It consisted of N.C.O's and orderlies selected from regiments, who were employed in regimental and other hospitals. The whole organization eventually came under *The Medical Staff Corps*, and ultimately developed into *The Royal Army Medical Corps*.

THE ARMY SERVICE CORPS

As one more proof that the authorities had been really shaken by events in the Crimea, *The Land Transport Corps*, which had been raised for the war, continued in existence as *The Military Train*. This provided transport for the army, while the Commissariat Department was responsible for rations, forage, fuel, etc., until 1888, when they were amalgamated to form *The Army Service Corps*. (The Indian Army equivalent was called *The Supply and Transport Corps* or S.&T. [nicknamed the 'Sausage and Tumtum (native cart) Corps'], a name which more clearly described the combination of the two functions.)

CIGARETTES

Cigarette-smoking dates from the Crimea, where the soldiers acquired a liking for it from the Turks, and continued to make their own 'fags' after they came home. (Fag-end is a naval word, meaning the untwisted end of a rope.) No one then imagined that a habit of such apparent triviality would develop into a problem of international importance, or that later on a Chancellor of the Exchequer would come to regard it as an act so criminal that it required the infliction of a tax in the region of 1,200 per cent *ad valorem*.

PLATE XIII

(29)

1829-34

| The Royal Artillery (Foot)

Gunner, 1829 | The 19th or 1st Yorkshire (North Riding) Regiment. Now The Green Howards

Private, 1830 | The Coldstream Guards

Sergeant, 1830 | The 43rd or Monmouth-shire Regiment (Light Infantry) Now 1st Oxford and Bucks Light Infantry

Private, 1834 | The 60th Rifles

Rifleman, 1834 |

(30)

1833

| The 14th Light Dragoons Later 14th Hussars

Sergeant | The 15th Hussars

Trooper | The Royal Horse Guards

Trooper | The 9th Lancers

Sergeant | The 6th Dragoon Guards

Trooper |

(31)

1845-68

| The 56th or West Essex Regiment. Now The Essex Regiment

Sergeant, 1845 | The 68th or Durham Regiment (Light Infantry)

Private, 1845 | The Scots Fusilier Guards. Now The Scots Guards

Guardsman, 1868 | The 66th or Berkshire Regiment. Now 'Royal'

Private 1855 | The Royal Engineers

Sapper, 1868 |

PLATE XIII

Figs. 29, 30 & 31

PLATE XIII (30) 1833

Being of the same period the notes on Plate XIII (29) are combined with those regarding Plate XII (26), page 141.

William IV, 1830–7, who was at first mainly concerned with the navy, soon began to be very interested in the army, and made several changes in the uniforms. He decided that, as red was the national colour, the whole army must wear it, with the exception of *The Royal Artillery* and the Rifle regiments. This change was made between 1830 and 1832, with the result that light dragoons and lancers wore red coatees until 1840, when they reverted to blue. Hussars surmounted the difficulty by wearing red pelisses.

About this time all ranks of cavalry regiments were provided with coatees of scarlet cloth, which superseded the old red colour. (This did not affect the infantry until much later.)

The seven regiments of Dragoon Guards (the original regiments of Horse), and the three heavy dragoon regiments—*The Royals* (1st), *The Greys* (2nd), and *The Inniskillings* (6th), had always worn red, since the early eighteenth century. *The Royal Horse Guards* was the only one of the old regiments which had always worn blue, and they continued to do so.

The Household Cavalry wore bearskin grenadier caps from 1821 to 1842, with an interval from 1827 to 1832, during which they reverted to helmets. *The Royal Horse Guards*, however, did not adopt the grenadier cap until 1833.

The wearing of cuirasses, by *The Household Cavalry*, was revived for the coronation of George IV, in 1821, and thereafter they were worn continuously.

The red shako was a regimental peculiarity of the *15th Hussars*, and each light cavalry regiment had its own distinctive method of arranging the cap-line and 'flounders' (tassels, shaped like flat fish). The 15th was the first regiment of light dragoons, raised in 1759, and was known then as Eliott's Light Horse, after Colonel Eliott, afterwards Lord Heathfield, of Gibraltar renown. On its formation the whole regiment consisted of London tailors, who were then on strike, and they so distinguished themselves at the battle of Emsdorf, 1760 (see Chapter II), that they were given the title of the 15th, or *King's Own Royal Light Dragoons*. They became hussars in 1807.

The lancers' uniform was copied from that of the Polish lancers, who fought on the French side in the Napoleonic wars, the peculiar 'mortarboard' cap being its most characteristic feature. (It will be remembered that, during the recent war, Polish officers in England wore a forage cap with a 'mortar-board' top.) The uniform was also very similar to those of the German lancers, or Uhlans. At various times, from 1816 onwards, the *5th, 9th,*

1 2*th*, 16*th*, and 17*th Light Dragoons* were converted to lancers, and the 21*st Hussars* became lancers in 1897.

George IV, 1820 to 1830, was another monarch who made a particular hobby of uniforms, and one of his foibles was to insist on the upper garments being almost skin-tight and fitting without a wrinkle. It is said that the piping along the seams of the lancers' coatees, and later tunics, was due to his pedantry when inspecting a new design in the fitting stage.

The Carabiniers were so named from the carabine, or long Horse pistol, with which regiments of Horse were armed in early times. The heavy cavalry had worn the bearskin-crested helmet from August 1822, and in 1829 all ranks adopted a single-breasted version of the new coatee. The facings of Dragoon Guards were of velvet and those of heavy dragoons of cloth. Light dragoons and lancers had very short tails, and the heavy regiments long ones. The striped girdle, which was purely decorative, was discarded in 1827 by heavy cavalry, but lancers and light dragoons continued to wear it.

PLATE XIII (31) 1845–68

This illustration shows the differences in uniforms before and after the Crimean War, which were very considerable.

The most noteworthy changes just before the war were the abolition of the old crossbelt equipment in 1850, and the rearming with the Minié rifle in 1854. The bayonet was now carried in a frog attached to the waistbelt, but everything else was on separate slings and the pack-supporting straps had no connection with the belt, so the improvement in comfort can only have been small. The waistbelt did, however, hold things together and prevented the cartouche box, bayonet, water-bottle, etc., from walloping up and down when a man was doubling.

In December 1845, white duck trousers were discontinued for home service. One supposed reason was that the constant washing which was needed, without proper facilities for drying, was causing many cases of rheumatism.

In 1844 the Albert shako replaced the previous one, and was worn also by fusiliers and grenadier companies, as bearskin caps were then abolished, except for the Guards and *The Scots Greys*. In 1845 sergeants' sashes, which had had a central stripe of facing colour since 1768, were replaced by plain crimson ones.

Service dress in the Crimea consisted of full dress, minus plumes and head-dress ornaments and with waterproof cap covers. This dress was generally worn in action in the early part of the war, but at other times 'pork pie' and 'pill-box' caps and stable jackets were allowed and officers wore frock coats. Booted overalls were the issue for mounted troops, but knee boots were also worn. The supply system collapsed during the war and it became a case of wearing whatever was available.

Photographic records show numerous oddities—officers wearing 'pea jackets' (from which the British Warm originated), poshteens, fur caps, even civilian hats and jackets, and much of it in rags.

Two primary causes, operating during the Crimean War, resulted in fairly drastic changes in uniforms—first the inefficiency of the supply system, which inevitably resulted in a general relaxation in dress, and secondly the publicity given to the army by the newspapers, and the consequent public indignation at the out-of-date uniforms the men had to wear. There were complaints about the tightness of the coatee, the high stiff collar and stock, the tall hard shako and the number of straps across the chest, which restricted a man's breathing when he had to double and fight with the bayonet, or carry out long marches.

The main results were the substitution for the coatee of a tunic with a low collar and a lighter and smaller shako. These changes were made in 1855 —showing the speedy result of publicity.

The new shako was similar in shape to the French *képi*, probably a compliment to our allies, who had for so long previously been our enemies. In any case, styles still moved from East to West and most of our innovations in dress came from continental armies, the victorious ones always leading the fashion. The ball tuft on this shako reverted to the old red and white (St. George's) colours, for the centre companies of infantry, and Rifles and light infantry had black and green respectively. Fusiliers wore white plumes of the light dragoon type, but about 1865 they were issued with otter- or racoon-skin caps, which they wore until 1914.

The new tunic was long and sloppy but reta ned some of the characteristics of the coatee. It was double-breasted for the first year and it had slash cuffs, the slash now of facing colour instead of red as formerly. The black stock was still worn, but with a much lower collar. Brass buttons were made universal and were evenly spaced for all regiments except the Guards. Coloured piping (white for infantry) was put round the edges to relieve the bareness, now that the lace (or rather tape) loops had gone.

The Guardsman's uniform, illustrated, has scarcely altered up to the present day (except for the weapons and the whiskers), as the Guards have kept the slash cuffs. (*The Royal Marine Light Infantry* also wore these for a few years before 1914.)

The 56th was known as 'the Pompadours', from its facings of a purple named after the Marquise de Pompadour (1721–64). This colour was worn also by the 59th, now *2nd Battalion East Lancashire Regiment*, and the 56th appear to have first worn it in 1764.

The gosling green of the 66th was also an unusual colour, which nearly disappeared from the army after the 1914–18 war, when *The Northumberland Fusiliers*, the last to wear it, became a 'Royal' regiment. The regiment, however, was able to prevent this by obtaining special permission to keep their traditional facings.

The Royal Artillery and *The Royal Engineers* wore busbies from 1855, until the introduction of the spiked helmet in 1878, the R.A. having a red busby bag.

Highland regiments, in 1855, replaced the coatee with a doublet, similar to the modern one, except that it was double-breasted. They wore white spats over hose, which now had turned-over tops, and the sporran had assumed its modern proportions.

The general rule regarding gloves was that, from the army's earliest days.

all mounted men and officers and sergeants of dismounted troops wore them when in full dress, or anyhow when on ceremonial parades. At other times it was a question of regimental orders. Contemporary illustrations, however, show some variation on this point.

Flank companies were abolished in 1862, as the training of the other companies was extended to include their functions, and it was no longer considered an advantage to have the best men concentrated in two companies of each battalion.

CHAPTER VII · 1857-8

THE BENGAL ARMY, RESULTS OF BUREAUCRACY

The next serious military undertaking was once more in India 'John Company' had a native force of over 300,000, two-thirds of them being in the Bengal Army and mostly 'Purbiahs' enlisted from Oudh. For quite a long time the discipline among them had been indifferent, and orders issued by the Company had contributed a great deal towards this, as they were continually restricting the powers of the British officers, thus giving an impression of weakness to the sipahis. An Asiatic, descended from countless generations who lived under tyranny and ill-treatment, has great difficulty in distinguishing between kindness and timidity, and once he thinks he detects the latter he feels that his chance has come. The Afghan massacre and our Crimean deficiencies were also used by agitators to show that our power was declining.

The well-known incident of the new cartridges for the Enfield rifle, with which the sipahis were being rearmed, was evidently not the cause, but merely the excuse for the final outburst of propaganda which produced the Mutiny. The cartridges were encased in greased paper and the ends had to be bitten off, so that the powder could be poured down the barrel. The remainder, containing the wad and bullet, was then forced home with the ramrod, the bullet also having to be lubricated to enable it to be driven down the rifling without undue effort. The agitators spread the rumour that this was a deliberate attempt to defile the religious castes of the sipahis and then force them to become Christians. They said the grease was composed of the fat of pigs and bullocks—the former an unclean animal according to the Mussulmans, and the latter a sacred one to the Hindus. Though this convenient story had already been nullified by an order permitting native troops to make up their own lubricant, it still served its purpose.

CHURCH PARADE AT MIRATH, 1857

One of the first mutinies was at Mirath, and was timed for church parade on Sunday, 10th May. The British troops however, were warned and prevented from marching to the church.

159

Amazingly the Station Commander failed to react and the mutineers went round the cantonment, murdering officers and women and children, and firing the bungalows, after which they marched off to Delhi. (This affair was the origin of the standing order under which all British troops in India from then attended church parade with arms.)

UNSUSPECTING COMPLACENCE

There were only about 40,000 British troops in the whole of India, a country of immense distances, where railways and telegraphs were hardly beyond the embryo stage, and roads were by no means first class. In those days regiments often remained in the country for twenty years or more (those of the Company never went out of India) and the men settled down with their families to make it their home. They became 'Anglo-Indians', many of them acquired a colour as dark as a native and the majority, after finishing their service, did not return to the United Kingdom, but carried on with some civilian job in India.

When the Mutiny came the families were one of the army's greatest worries, as there was no safe place to send them to, nor any escorts that could be spared to accompany them, so through force of circumstances they had to share in all the dangers and hardships of war.

Military fitness was maintained by constant warlike expeditions arranged, when possible, for the 'cold weather'. The regiments marched from their stations, often for many days, to join a Field Force, and then probably had some very exciting and arduous times. But, once back in a permanent station, there was an atmosphere of settled tranquillity, induced by the organized system of life, the ordinary affairs of the families, who all knew each other, and the fact that each station was such a self-contained community, owing to being probably a hundred miles or more from its nearest British neighbours. Every bungalow and every stall in the bazaar was familiar, and on a hot afternoon with most people taking their siesta, it seemed as peaceful as York or Canterbury.

It seems that the civil officials of the Company, and the officers of their army, also had this unwarranted feeling of security. Most of them were not watching for trouble, and would have hated to suspect their trusted sipahis of anything so uncalled-for. In addition senior officers and officials were often very old, and after so many years in an enervating climate were not mentally or physically fit for taking the rapid decisions and drastic actions necessary in a crisis. To make things worse, many of the younger and more efficient officers had been seconded from their regiments to posts in the governments of the recently acquired provinces.

So the mutinous sipahis of Mirath marched away in good order, with bands playing, surprised and elated at their easy success and, though there were some 2,000 British troops available, there was no serious pursuit.

News travels among the natives with surprising speed, and this quickly led to other outbreaks in far distant places. The Bombay and Madras Armies did not join in, but were naturally viewed with suspicion, and Punjabi and Sikh volunteers were the main reinforcements available, until many months later, when troops began to arrive from England. These had to travel round the Cape in sailing, or steam-and-sail ships, the voyage usually taking from three to four months, as the Suez Canal was not opened until 1869. A few reinforcements on the way to China were diverted by the Governor at Cape Town and arrived fairly soon after the mutiny began. (Until 1869, St. Helena, first acquired by Oliver Cromwell, was an important depot for all ships sailing to East Africa, India, and the Far East, but from then on it gradually declined and assumed a forlorn and impoverished appearance.)

ORGANIZING A WAR WITH SKELETON FORCES

As the emergency developed the right men gradually found the jobs for which they were suited, and brought their personalities to bear. Names such as Sir Hugh Rose, Sir John Lawrence, Chief Commissioner of the Punjab; his brother, Sir Henry Lawrence, the defender of Lucknow, Outram, Havelock; Sir Colin Campbell, Nicholson, Hodson, Roberts, and others, are bright spots in history and examples of the best types of officers and administrators.

The whole story was one of resolution and audacity pitifully lacking in resources, but backed by small numbers of reliable and enduring British soldiers and loyal sipahis, many of whom earned most honourable places in the annals of the army.

First the whole campaign had to be planned. Besieged garrisons must hold on at all costs, while columns had to be scraped together to relieve them as quickly as possible, and others to attack the strongholds of the mutineers. The most important was Delhi, their headquarters, where they had set up as king the last of the Moguls, an ancient drug-sodden puppet, who nevertheless formed a rallying point; Jhansi where the Rani was a red-hot Amazon warrior who fought in battle and was a great organizer of rebellion; and various lesser hotbeds.

The fighting extended from Bengal to the United Provinces and the Central Provinces, as far west as the state of Indore, and the experiences of these columns would fill a large book. They marched incredible distances, many dying from heat-stroke, cholera and dysentery, and fought action after action, normally against odds of four or five to one and often more. (There was no chlorinating of water in those days and men distracted with thirst, drank from filthy, stagnant pools and polluted streams. Nor were there any modern malaria precautions, and it is doubtful whether even the cause of the disease was known then.)

JHANSI

One instance of these unequal battles occurred during the siege of Jhansi, when Tantia Topi came to relieve the Rani with 22,000 men and 28 guns. Sir Hugh Rose decided to continue the siege and deal with him at the same time, and for this purpose he was able to detach only 1,500 men, 500 of whom were British. In spite of odds of nearly fifteen to one, Tantia's army was soundly beaten and driven across the Betwa river in extremity of disorder. Sir Hugh Rose then successfully assaulted the fortified town and the fortress, using one brigade against 11,000 defenders, who had plenty of artillery and were ensconced in massive and well-designed granite fortifications, perched on a towering rock.

This was typical of the work of all the columns. Two or three hundred men would always attack thousands of the enemy and in nearly every case they succeeded. As Lawrence said when Anson, the C.-in-C., doubted the possibility of recapturing Delhi: 'Where have we failed when we have acted vigorously? Where have we been successful when guided by timid counsels?'

THE SPIRIT OF THE MUTINEERS

Throughout the period of hostilities the mutineers normally fought well and stubbornly and, owing to their British training and equipment, were far superior to the private armies of disloyal Rajahs. On many occasions they nearly won, and there were many mutinous sipahis who performed deeds worthy of the V.C. But leadership and co-ordination were not their strongest points. Against individuals they would behave excellently, but often the sight of a British regiment charging in close formation caused them to panic.

PRIVATE CAVENAGH'S EXPLOIT

But there are times when even the best troops are temporarily appalled and hesitate, while the fate of an action, and their own, hangs in the balance. At such moments their deep-rooted discipline and pride will prevent a panic, but to get them moving some inspiring feat of leadership becomes necessary.

Such an instance occurred in a battle at the village of Unao, near Cawnpore, during Havelock's first relief of Lucknow. Men of the 78th, the 64th, and the Madras Fusiliers, now *The Seaforth Highlanders*, *The North Staffords*, and *The Royal Dublin Fusiliers*, were held up by heavy fire from sipahis standing behind a long wall. There was uncertainty and temporary inertia and the men could not bring themselves to advance.

Then one man, Private Cavenagh, sacrificed himself to break the spell. He rushed forward alone, leapt on to the wall, and down among the mutineers. He killed two and then was hacked to pieces by their swords. This both shamed and excited the waiting men to such a pitch that they charged forward and cleared the village without further delay.

THE SIEGE OF DELHI

A most important part of the plan was to besiege Delhi, or at least threaten it until more definite action became possible. This was done under most difficult conditions, the force outside being only a fraction of the strength of the enemy and liable itself to become the besieged at any time. It was not large enough to surround the city, but had to encamp along 'the Ridge', which was about two and a half miles long and two miles north of the city.

The mutineers could come out of Delhi when they chose and they made several attacks on the camp and on reinforcements arriving from the Punjab, along the Grand Trunk Road. Their most spirited attack was on 23rd June 1857, the 100th anniversary of Plassey. They had been well keyed-up by the Pandits, who told them that the astrologers, in whom they believed implicitly, had prophesied that the British Raj was only to last exactly one hundred years; but, like their other sorties, it failed after perilous moments and hard fighting.

TWO V.C'S

On 9th July the 8th Native Horse got right into the camp, having been mistaken for the 9th, whose uniform was almost the same and who were with the British force. They were cleared out, but during the confused fighting among the tents, in a tropical downpour of rain, two V.C's were won.

Lieutenant Hills (afterwards General Sir Hills Johnes), in command of a section of artillery, mounted his horse as the mutineers galloped towards his guns and charged them single-handed in the hope of giving his gunners time to come into action. He cut down one sowar and was then thrown to the ground and his horse rolled over him. The main body of cavalry galloped on.

Just then Major Tombs, his battery commander, came running up and saw a sowar on the point of killing him. He dropped this man from about thirty yards with his revolver. Hills's sword was lying some yards away and before he could get it he was attacked again by two mounted mutineers and one on foot. He just managed to reach his sword and slashed one man with it, killed another with his pistol, and seized the lance aimed at him by the third. After a struggle he managed to cut down the sowar with the lance, but was bleeding badly from his head and was again attacked, and when Tombs reached the spot and rescued him he was fighting with his fists. They were both awarded the V.C.

NICHOLSON'S ARRIVAL

Things were not going well in August. There were something like 30,000 mutineers in the city, while the besiegers had only a small force containing no more than 4,000 British. Cholera was rampant and had killed three Generals, 2,500 men were sick and the remaining senior officers did not feel that there was any immediate possibility of carrying out an assault.

At this low ebb Brigadier-General John Nicholson arrived with a movable column from the Punjab and a train of siege guns from the arsenals at Philur and Ferozepur. A large force of mutineers tried to obstruct him at Najafghar, a few miles out on his road, but were driven back after very severe punishment.

Nicholson was a man who was greatly respected in the army as a daring leader, a sound General and a man who thoroughly understood native psychology and held a position similar to that of Lawrence of Arabia in recent times. 'Nikolseyn Sahib' became, in fact, a sort of saint, and his name was known and revered, or feared, among millions of natives. His arrival with reinforcements, and especially the guns, gave a fresh spirit to everyone and preparations for the assault were soon put in hand.

THE ASSAULT

On the 14th September, after a three days' bombardment, the attack was made by five storming parties, Nicholson's column being the one which entered by a breach made in the Kashmir bastion. The Kashmir gate was assaulted by 240 men of the *52nd Light Infantry* with some native infantry, under Colonel Campbell.

The men attacked with great ferocity as many had lost wives

and children in the massacres which the natives had perpetrated and were bitterly resolved to take revenge. Often as a man drove his bayonet through the guts of a mutineer, he would grunt, 'That's for Mary', or 'That one's for Tommy', and pass on grimly to the next native in front of him.

Nicholson's column, after advancing along Rampart Road inside the city walls, having taken the Mori bastion and the Kabul gate, were checked by guns firing grapeshot on the ramparts and in the road. They took and spiked two of them, but the third brought them to a standstill, after many had been killed. (To spike a gun a musket ramrod was forced into the touch-hole and snapped off.) Nicholson would not wait for the gun to be outflanked, as some one suggested, but dashed on towards it, calling the men to follow. Almost at once he was shot through the chest, probably by one of the many snipers on the roofs, and died a few hours later. He was thirty-five years old and might have done great things had he lived.

There is now a tablet on the central pillar of the archway of the Kashmir gate, telling how Bugler Hawthorn of the *52nd Light Infantry* won the V.C. He was with the demolition party—two officers, four sergeants and seven sappers of *The Bengal Sappers and Miners*, who had to work under heavy fire at very close range and were nearly all killed. The last survivors just managed to blast in the gate and Hawthorn, while bravely attending to the wounded under fire, sounded the 52nd regimental call and 'Advance'. Actually his bugle was not heard owing to the din of firing, but the 52nd rushed forward on seeing the flash and smoke of the explosion.

SNIPERS AND SAPPING

After clearing the ramparts and outskirts, the warren of narrow alleys in the native city and bazaars enabled snipers to inflict such a number of casualties that it became necessary to resort to sapping a way through the buildings. This process took several days, during which holes were broken or blasted through the walls of the houses so that the troops were enabled to advance the length of one street at a time under cover.

HODSON'S EXPLOIT

When the city was completely occupied Lieutenant Hodson, of Hodson's Horse, took fifty of his sowars and rode out to the tomb of Hamayoun, one of those large ornate buildings which were often erected in memory of native rulers, where the old Mogul and his court and his most loyal and fanatical followers had taken refuge. Hodson rode straight into the armed and surly looking crowd gathered round the building and demanded the surrender of the king. The natives were so taken aback at his bold entry that the king came out without any trouble and was removed into custody.

Next day Hodson took a hundred men, posted them round the tomb and ordered the surrender of the princes who still remained there with several thousand armed retainers and sipahis. The princes expressed their resentment by taking a long time and finally being driven out in their carriages. Hodson made them dismount into the roadway and himself shot each one. He then had the bodies thrown down in the Chandni Chauk (Silver Street), the main bazaar of Delhi, for all natives to see the fate of those who, a few months before, had murdered British women and exposed their bodies on this same spot. It was a time for deeds, not words and procrastination, and the princes got no more than they deserved. It no doubt saved many lives which their execution, after a long and delayed trial, would not have done, and Hodson, knowing this, did not even consider the possible effect on his own career.

REGIMENTS AT DELHI

Some of the regiments which took part in the siege of Delhi were: the 75th, now 1st *Gordon Highlanders*, the 1st and 2nd Bengal Fusiliers, later *The Royal Munster Fusiliers*, *The King's Royal Rifle Corps*, the 8th, now *The King's Regiment (Liverpool)*, and the *9th Lancers*. The remainder were natives from the Punjab and Gurkhas.

THE SIEGE OF LUCKNOW

The fall of Delhi was a great step forward, but it was not until the third battle of Cawnpore in December 1857 that the British were able to feel that the super-critical time was ending and the tension lessening. They could then concentrate on mopping-up expeditions, which continued until April 1859. (In that battle Sir Colin Campbell, with a force of under 6,000, routed a native army which outnumbered him by five to one—about the usual odds.)

Between May and December many atrocities were committed by the natives and immortal defences were made by besieged garrisons, the most memorable being that of Lucknow, in which the 32nd, now *The Duke of Cornwall's Light Infantry* and the 84th, now *The York and Lancaster Regiment*, took a leading part.

Lucknow, the capital of Oudh, was a city filled with palaces and gardens, many of which figure in accounts of the fighting, as they dominated the approach routes—such as the Dilkusha Bagh (Heart's Content Garden; Kush = 'cushy' in army language), the Sikander Bagh (Alexander's Garden), the Kaiser Bagh (Emperor's Garden), etc. The Chuttermunzil, one of the palaces, afterwards became a British club.

The defence was organized by Sir Henry Lawrence, Chief Commissioner of Oudh, who was one of the few who, while hoping for the best, had prepared for the worst, had accumulated ample stores and had all the tactical details worked out. All this he left as a handsome legacy to his successor, Colonel Inglis, as he himself was killed two days after the siege began by a shell which burst in his room in the Residency.

The mutineers advanced on Lucknow in high spirits, after the surrender of Cawnpore. Lawrence went out to meet them with a small force and fought an action at Chinat, which was the nearest approach to a disaster. On his return he had to blow up the Machchi Bhawan, an old fortress he had meant to defend, and occupy only the Residency and its grounds and adjacent houses, an area of about forty acres.

The garrison, in addition to the 32nd, consisted only of 220 volunteers and 750 loyal sipahis. They had 1,300 civilians in their charge, including army and civil families, and the enemy's strength varied from 30,000 at the lowest, up to about 100,000. For over four months these large numbers were kept occupied and prevented from joining the mutineers at Delhi, where they might have turned the scale.

Every building was made into a strong point and it was a case of almost permanent 'stand to', only a few men at a time being allowed to feed and rest. The enemy were in loopholed houses about thirty yards outside the perimeter and possessed artillery. (Fortunately in those days a cannon shot hitting a wall usually only knocked out a few bricks whereas modern shells would soon have destroyed all the buildings.)

Sniping by the mutineers was constant, but there was very effective retaliation to this, especially by the officers, firing from the roof and windows of the Mess bungalow.

There were numerous assaults, such as the one on 20th July, when the mutineers sprang a mine and about 7,000 of them tried to get into the Residency. They made repeated efforts for hours, while every man of the garrison fired as fast as he could. Eventually they had to give up. Lieutenant Loughnan, of the 13th Native Infantry, with about twenty-five men, half of them temporary Civil Servants, bore the brunt at Innes's house, and gave them such a strafing that they kept quiet for about three weeks afterwards.

Cholera, the frequent killing and wounding of women and children, and the 'hot weather', were not calculated to raise morale, but everyone stuck it with no more than normal healthy grousing.

On the 25th September, Havelock and Outram fought their way in and were much surprised to find the garrison still alive. Their force only brought the total strength up to about 3,000, and all they could do was to reinforce the garrison and hang on until, six weeks later, Sir Colin Campbell arrived with a stronger column, again having to fight all the way. He removed all the civilians, the stores and a large amount of money which had been accumulated in the treasury, in a convoy ten miles long, leaving Outram to follow with the rearguard. The city was then left to the mutineers until March 1858, when Sir Colin came back and retook it. From that day, until the Dominions of India and Pakistan were set up, the Union Jack flew over the ruins of the Residency, and was the only flag in the Empire which was never lowered by day or night.

Sir James Outram was senior to Havelock and reached Cawnpore in September to supersede him, just as he returned to camp from his ninth successful battle. Outram decided not to deprive him of the command until they entered Lucknow, and so accompanied the column as Chief Commissioner of Oudh, with the rank of private in the Volunteers, but Havelock unfortunately died of cholera a few days after they reached Lucknow. Sir Colin Campbell was the son of a Glasgow carpenter, and is an instance, rare in those days, of a man with small beginnings rising to be a General. He was a veteran with a great reputation, having served in nearly every battle since the Peninsular War. He left England at twenty-four hours' notice to take Anson's place, after his death, as C.-in-C. Forces in India.

LIEUTENANT HAVELOCK

An incident, during the first relief of Lucknow, shows how the personality of one man can affect the course of a battle. Havelock's plan was to cross the Charbagh (Four Gardens) bridge in order to gain access to the Residency without going through the tortuous lanes of the poorer quarters. The 5th, now *The Royal Northumberland Fusiliers*, were held up at the bridge by six enemy guns and were ordered to lie down and wait for Major Maude's battery to deal with them.

Maude had only room to unlimber two guns, which could not

cope with the enemy's six, and many of his men were being knocked out. He shouted to Havelock, son of General Havelock and his A.D.C., who was watching the operation: 'For God's sake DO something!' Havelock rode off in haste to General Neill, the column commander, and asked for permission to rush the bridge, but Neill said he would not do it without Havelock's orders. So young Havelock rode away as if to ask, went a short distance out of sight and returned at a gallop. 'You are to carry the bridge at once, sir,' he said. He joined the first attacking party, and he and a corporal were the only men at the head of the column who survived the first discharge of grapeshot. Leading the Fusiliers on, before the enemy could reload, he took the guns and cleared the way for the next advance.

THE MASSACRE AT CAWNPORE

Neither Lucknow nor Cawnpore was to be compared with Delhi in importance, nor in the number of casualties involved, but owing to the tragic events at Cawnpore it has been given a more dramatic place in history. The massacre, which wiped out the garrison, is still remembered as the most outstanding example of Oriental treachery and sadistic cruelty during the Mutiny.

When the Mutiny broke out at Cawnpore the garrison, under Major-General Sir Hugh Wheeler (aged seventy), was composed of about 300 combatants, made up of gunners, detachments of the 46th, now *The Duke of Cornwall's Light Infantry*, and the 84th, now *The York and Lancaster Regiment*, some loyal sipahis and about 500 women and children, including 300 Eurasian children. Incidentally more than 70 of the men were sick, and Wheeler, knowing that Lucknow was more important, had sent some of his troops to reinforce it.

They occupied a ridiculous and pathetic little entrenchment outside the city, which consisted of a few huts surrounded by an earth rampart about five feet high. Wheeler had this constructed and moved out to it, rather than defend the walled and fortified magazine in the cantonment, because he thought that if he removed the sipahis quartered in it, a fresh outbreak of mutiny would be precipitated.

There they lived on a daily ration of a few ounces of flour and lentils, constantly under fire from guns and muskets, with the men 'standing to' most of the time to repel the frequent attacks of the mutineers. It was the month of June when the heat is so great that life is barely tolerable even in peace-time nowadays, with the modern amenities of ice and electric punkahs and no outdoor work between about 10 a.m. and 4 p.m.

The greatest privation was caused by shortage of water, there being only one well, which was in an exposed position and was kept under observation by snipers and often fired at with grape-shot. As it was sixty feet deep, drawing water was a slow and dangerous job, and there were many casualties at this place which could only be visited at night. John McKillop, a Civil Servant, who was lame, took charge of it and did noble work until he was killed, but there was never enough water, the children were in a pitiful state and adults hardly any better.

About 250 people died or were killed in three weeks and the remainder reached such a state of exhaustion and weakness that they could not hold out much longer.

When their position had obviously become hopeless the Nana Sahib (adopted son of the last Peishwa of Poonah), who was the local leader of the mutineers, made an offer to Wheeler, if he would surrender, to provide boats and guarantee safe conduct to Allahabad. Wheeler had been on good terms with the 'Nana' before the trouble started, but knew that he had a grievance against the government and doubted his philanthropic intentions. Unfortunately Captain Moore, who had been his right-hand man during the defence, influenced him to accept in order to release the civilians from the unbearable conditions.

They moved out at sunrise on 27th June to the Chaura Ghat, a landing place at the side of the Ganges, where wide paved terraces, constructed in a high bank, led down to the water. On the sides of the river were bushes and long grass, and some small stone buildings stood above the terraces. (This place is now known as 'the Massacre Ghat', and still looks much as it did on that day.)

On the river were a number of native boats, with the usual thatched roofs for protection from the sun, containing native boatmen in them, and the survivors of the garrison, thankful that their ordeal was, as they thought, over and that families were allowed to remain together, embarked more or less unsuspectingly. When the sick and wounded had been carried on board and everything was ready, there was an unexpectedly long interval, during which the Nana was probably gloating in a leisurely manner over the success of his plan.

Eventually a bugle sounded. Then the boatmen, who all had small cooking fires, set alight the roofs of the boats, threw away the oars and jumped overboard. While the passengers, now fully aware of treachery, made haste to put out the flames and push off the boats, musketry and artillery fire crashed out from the river banks. This continued until the now blazing boats were a shambles of dead and wounded. Only one boat got away and four men reached safety, after many adventures.

Then the 'cease fire' was sounded and native cavalry rode into the shallow water to sabre the survivors.

Finally about 200 pitiful, bloodstained and bedraggled creatures, many of them wounded, were herded back to Cawnpore and shut up in two small buildings. Here they existed in foully over-crowded misery for a fortnight, some dying each day, until in the end their fate was settled by the Nana's apprehension at the victorious approach of Havelock's column. When they fought their way in, three days later, all that was found of these 200 women and children was a mass of mutilated corpses in a well, and the floor and walls of their prison were literally soaked and covered with blood. The troops were naturally infuriated at this discovery and many took some small souvenir of the victims, such as a button, a lock of hair, or a scrap of cloth, and wore it inside their tunics to remind them always of the vengeance they had sworn to exact.

RETRIBUTION

The idea of collective retaliation is one of the problems of the present day, as shown by the many examples of barbaric revenge in the recent war. Obviously, it is completely unjust from the individual's point of view, but it arises from a deep and ancient instinct. In the early days if members of a tribe committed such crimes it was more than likely that others of the same blood would repeat them if they had the chance. Therefore the soundest plan was to hold them all equally responsible, and exterminate them as far as possible, to prevent a recurrence. After all, in a war all were equally involved. For those who did not bother to think it out, a strong motive was that in order to fulfill the primeval desire for vengeance, the criminal's nearest relation was the next best person to punish if one could not get the man himself.

As might be expected after Cawnpore the men, of all regi-ments, showed little mercy to the mutineers. One instance of retribution occurred in the assault on the Sikander Bagh, at Lucknow—a large walled and fortified enclosure, inside which its garrison of 2,000 mutineers was exterminated with rifle and bayonet.

Nemesis also caught up with the Rani of Jhansi, who had com-mitted massacres of men, women, and children, before she was besieged and escaped from her fortress. She was eventually killed in action, dressed as a cavalry sowar, by a trooper of the *8th Hussars*.

A number of the most deeply incriminated instigators of mutiny, in various stations, were executed in a somewhat primitive manner, immediately after their revolts had been frustrated, in order to impress the spectators and discourage emulation. The method was to hold a ceremonial parade of the garrison, including units which might be contemplating mutiny, formed in three sides of a square. On the fourth side was a line of guns, each with a beam lashed on at right-angles to the barrel. The criminals were led out and bound to the beams, with their backs to the muzzles, and on the command 'Fire!' they were blown to pieces.

THE END OF THE COMPANY

In 1858 the East India Company was abolished, and India, including the Indian Army, was taken over by the Crown. There were reforms in the native army, including the abolition of most of its artillery, and an increase in the proportion of British troops stationed in the country. The class company system was introduced, and battalions composed half of Mussulmans and half of Hindus, who were previously never agreed upon anything, united under British officers, worked excellently together and reached a high standard of efficiency. What will happen now that this unifying force is removed from India, is a major problem.

The old British regiments in the service of the Company were taken on to the Army List in 1860. They were the 19*th*, 20*th* and 21*st Hussars* (the last converted into lancers in 1897), *The Royal Munster* and *Royal Dublin Fusiliers*, and the second battalions of several infantry regiments.

PLATE XIV

(32)

1857

The 52nd Light Infantry	The Royal Artillery. (Foot)	Infantry of the Line
Colour-Sergeant (Service dress, India)	*Sergeant-Major (undress, India)*	*Sergeant-Major ('Hot weather' dress, India)*
Bandsman (full dress)		*Private (marching order)*

(33)

1840–60

The 4th Dragoon Guards	The 14th Light Dragoons. Later 14th Hussars	The Royal Horse Guards	The 2nd (Royal North British) Dragoons	The 9th Lancers
Trooper, 1859	*Trooper, 1860*	*Trooper, 1860*	*Trooper, 1854*	*Trooper, 1840*

(34)

1881

The Royal Field Artillery	The Highland Light Infantry	The Lancashire Fusiliers	The Queen's (Royal West Surrey Regiment)	The Seaforth Highlanders
Bombardier	*Lance-Corporal*	*Corporal*	*Sergeant*	*Sergeant*

PLATE XIV

Figs. 32, 33 & 34

PLATE XIV (32) ARTILLERY AND INFANTRY. 1857

In the Indian Mutiny a variety of dress was worn, in addition to the new tunics, etc. According to a description by Bugler Johnson of the 52nd, who was present, his regiment wore khaki, with shirts outside in the native fashion, the old equipment and khaki cap covers. With beards and deep sunburn their appearance could not have been very different from that of the desert patrols of the 1939-45 war, who looked very much like Arabs. The topee made its appearance at this time and was issued to all ranks in 1858.

The mutineers who, of course, began the war in the Company's uniforms, soon relaxed their standards, substituted *dhotis* or *pyjamas* for European trousers, threw away their hard shakos and wore puggarees or no hats. Their red coatees, British Colours and British bugle calls and words of command must have given a very odd effect when they were the enemy.

For further information *re* khaki, see notes on Plate XV (38).

The two Sergeant-Majors, whose badge of rank then was a crown over four inverted chevrons, illustrate other types of uniform worn in India—the shell jacket, for the 'cold weather', with booted overalls, as worn in the Crimea, and the white drill edition of the new tunic, for the 'hot weather'.

The bandsman is in ordinary home service dress, white tunics being a peculiarity of infantry bandsmen. Wing epaulettes, having gone with the old coatee, had not yet been restored to the bands. The green (Light Infantry) plume on the shako was so long that it was fastened in by a loop.

The equipment worn in marching order remained as in the Crimea and, as a result of recent active service, the 'pork pie' forage cap was sometimes permitted in place of the shako.

PLATE XIV (33) 1840-60

After the Crimean War changes were made in cavalry dress as in the infantry. The loose tunic replaced the coatee and 'booted overalls' (as shown on the Trooper of the 14th), were worn by all mounted troops (except *The Household Cavalry*, who retained their tall jack boots). They disappeared in 1871, when knee boots and pantaloons took their place.

Light dragoons wore the new pattern shako, with a red and white plume and a tunic with five pairs of frog loops, which was the same as that for hussars, except that the latter had six pairs of loops. Pelisses were abolished and only officers and sergeants wore sabretaches. In 1852 heavy cavalry adopted the same type of helmet as those now worn by *The Household Cavalry* and chin-chains replaced chin-scales. The large 'flounders', terminating the cap-lines of light cavalry, were discontinued in favour of rather insignificant acorn tassels, and plain shoulder-straps took the place of epaulettes. In 1849 two yellow stripes were ordered to be worn on the overalls by light cavalry. (The 13th, however, seem to have invoked the long-dead custom of regiments with buff facings wearing buff equipment, etc., and wore buff stripes up to 1914.)

The scarlet cloak (on the Dragoon Guard) is of the old type worn by regiments of Horse in the eighteenth century, and still worn by *The Life Guards*. Sleeves were added to it in 1796. The heavy cavalry line regiments were ordered to wear blue greatcoats and capes in 1859.

Owing to their very hirsute appearance at this period one might get the impression that most of the men were middle-aged or old, but this is not correct, as the system of enlisting for life ended in 1847.

PLATE XIV (34) ARTILLERY AND INFANTRY. 1881

The helmet, introduced in 1878, was of German type and resembled the 'pikelhaube', except for being slightly taller and not so square. It has been much criticized for its lack of artistic merit, not to mention its origin, but it continued to be the universal head-dress until 1914. (There was always a 'universal' head-dress, as far back as the tricorne hat, but with each one there was an increasing number of exceptions.) 'Royal' regiments had red backing placed under the regimental number or badge in the centre of the star-plate.

The Highland Light Infantry retained the shako, which is still their full dress head-wear.

The fusilier's cap, made of racoon or sealskin, had a distinctly different shape from that of the Guards' bearskin, reminiscent of the time when the mitre-shaped caps of the early fusiliers were smaller than those of grenadiers. The title of the 20th was changed to *The Lancashire Fusiliers* on 1st July 1881, having previously been *The East Devonshire Regiment*.

The tails of the highland bonnet grew longer as the century progressed and the ends were now level with the collar. Later they came down to the shoulder.

In 1868 slash cuffs were replaced by plain pointed ones which, in some regiments, were surmounted by a knot of white braid, and Scottish regiments wore a gauntlet cuff something like the Waterloo one, but rising to a point on the outside. An order was issued in 1881 that chevrons were to be worn only on the right sleeve. Previously light infantry and fusiliers had worn them on both arms.

Regimental buttons (other ranks) and belt-lockets were replaced by the universal pattern about 1878. The madder-red tunics worn by corporals and privates were abolished in 1873, and from then all ranks wore scarlet.

An improved equipment had been issued in 1868, with the weight of the greatcoat (carried on the shoulders), and the two ammunition pouches (worn on the waistbelt and each containing 20 rounds), supported by a pair of braces connected to the belt at both ends, and to some extent balancing one another. The haversack and water-bottle still hung from separate slings, which constricted the chest, as before. The valise or pack was, for a time, carried in a curious manner, suspended on the buttocks, with supporting straps attached to the front buckles of the braces. (The Slade-Wallace equipment, 1873-89.)

Also, rather oddly, black pouches were worn on white equipment. Custom dies hard in the Army and this was probably due to the fact that the old cartouche box had been black (so as not to show greasy finger-marks from the lubricant on the paper cartridges) attached to a white crossbelt. The extra pouch carried thirty rounds for the Martini-Henry rifle, issued in 1871. There were several types of sword-bayonet at this date, some with long wavy blades, but the ancient triangular-bladed type still predominated.

The short leather anklets were the same style as those which were brought out of store for *The Home Guard*, during the 1939-45 war, and exactly the same shape as those of the 1937 equipment.

In 1881, with the introduction of the Cardwell system (see Chapter VIII) all English infantry regiments, apart from 'Royal' ones, were ordered to wear white facings, Scottish regiments, yellow, and Irish, green (the colours of the 'fields' of their national flags), thus obliterating the old distinctive facings, among other traditional features which went with the Crimean War. This was done to avoid the complications which would have arisen when two regiments with different facings became 1st and 2nd battalions of the same regiment, and later on a great many of the old facings were restored. At the same time badges were invented for all regiments which did not possess them, and the numbers disappeared.

The following line regiments had badges before 1846: 1st to 9th Foot, 18th and 27th Foot, and fusilier and highland regiments. Light infantry and Rifles wore the horn as a cap badge. In addition there were many semi-official badges, as regiments were then allowed to put thier own devices on their shako plates.

CHAPTER VIII · 1859-80

MINOR WARS

After the Mutiny several minor wars occurred in widely separated parts of the world. In 1859 there was another war with the Chinese, who had failed to observe treaties made with us. It involved a landing at the Taku forts and an advance to Pekin, where the emperor's palace was destroyed. The battle honour 'Taku Forts' is borne by *The Royal Scots*, *The Queen's*, *The East Surreys* and *The King's Royal Rifles*; and 'Pekin, 1860' by the last named and *The Wiltshires*.

THE CROWN OF THE KING OF KINGS

In 1868 Sir Robert Napier led an expedition to Magdala, in Abyssinia. Troops were sent from India to march and fight through nearly four hundred miles of unknown and roadless tropical mountain country, using for transport mules, elephants and camels. The crown of Ethiopia was brought back as a trophy and was restored to Haile Selassie when the Duke of Gloucester attended his coronation in 1928. *The Cameronians*, *The Duke of Wellington's*, *The Sherwood Foresters* and *The King's Own Royal Regiment* (*Lancaster*) took part in this campaign.

THE ASHANTI EXPEDITION

In the Ashanti War of 1873, Wolseley advanced from the West African coast, through tropical jungles, to Kumasi. The purpose of the expedition was to avenge a series of native outrages, which had included the murder of a British official whose skull was used as a drinking cup by King Coffee, and to put a stop to habitual massacres and daily human sacrifices. There were two successful battles, at Amoaful and Ordashu. The battle honour 'Ashanti' appears on the Colours of *The Black Watch* and *The Royal Welch Fusiliers*, and is borne by the Rifle Brigade.

IMPORTANT CHANGES IN THE ARMY—THE MARTINI-HENRY RIFLE

Some highly important and far-reaching changes were made in the weapons and organization of the army between 1870 and

178

1881. In 1871 the Martini-Henry rifle superseded the Snider, which had been in use since 1866 and was the first breech-loader. The Martini was a hammerless single loader, with an ejector worked by a lever behind the trigger guard. It was sighted to 1,000 yards and fired a heavy bullet with great stopping power. The recoil was correspondingly violent and black powder was still used. It was, however, a very big advance in the efficiency of killing machines.

In 1870 the War Office Act was passed, which reorganized the control of the army. Better barracks were built (some of the now-existing regimental depots, or I.T.C. barracks in the county towns were among these), pay was increased a little, food was improved, canteens also received attention, and organized games and recreations became a part of the general scheme. One could say that the soldier's conditions of life were improving.

The system of purchasing commissions and promotion, under which an officer paid £450 for his first commission and up to £6,000 or £7,000 for promotion in the senior ranks, was at last stamped out, after having been in force since 1720. One instance of its abuses and absurdities occurred in *The Welch Regiment*, where there was a case of an officer being commissioned on the day of his birth and appointed as a company commander at the age of thirteen while, presumably, still at school.

THE CARDWELL SYSTEM

The most important change was the introduction of the Cardwell System in 1881, under which pairs of infantry regiments were united to form 1st and 2nd battalions of one regiment, with a county title (which was not a new thing), and a regimental district for recruiting purposes. Militia and Volunteer battalions were also allocated to each regiment and district. The main point of the system was that one regular battalion of each regiment was to be stationed at home and provide reinforcements for the other while it was overseas. (This made sure that at least one battalion would be up to strength.) It was definitely a sound scheme, but there was much dissatisfaction at the loss of identity and of the old regimental numbers and 'unhappy marriages' of regiments. The first twenty-five line regiments were not affected, as they already had two battalions each.

Another essential part of these reforms was the introduction of the short-service system—part 'with the Colours' and part in the Regular Army Reserve. Up to 1847 men had enlisted for life and had served until they were too old to be of further use. After that date the term of service had been ten years in the infantry and twelve in the other arms. Consequently there had been no trained reserve ready to be called up on mobilization.

WARS BETWEEN 1870 AND 1898

There were very few years when there was not a war going on in some part of the world, and from 1870 to 1898 the army was involved in the Second Afghan War, 1878–80, the Zulu War, 1878–9, the first Boer War, 1881, the Egyptian and Sudan Wars, 1882–5, the third Burmese War, 1885, the Tirah expedition, 1897, and the Sudan War, 1897. In Queen Victoria's reign there were altogether forty expeditions, large and small, in which British forces were used.

MAIWAND, 1880

The second Afghan War began as the result of another massacre. Sir Louis Cavagnari had been sent as Envoy to Kabul in 1878, to investigate and endeavour to counteract Russian influence which, it was thought, was becoming dangerous to India. After being there some time his quarters in the Bala Hissar (the citadel) were attacked by the Amir's ill-disciplined troops (probably at his instigation, although he used the ill-discipline as camouflage). Sir Louis and all his Staff and escort, numbering about eighty, were murdered. In an epic battle the detachment of the Guides, which formed his escort, killed 600 Afghans.

The battle of Maiwand, during the ensuing campaign, was another of those disasters which are, unfortunately, so frequent in our wars. However, against its murky background shines out one of the finest recorded examples of regimental discipline.

Brigadier-General Burrows, with six companies of the 66th, now the *2nd Battalion Royal Berkshire Regiment*, two Indian cavalry and two infantry regiments, and a troop of *The Royal Horse Artillery*, about 2,000 men in all, was sent out to reconnoitre when an Afghan force was reported to be moving on Kandahar. He discovered, too late, that he was confronted by a *lashkar* of about five times his own numbers, with modern guns and well armed with rifles. He was unable to manœuvre out of it, as the enemy was already across his line of retreat; the only alternative was to fight.

The Afghans were good shots at short range and very aggressive fighters as long as the prospects were good, and they knew from inter-tribal warfare how to make full use of the jagged hills and rock-strewn nullahs, with which their country abounds. Thus they had natural advantages over our troops who, though they were now in khaki, still knew more about the traditional methods of fighting than they did of mountain warfare, sniping, and fieldcraft. They still fired in volleys and fought shoulder to shoulder in solid ranks. The Indian regiments were composed, not of the classes now recognized as having the best fighting qualities, but of natives who were quite unaccustomed to frontier conditions and were no match for the hill men. They had heard so many gruesome tales about these barbarous people that they had no great eagerness to meet them.

The brigade had marched twelve miles in the morning, in great heat and choking dust, and after being under fire for two hours, from thirty guns and numerous rifles, jezails and other weapons, the sipahis began to get nervy. Individuals tried to shelter themselves behind rocks and ceased firing so as not to attract the enemy's attention, and as things gradually became worse, a sort of despairing paralysis seemed to grip the minds and bodies of many of them. They appeared to have lost the power of action and entirely failed to respond to orders given by their officers.

The Afghans were greatly encouraged by this obvious loss of morale and still more by the withdrawal of a battery of native smooth-bore guns, after which they boldly rushed some companies, doing fearsome execution with their knives. They stabbed with an upward thrust, and the edge of the blade, which was held uppermost, was curved in such a way that it would slit a man's body right up to the breastbone. The sight of this was too much for the already shaky sipahis of other units and their inertia was suddenly broken by wild panic, which spread from company to company until it became a terror-stricken stampede.

The Indian cavalry, which had suffered heavily from shell-fire, refused to charge the Afghans, and finally made off like the infantry. *The Royal Horse Artillery* troop was out of ammunition and surrounded. They kept the enemy off with swords, hand-spikes and rammers, while they limbered up, and as soon as they were ready the drivers put the teams into a gallop to save the guns.

Only the 66th, after being overrun by the mob of flying sipahis, remained facing the enemy. They now had to become the rearguard and save the whole force from being annihilated. They fought it out while the Afghans drew nearer from all directions, massing up, but waiting until the British were sufficiently weakened for them to rush in without great loss to themselves. All this time bullets were cracking into the ranks and men collapsed to the ground with alarming frequency.

They made several short withdrawals in the direction the main

body had taken, and at each stand their numbers were much reduced. (Any wounded who were left would be killed and then
mutilated, but things were so desperate that it was impossible to
spare enough men to move them all.)

During the retirement one party, about a hundred strong, had
to take up a temporary position in a mud-walled garden, where it
became surrounded by great numbers of Afghans and was cut
off from the remainder. The men fought on undeterred, though
losing very heavily, and eventually their situation became hopeless. The enemy were closing in by thousands—mounted and on
foot—waving Standards and yelling their fanatical war cries, but
they were too cunning to charge, knowing that the end was near,
and crowded round at a respectful distance, whilst they tried to
finish the job with rifles.

At the last only eleven men were left in action, most of them
wounded, all exhausted and completely ringed-in by the enemy.
Each man knew that all hope had gone, so they decided to end it
in the same spirit with which they had fought throughout the
interminable day. They charged together into the nearest Afghans,
bayoneted a few, and disappeared beneath the knives and tulwars
of the gleefully howling savages.

The remainder of the 66th continued to retreat very slowly,
thinking that, while they did so, the fleeing rabble would be put-
ing a few miles between itself and the enemy. Every time a company halted and faced about for a fresh stand, its ranks were
visibly reduced. A man would instinctively glance round and
something of this sort would pass through his mind: 'The Captain's gone this time—and the Colour-Sergeant. That old ——,
Sergeant ——'s in command now. Bill's lying back there, and
Bert looks as if his number's up. Here they come again, blast the
——s. Wait for it, and aim low.' It was a great test of endurance
and will-power, and the men were, like the ammunition, almost
finished when, at last, the pressure of the enemy began to ease.

Out of a total strength of 488, the 66th had 308 casualties, of
which only thirty-three wounded came back. Thus a fine regiment
had nearly ceased to exist, but it had shown that discipline (which
someone aptly described as 'organized unselfishness') when
backed by the right spirit, can enable men to rise above bodily
fears and sufferings, and perform almost super-human tasks. By
its sacrifice the regiment had preoccupied the enemy long enough
to prevent the general massacre, which otherwise must have taken
place, and made a deep impression on the Afghans, adding greatly
to their respect for British troops for many years afterwards.

ROBERTS'S MARCH TO KANDAHAR

Apart from this disaster the war was successful and during its progress Sir F. Roberts, V.C., then a Major-General, commanding the Kurram Field Force, proved his outstanding ability and rose to a number one position in the confidence and affection of his officers and men, and of the nation.

His march from Kabul to Kandahar, in August 1880, has often been quoted as a model operation. The force consisted of 10,000 men, with camp followers (which are indispensable in India) and about 8,600 mules, ponies and donkeys, carrying the baggage and the pack guns. No wheeled transport was used, owing to the rough country to be traversed. They covered 303 miles in twenty days, the average day's march being about fifteen miles. This may not seem an extraordinary feat, but when one considers the heat and dust in August, the mountainous rocky country and the long column which had to be protected every moment against possible surprise attacks, not to mention the numerous native servants, drivers, etc., who were not soldiers but had to keep up with the troops, it was undoubtedly a record achievement. This fifteen miles was an average, too, which meant that it was done every day, and actually there was only one rest day in the whole period. The daily programme, quite a normal one in 'hot weather' operations, was 'Rouse' at 2.45 a.m., march off at 4 a.m., and reach the camping site for the night at about 4 p.m., the tail of the column arriving about an hour later.

Roberts himself had fever most of the time, but on the day after the end of this march, he fought the battle of Kandahar, and gained the smashing victory which ended the war.

EARLY MACHINE-GUNS

An early type of machine-gun, invented by Doctor Gatling of Chicago, was used in the Afghan war, and also in Egypt shortly afterwards. It consisted of a number of rifle barrels, bound together like a faggot, and mounted on wheels, with a firing mechanism worked by turning a handle similar to that of a barrel organ. It usually jammed at critical moments, and was not a great success. (The first efforts with this type of weapon date back to the fifteenth century, when it is recorded that a number of muskets were mounted, bound together, on a wheeled carriage. Other experiments followed but did not come up to expectations, and the project was abandoned.)

ZULU MILITARISM

The main preoccupations of the army for the remainder of the century consisted of a series of wars in different parts of Africa.

The Zulus were a savage, but highly militarized nation, and among African tribes they had long been invincible. They were well organized, were formed into regiments, which had distinctive uniforms—if ostrich feathers and skins may be so described, and discipline was probably as rigorous as any army has ever known. Disobedience of an order inevitably meant death in some ingeniously unpleasant form and recruit training involved such exercises as capturing a lion alive, or treading out a bush fire with bare feet, as part of the daily routine. The system was most thorough and even went so far as to compel the men to live in regimental kraals, as European troops live in barracks. Their arms though, apart from a number of miscellaneous rifles and muskets, were just their native weapons—throwing and stabbing assegais and knobkerries, and they carried cowhide shields. They were magnificent animals and quite fearless, and if they could catch a party of regular troops unaware, it was a poor prospect for the troops.

They were very arrogant and resented European colonization in Africa and wanted to lead in a war of all the native tribes to exterminate the comparatively small number of white men in the country. The war came after years of tension, during which the Boers suffered and committed atrocities and were defeated in various minor expeditions. In spite of all efforts to settle things peaceably, Cetewayo, their king, remained exceedingly insolent and evidently intended to invade the Transvaal. So, in the end, the British, under Lord Chelmsford, took the initiative and four columns marched into Zululand.

Events followed the pattern so often repeated—underrating the enemy, lack of preparation, disasters, and finally, crushing victory.

ISANDLWANA, 1879

For the second time in their history (the first was at Chilianwala, in the Sikh War, 1849), the 24th, now *The South Wales Borderers*, was almost completely wiped out. Six companies were left, with some native troops, in charge of the camp at Isandlwana (the little hand), while Chelmsford took out the main force to find the Zulu 'Impis', and were suddenly rushed by about 20,000 Zulus, when unsuspectingly issuing the midday meal. Practically every man was killed, and when the column returned after dark, it found nothing alive, the camp littered with gruesome remains, and all their transport and stores gone or destroyed. Horror was added to the spectacle owing to the fact that the Zulus always ripped-up the stomachs of dead and wounded men, as they had a superstition that if a body was left to swell up in the sun, their own would do likewise. This resulted in their being even more thorough in war than the modern exponents of totalitarianism.

The usual procedure in South Africa, when halted for a night, was to form a 'laager' by lining up the ox-waggons head to tail, in a circle, and interlocking the dissel-boom of each under the body of the one in front of it, thus forming a sort of stockade, which prevented the enemy from being able to rush the camp. (A similar method was used during the Indian Mutiny, using bullock carts.) This had not been done, and a further advantage to the enemy was that the reserve ammunition boxes could only be opened by unscrewing them. In addition, it appears that the picquets, if there were any, could not have done their job, as, although Zulus had been in the neighbourhood for some hours, there seems to have been no warning of the attack. Only six men of the 24th escaped, and the bodies of Lieutenants Melvill and Coghill, the former with the Queen's Colour tied round his body, were found with several dead Zulus, at the Buffalo River. Around the camp at Isandlwana 1,000 Zulu bodies were counted—circumstantial evidence that, regardless of their hopeless situation, the 24th had died fighting it out to the bitter end.

RORKE'S DRIFT

On the same day a detachment of 104 men of the 24th at Rorke's Drift, a few miles away, under Lieutenants Bromhead of the 24th, and Chard, of *The Royal Engineers*, was attacked by 3,000 Zulus fresh from their victory at Isandlwana, and beat off repeated rushes for about twelve hours—from early afternoon until about 4.30 a.m.

This detachment was in charge of stores and a small hospital and the two officers had organized a defensive perimeter, making a slight breastwork out of sacks of mealies, tins of biscuits, etc. During the action the hospital caught fire and there were many moments of extreme peril, but in the end they had killed 350 Zulus and had lost 17 killed and 10 wounded.

Within twenty-four hours the 24th lost altogether 590 men and 21 officers killed. Lieutenants Bromhead and Chard were awarded V.C.s, and in memory of these two actions the regiment has the distinction of bearing a wreath of silver laurels attached to the King's Colour.

ETSHOWE, AND ULUNDI, 4TH JULY 1879

Another of the columns, under Colonel Pearson, narrowly escaped disaster and was besieged for two months at Etshowe, where rough defences had been constructed to form a depot camp. There were other indecisive battles at Inhoblane, where Colonel Sir Redvers Buller won his V.C., and at Kambula, where a strong Zulu attack was beaten off. All this was considered, at home, to be so unsatisfactory that Colonel Sir Evelyn Wood was sent out to supersede Lord Chelmsford but, before he arrived, Chelmsford had restored his tarnished laurels to brilliance by winning the battle of Ulundi, which shattered the Zulu army.

This battle was fought with the whole British force, numbering about 5,000, formed in one large hollow square, transport, etc., inside, and guns in the firing line—they had only about four. The cavalry also went inside during the attack.

The Zulus—about 20,000 of them—first worked themselves up with war dances, drum-beating with rhythmic chants, and native beer, and then advanced in their usual crescent formation. The intention always was for the horns of the crescent to lap round the flanks of the enemy, while the centre made the main attack, and behind the centre was a reserve which could reinforce in any direction. Being practically naked and as tough as wild animals, they could move almost at the speed of cavalry, and the sight of men being mown down by rifle fire or blown-up by shells usually did no more than increase the ardour of their savage minds. (One of the queerest and most sinister sights of this campaign must have been the Zulu 'Impis' moving across country in formation, looking for their enemy. They could be seen from the tops of the hills when they were several hours' march away.)

In this battle things were better organized on the British side and the ground was of their choosing. The Zulus had also lost some of their confidence after their repulse at Kambula, and the attack was less orderly than in earlier battles and was broken up finally when the leading men were about thirty yards from the square. The 17th Lancers and *The Irregular Horse* then galloped out and completed their disorganization. Many of them fought like panthers, turning on the cavalry, seizing lances, and assegaiing men or horses, but they were driven off and altogether about 1,000 were killed. The regiments forming the square were the 13th, 34th, 58th, 80th, and 90th, now *The Somerset Light Infantry, Border Regiment, Northamptons, South Staffords*, and the *Cameronians*.

Cetewayo, who was commanding in the battle, fled to a mountain cave and was afterwards captured by men of the *K.D.G.s.*

PLATE XV

(35)

1846

The 7th Hussars
Officer

(36)

1850

The Grenadier Guards
Officer (State dress)
Sergeant (drill order)

The 60th Rifles
Field Officer

(37)

1855

The 11th or North Devonshire Regiment. Now The Devonshire Regiment

Officer (shell jacket)

The 48th or Northamptonshire Regiment
Field Officer

(38)

1880

The 81st Regiment. Now The Loyal Regiment

Officer, Sergeant and Private (Service dress, India)

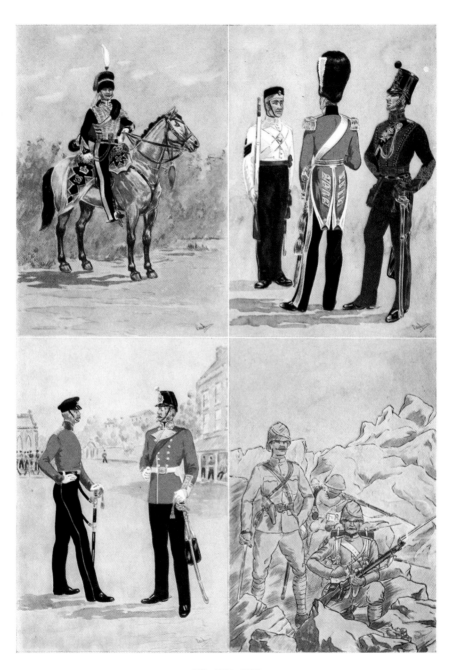

PLATE XV

Figs. 35, 36, 37 & 38

PLATE XV (35) THE 7TH HUSSARS. OFFICER. 1846

The Dress Regulations of 1846 give the following meagre information regarding hussar regiments: Pelisse—blue. Fur—regimental. Waistcoat—scarlet. Cap—busby of regimental fur. Hussars wore the shell jacket until 1855, and it is still the full dress of *The Royal Horse Artillery.*

The orders of 1830 had not reduced the amount of lace worn by hussar officers, but thereafter all regular regiments wore gold lace. The chest and the front of the pelisse were entirely covered, by interspersing 'bright Russia braid' between the 'dead gold' cord, and the weight must have been quite considerable—not to mention the cost.

General rules regarding light cavalry head-dresses at this date were: light dragoons—shako; officers—white cocktail feathers; other ranks—white horsehair 'hangover' plumes. Lancers—lancer caps; officers—black cocktail feathers; other ranks—black horsehair 'hangover' plumes. Hussars—busbies; officers—white feathers with red bases, larger than those of other ranks, but much shorter than those worn from about 1890, which were 13 inches high.

The pistols, for so long carried by all ranks of cavalry, were abolished in 1840 for ranks below Sergeant-Major.

Hussar regiments seem to have reverted to busbies (instead of shakos) at various dates, between about 1840 and 1860. As one instance, the 15th did so in 1857.

PLATE XV (36) THE GRENADIER GUARDS, 1850. THE 60TH RIFLES, 1850

Shortly before the Crimean War, when appearance was still the most important consideration in designing a uniform, the ugliest and most maligned article of dress which had yet appeared was the 1844 shako, known as the 'Albert pot' (named after the Prince Consort).

The white shell jacket was worn by the Foot Guards and highland regiments, in drill order, and gave a smart appearance. It seems to have been a survival of the sleeved waistcoat, which was formerly worn for fatigues. The cap was rather similar in appearance to that worn by the Germans in 1914, and to the unpopular Broderick cap, of the early twentieth century. Sergeants' caps, in *The Grenadier Guards,* had gold lace bands and those of the lower ranks red.

The officers, when in state dress, wore gold-laced trousers (as those of other regiments did before 1829) and gold and crimson sashes, with very long tassels. Each regiment had its own 'skirt ornaments'—in this case grenades, for fastening the turned-back corners of the coatee.

Rifle regiments (officers) continued to wear the shell jacket, copiously corded and laced. This and the barrelled sash and the pouch belt, maintained the similarity between their uniforms and those of hussars. In undress officers of the 60th wore a plainer shell jacket, with only five loops across the front, no sash and the round, peaked cap. The Albert shako was worn by all units which had the previous shako, except the hussars and *The Royal Horse Artillery*, who wore busbies.

PLATE XV (37) OFFICERS—INFANTRY REGIMENTS. 1855

In the changes of 1855, officers' uniforms became positively austere in comparison with what they had once been. Incidentally, it has been regarded by many as one of the ugliest periods in British history, with regard to many aspects of life—dress, furnishing, architecture, etc.

There were two slight changes in the 1855 shako, in 1861 and 1869, but the most noticeable difference was that from 1861 Lieutenant-Colonels and Majors wore two rows and one row of gold lace round the top, respectively.

Epaulettes were abolished in 1855 and, in their place, officers wore only a twisted crimson cord and button, to retain the sash on the left shoulder. Lapels, lined with facing colour, but without lace, were a half-hearted reversion to Waterloo traditions. They were turned back only to the third button and had to be buttoned across when on duty. They disappeared in 1856, when the tunic was made single-breasted. Rifle regiments wore a green tunic, officers having loops like those of Hussars.

The sword was now worn on slings from a waistbelt by all officers.

The distinctions of rank were revised in 1855, as follows:

Field Officers. Lace at top and bottom of collar, on edges of skirts, and cuff slashes, and lace buttonholes on skirts and slashes. Two rows of lace round the cuffs.

Company Officers. Lace at top of collar, one row on cuffs, lace buttonholes as above.

Badges of rank, now placed on the collar, were:

Colonel—crown and star; Lieut.-Colonel—crown; Major—star; Captain—crown and star; Lieutenant—crown; Ensign—star.

The repetition must have been quite confusing, as one had to look at both the lace and the crowns and stars to decide on the rank of an officer.

Gilt-hilted swords and leather scabbards with gilt mountings continued in use until 1866, when steel scabbards were ordered, and the sword hilts were plated to match.

In 1848 the shell jacket, which had long been in use overseas, and was worn by all ranks in the Sikh War and other campaigns in India, took the place of the blue frock coat. The latter was, however, revived in 1855, with a plain stand-up collar and double-breasted.

PLATE XV (38) SERVICE DRESS. INDIA. 1880

Khaki (the Persian word for dust-colour), originated in India in the 1840's, and was worn by a few British units during the Mutiny—among them the 32nd and 52nd Light Infantry. Regiments dyed their own white clothing by using a variety of substances such as coffee, curry powder, mulberry juice, etc., and produced a number of different shades and some blotchy effects which might have appealed to modern airborne troops. The soldiers of that era did not take kindly to it, and felt so scruffy that they refused to 'walk out' in khaki, but spent the evenings in the canteens, with the result that there were many cases of drunkenness. After the Mutiny it was agreed that it was not a smart enough dress and it went out of use for several years, white drill again being the normal summer dress in India, but it was worn again for the Afghan War, 1878.

The Sam Browne belt was invented about 1860, by General Sir Samuel Browne, V.C., who had lost an arm and so thought out a more convenient method of carrying his sword and revolver. The present pattern differs only very slightly from the original which has been preserved by *Sam Browne's Cavalry (12th Frontier Force) Indian Army*. It came into general use for officers of the British service in the wars of 1870–80, and is now worn also by Warrant Officers, Class I, and has been adopted by nearly all the armies of the world. It was generally worn with two braces until the South African War of 1899, and a few regiments retained these up to 1914—among them the 60th *Rifles, The Rifle Brigade*, and *The Cameronians*, but now almost the only units still wearing the two braces are *The Oxford and Bucks Light Infantry* (who have special regimental patterns) and *The Cameronians*. The Dress Regulations of 1911 said that there should be two braces, but that the second one was only for use when wearing a revolver

CHAPTER IX · 1881-98

THE FIRST BOER WAR, 1880-1

To give a true picture, the bad as well as the good must be recorded, and this war was definitely not a thing of which to be proud. It was fought because the British, after giving many warnings, were completely dissatisfied with the Boers' methods of administration in the Transvaal, and wished to annex it in order to govern it properly. But, from beginning to end, there was no real determination to carry out this purpose, and everything went wrong. Very small numbers of troops were employed and were used in a way that could only bring discredit on them and on the country.

There was military inefficiency as well, and the first example of this was evident at Bronkhorst Spruit, where a small column, moving to Pretoria, marched with a band playing, baggage vehicles straggling for miles, and none of the usual 'protection'. The Boers lay in ambush and, when the column arrived, sent a warning letter to the Commanding Officer, saying that they did not consider that a state of hostilities existed, but that if he crossed the border, it would be regarded as an act of war. The warning was ignored; the Boers shot up the convoy and, in ten minutes, killed or wounded 155 men, and captured the remaining 104. They behaved with faultless chivalry after this and did all they could for the comfort of the wounded.

Next came the disaster at Laing's Nek, when the British attacked the Boers in position on a ridge near Majuba Hill, and were decisively repulsed. There were many acts of outstanding bravery by men of the 58th and 60th (*Northamptons* and *King's Royal Rifles*), but, unfortunately, the red coats of the 58th and their close-order training made them easy prey for the men who lived on the veldt, who were good shots and accustomed to concealing themselves when hunting big game. Again, after this action the Boers cared for the wounded as well as they were able.

MAJUBA HILL

One more unsuccessful action was fought at the Ingogo river, where the British had 139 casualties and the Boers 14. Then came the final calamity at Majuba Hill.

For some reason not very clearly recorded, General Colley, who was killed in the action, marched about 400 men up this precipitous, 6,000 foot kopje, at night, to occupy the summit, which overlooked a Boer laager on an adjacent nek.

The men were exhausted by their climb in darkness, through boulder-strewn scrub and steep ravines, the last part of which had to be done on all fours as it was almost perpendicular. All the various detachments which formed the force were mixed up, and nothing was done to sort them out. In fact there was no action of any kind, apart from posting some men round the circumference of the broad, saucer-shaped top of the hill, and the remainder were allowed to sleep in the central depression.

Complete inactivity reigned during the whole morning, while the Boers, seeing men on the skyline, first thought of moving to safety, but later decided to attack and began to infiltrate silently and invisibly up the sides of the hill. They posted a covering party of marksmen, who fired at any soldier they saw, and quietly developed their attack as if they had been stalking game. Quite often a man showed himself on the hill, and the sniping which followed each exposure should have been sufficient warning of coming events.

The Boers reached the edge of the plateau while the reserves and supports were still sleeping in the centre, and opened accurate close-range fire. Mixed up and still half asleep, these troops were ordered into the firing line, but they quickly lost their nerve under this telling fire, hesitated, scattered, and finally fled in headlong panic, down the side of the hill, followed by the remainder of the force. The Boers lined the edge and took pot shots at anything that moved in the bushes and long grass below them. The British casualties numbered 283 and great damage was done to prestige and morale.

There were some, besides officers, who did not succumb to the ghastly infectious madness of panic—a hideous spectacle, fortunately extremely rare in the annals of the British Army. There was a group of Gordons under Hector McDonald, who stuck it out until quite surrounded, and an officer and an orderly of *The Royal Army Medical Corps*, who coolly continued their work after being wounded, and others who only followed the rout slowly on seeing that matters were beyond hope. But, like the whole war, it was one of our most disgraceful exhibitions.

One of the worst omissions was the failure to sort out the units before the men were allowed to rest. A soldier hates being with a strange unit and, at first, trusts no one, which is, perhaps, an unforeseen result of always being taught the admirable belief that

N

no unit is as good as his own. Of course units have been unavoidably mixed in many battles, but it is a fact that during the recent war the majority of soldiers under sentence in military prisons, if questioned, began their story with an account of being sent to a strange regiment. Had this point been better appreciated by the officers the story of Majuba might have been different, in spite of all the other sins that were committed.

The end of the war was no better than the rest of it, as peace was concluded soon after Majuba and without any further effort, while Lord Roberts was on his way with reinforcements.

COLOURS NO LONGER TAKEN ON SERVICE

Majuba was the last occasion on which Colours were carried in action. From then on, when a regiment was about to embark for foreign service, the Colours were ceremonially laid-up in the local cathedral or church.

THE EGYPTIAN WAR, 1882

The Household Cavalry and the *Guards* took a prominent part in the Egyptian and Sudan Wars, and the three regiments of each, then existing, bear the battle honours 'Tel-el-Kebir', and 'Egypt, 1882', the Foot Guards having in addition 'Suakin, 1885'.

In 1881 Egypt was ruled by the Khedive, or Viceroy of the Sultan of Turkey, who asked Great Britain to deal with a very serious rebellion under Arabi Pasha.

The latter was a colonel in the Egyptian Army, who had started a violent agitation based on the slogan 'Egypt for the Egyptians', and had the backing of 60,000 troops. Murders of Europeans and other outrages occurred in Alexandria, where he strengthened the forts and mounted additional heavy guns to menace the British ships in the harbour. Because of our great interest in Egypt and the Suez canal, it was decided that this could not continue and action was taken.

After due warning the fleet bombarded Alexandria, and Sir Garnet Wolseley, who was sent out as Commander-in-Chief of the expeditionary force, deceived Arabi into thinking that he intended to land there in force. He actually put one division ashore, but later moved all his transports by night to Ismailia, about halfway down the canal, and advanced by land from there towards Cairo.

THE MOONLIGHT CHARGE

The first fighting was at Kassassin lock, which had to be seized in order to control the supply of drinking water in the

Freshwater Canal, which the Egyptians had cut off. This is a small channel which runs from Ismailia towards Cairo and was the main reason for the choice of route, as the desert contained no other water supplies worth mentioning. General Graham, after capturing the lock, was heavily attacked, but was relieved by Drury-Lowe's cavalry brigade—one squadron each, of the 1*st* and 2*nd Life Guards* and *Royal Horse Guards*, and the 7*th Dragoon Guards*, which arrived after dark, while the attack was still going on, and drove off the Egyptians by its celebrated 'moonlight charge' across the desert.

TEL-EL-KEBIR

The main battle, which decided the war, was at Tel-el-Kebir, a small town a few miles from Kassassin, along the Port Said–Cairo railway, and the desert battle ground was close to the station. (In 1914–18 and in 1939–45 there were enormous reinforcement camps in this area, which was probably chosen again on account of the Sweetwater canal, although the water would have needed much purification and extraction of dead donkeys, etc.)

The force, about 13,000 strong, reached a point about five miles from Arabi's position, without being detected. They marched from there at 1.30 a.m., and as there were no landmarks their direction was kept entirely by compass bearings and the positions of the stars, which was no simple matter with so large a force, but the only incident was when the Highland Brigade nearly started a private war. Owing to the centre having halted, and the whispered order not being passed to the flanks, the outside regiments continued to advance, keeping touch with the centre and gradually converging. They eventually came face to face and very nearly mistook each other for the enemy. Had they fired, the whole surprise effect would have been ruined.

Just before dawn some Egyptian picquets fired. Then a bugle roused the whole camp and fire broke out from four miles of trenches and redoubts. But everything went according to plan. The infantry went in cheering, in solid ranks, in the good old style, and in about half an hour cleared the whole position with the bayonet. There had been no artillery bombardment, as it was a surprise attack and there was some tough fighting before it was over. But once beaten the 25,000 Egyptians made no effort to rally, and simply fled, without stopping, until they got to their homes and turned themselves back into civilians.

Next day the cavalry marched forty miles and entered Cairo, where they captured Arabi. The whole war had lasted less than two months and was a model of good Staff work and organization.

Sir Garnet had said, before he left England, that he would beat Arabi at Tel-el-Kebir, about the 13th of September, and he did so on that very day. The total force used in Egypt was about 40,000 strong, including 8,000 Indians.

The Egyptians were armed and trained, by the Turks, on European lines, but were not specially tenacious and had loathsome Oriental habits, such as mutilating the dead and wounded. They fought well at times, but their officers did not excel in leadership.

THE FIRST AUTOMATIC MACHINE-GUN

At this period, in addition to the Gatling gun, another infantry weapon known as the Nordenfeldt gun, which had five barrels placed side by side, was used. The Gardner gun, of similar construction, was also used, but none of them was very efficient and in 1883, Hiram Maxim, an American, invented the first automatic gas-operated machine-gun, which, with slight improvements, became the Vickers gun. He was also the inventor of the Pom-Pom, used in the second Boer War, which fired belts of one-pound shells.

THE KHARTOUM EXPEDITION, 1884

The responsibilities acquired in Egypt in 1882 led to our being involved in wars in the Sudan, which Egypt was attempting to rule with British help.

About 1883 the Mahdi (Messiah) took control of the savage tribes in the Sudan and, being quite a genius at desert warfare, caused a great deal of trouble. This included the massacre of 11,000 Egyptian troops under Colonel Hicks, after a three days' battle, the success of which left no doubt about the Mahdi's divine origin, and fanatical recruits crowded in to join him. After this, the British Government short-sightedly decided to evacuate the various small garrisons in the Sudan and leave it to the Mahdi. General Gordon was sent out to conduct this operation.

He was besieged in Khartoum and after lengthy procrastination an expedition was sent to relieve him, the delay having been caused by Gladstone's anti-imperial and pacifist views, and his refusal to provide the troops or the money.

Sir Garnet Wolseley was in command and moved his force in two columns, one up the Nile and the other partly across the desert. The latter had to follow the ancient camel routes, so as to obtain water at the few oases, which were the only sources of supply. The men suffered greatly from heat, dust, thirst, and eyestrain from the glare of the desert, as well as from sand-fly fever and all the other normal inconveniences of a tropical climate. They fought two battles, at Abu Klea, and Abu Kru and, in the end, had to turn back after Gordon and about 4,000 people had been killed in a night of massacre on 25th January 1885, while the relief force was only a few miles away.

In the force were a camel regiment formed from the cavalry, the Guards and *The Royal Marines*, one known as the Light Camel Regiment; and another as the Mounted Infantry Camel Regiment (they were actually all mounted infantry), as well as horsed cavalry, horse artillery, a field hospital, and the inevitable baggage camels. The infantry were *The Black Watch, The Gordon Highlanders, The Royal Sussex, Essex, Royal Irish*, and *Royal West Kent* regiments.

END OF RED COATS

This was the last war in which red coats were worn, and already the exigencies of desert war were hurrying the transformation— khaki breeches, shirt-sleeves, grey 'frocks' for the camel regiments, etc. Probably some khaki drill jackets were worn but, true to type, the War Office held out to the last against making it universal, though it had been worn for about thirty years in India.

Weapons were the Martini rifle and carbine, primitive machine-guns and field guns. Even these could not always stop the frenzied rushes of the Arabs and, at Abu Klea, they broke into the middle of the square and for some time there was a desperate mêlée inside it. The troops dealt manfully with them and few got out again, but the British position was very precarious for a time. When it was over more than a thousand dead Arabs were counted.

SQUARES

The square was the usual formation in savage warfare of this type—not regimental squares, such as were used at Waterloo, but one large square containing the whole column, minus its protective screen of cavalry, scouts, etc., which, however, often came inside during an attack. If fighting was expected the column would march in square formation, this being quite possible in the open desert, where there were no confining roads.

ZAREBAS

The nightly drill in this country was to construct a zareba, or thick thorn hedge, such as natives in Egypt, India, etc., use to protect their cattle at night from thieves and carnivora, but if there were no thorn bushes to use, a parapet was made from the camels' loads. (The thorn barrier may have given the idea to the inventor of barbed wire.) Inside the zareba the arrangement was much the same as in the square—fighting troops and guns lined round the perimeter, and all the 'odds and sods' and the camels in the middle. There were sentries all round the perimeter, and every man slept at his battle station.

THE ENEMY

The enemy differed from the Egyptians in much the same way as the Pathans do from the Bengalis. They were wild, tough, fanatical, fighting, looting savages—armed mostly with primitive weapons, but brave and fearless, and very numerous. Like others of their kind, they had their own tricks of warfare, a favourite one being to sham death, and then leap up and shoot or knife a man in the back, or hamstring a horse. They also mutilated the dead and treated prisoners barbarously.

THE BATTLE OF OMDURMAN, 2ND SEPTEMBER 1898

After thirteen years of anarchy and desolation in the Sudan, it was decided that the job which had been thrown up in 1885, must now be finished. The battle of Omdurman was the grand finale, and was fought within sight of Khartoum, where Gordon met his end and British influence seemed to have died also.

Kitchener (afterwards Lord Kitchener of Khartoum) was in command. Outwardly a grim and ruthless man, he had the reputation of being a great organizer, and his watchword was 'Thorough'. He had spent many years in Egypt and the Sudan, and it was in this campaign that he gained a name which was enhanced owing to the fact that Gordon, after his death, had become a national hero and martyr—and Kitchener was his avenger. Actually his method was to run a 'one man show' after breaking-up much of the established organization, to listen to no one's advice, and keep most of his plans to himself. In later wars in other countries with which he was not familiar, this system was less successful. He now commanded a force of 22,000 British, Egyptian and Sudanese, with 44 guns and a number of Maxims. The British were all in khaki drill and were armed with Magazine Lee Metford rifles, using smokeless cordite (invented in 1889), which for the first time banished the old problem of the target disappearing in a cloud of smoke after each volley. (The M.L.M. rifle had a magazine holding five rounds, which had to be put in separately, as chargers had not then been thought of.) One memorable thing about this battle is that it was the last time line formation and volley-firing were used.

The Khalifa (successor to the Mahdi) had between 40,000 and

50,000 men, consisting of about 10,000 very inefficient riflemen, 2,000 Baggara horsemen, and the rest armed with swords, spears and shields. They had a few guns, which were badly served and had poor ammunition.

There had been one large-scale battle at the Atbara river, and about four months later, after waiting for the Nile to rise, so as to make full use of it for transport, the force advanced. A flotilla of gunboats moved up the river parallel with the troops, cleared the enemy from villages along the banks and protected the native boats carrying the stores.

Omdurman was the target of this expedition because this great hot, stinking city of mud houses and squalor was the headquarters of the Khalifa, where his followers lived in style, and from where he conducted his reign of terror, sending out raiding parties to loot, ravage and enslave the inhabitants of an enormous area.

When the force had arrived within range the challenge was given by shelling the stronghold with 5-inch howitzers, using the white dome of the Mahdi's tomb as the ranging mark, and shallow trenches and zarebas were constructed by the Nile.

As the shells crashed into the city, it was as if a hornets' nest had come to life and, after a spell of heated argument, the Arabs decided to come out and fight. The war drums sounded, and all along the seven-mile length of the town they streamed out into the desert and formed up on their Standards.

Then, most foolishly, but conveniently, they advanced in a mass over two miles long, to attack the British in their semi-prepared position, and had to cross 3,000 yards of open desert in broad daylight. Had they waited for darkness, an attack in such force by such fearless savages would have been extremely formidable, and the British advantage of superior weapons would have been greatly reduced.

The cavalry and the Camel Corps, who had been forward reconnoitring, had a difficult withdrawal, having to fire and charge repeatedly, and the Horse Artillery, accompanying them, lost so many horses that two guns had to be abandoned (minus their breech blocks).

The great army of dervishes pressed forward under the fire of the gunboats, the artillery and the maxims, losing heavily but undismayed. The riflemen were in front, then came the main body of spearmen and swordsmen, led by mounted Sheiks and numerous Standard bearers, the Khalifa's great black flag marking the centre. The mullahs intoned chants to work up their hatred of the infidels and promised an immediate heaven, filled with ravishing houris, to those who should be fortunate enough to be killed in battle. A second line consisted mainly of baggage camels and donkeys with a strong escort.

At about five hundred yards the British line opened fire and a little beyond this a sort of high-water mark was formed, which few were able to pass over. It became piled with lines and heaps of bodies, a specially large mound of them rising around the black flag. This was, of course, a selected target, but each time a bearer fell it was seized by another candidate for heaven.

In the British line rifles became too hot to hold, and frequent swops had to be made with the men of the reserve companies. There were some casualties caused by riflemen who had worked round among the sandhills, but they were not numerous.

The Dervish attack persisted, without success, for about two hours and then the dense masses began to trickle and finally to stream away. Personal bravery, however savage, had no chance against modern weapons, without being similarly armed and properly trained.

Kitchener then decided to advance on Omdurman, five miles distant, moving in echelon of brigades, but it had not been known that the Khalifa had still about 30,000 men hidden behind some rocky hills, and two attacks, each about 15,000 strong, suddenly rushed down on the marching troops. It was a very near thing for Hector McDonald's Egyptian and Sudanese brigade, which was caught on a flank, but in the end the result was as in the first attack.

Realizing their final defeat, most of the dervish leaders 'behaved like gentlemen' and took up positions round the flag, where they stayed until they were killed. Five hundred of the Baggara horse made a last desperate charge and were completely exterminated.

During the advance the 21*st Lancers*, riding to cut off a body of enemy, stumbled suddenly into an unseen khor (shallow ravine) containing about 1,500 enemy, who stood up to them, and in two or three minutes inflicted seventy casualties and killed 119 horses. The lancers went straight through the solid mass, which was about twenty deep, and re-formed on the far side, ready to repeat their effort. But, instead, they were ordered to give them carbine fire, which drove them out across the front of the infantry and gunners who wiped out most of them. It had been an extremely exciting incident. Many had been unhorsed and attacked on foot, and several V.C.s were won, when officers and men turned back into the stabbing, slashing mass to rescue them. Nearly every man and horse had some sort of wound, serious or slight, but they had met the sudden emergency with coolness and a fine team spirit and in recognition of this they were afterwards given the title 'Empress of India's'. (It will be remembered that they were originally one of the East India Company's regiments.) Lieutenant Winston Churchill, of the *4th Hussars*, took part in this battle, being attached to the 21*st Lancers* as a supernumerary.

This was the end of the Khalifa's tyranny over the Sudan, and he had lost about 10,000 killed and probably 15,000 wounded, against about 450 British casualties. It was a great and one-sided slaughter, but the enemy were people who could not have understood any other method, who had many nasty habits, and were completely barbarous to anyone unfortunate enough to be in their power.

A super-modern effect, in this land where scarcely a thing had changed from pre-biblical times, was made by the beams of the gunboat's electric searchlights, which swept the desert nightly, as a precaution against surprise attacks. Captive balloons were another novelty used by *The Royal Engineers*, for the first time on service.

PLATE XVI

(39)

1881

The Queen's Own (Royal West Kent
Regiment)

Officer (patrol jacket)

The Sherwood Foresters (Notts and
Derby Regiment)

Officer

Private (walking-out dress)

(40)

1882

Egypt

The Royal Field Artillery

Officer

The 1st Life Guards

Officer

The York and Lancaster Regiment

Private

(41)

1900

South Africa

The 14th Hussars

Officer and trumpeter

(42)

1910

Officers

The Gordon Highlanders (*blue frock*)

The Royal Scots

The Argyll and Sutherland Highlanders
(*white drill order*)

PLATE XVI

Figs. 39, 40, 41 & 42

With the introduction of the helmet, and the wearing of anklets, the silhouette view of an infantry officer became almost identical with that of a German officer.

The slash cuffs of the tunic were replaced, in 1868, by pointed ones with stripes and knots of gold lace, and in 1880 gold shoulder cords were ordered to be worn, on which the badges of rank were placed, instead of on the collar. These were again revised, as follows: Colonel—a crown over two stars; Lieutenant-Colonel—a crown over one star; Major—a crown; Captain—two stars; Lieutenant—one star. The rank of 2nd Lieutenant was abolished. (Ensigns and Cornets became 2nd Lieutenants in 1871.)

Lace on collars and cuffs varied according to rank until 1902. A Lieutenant-Colonel had two broad stripes on the cuff, with a narrow line of twisted gimp above and below. A Major had the same, except that the lowest line of gimp was not twisted. Captains had two stripes and Lieutenants one, with a line of untwisted gimp above and below. All officers' collars had lace round the top only, field officers having twisted gimp and company officers straight.

The Sherwood Foresters' old facing colour—Lincoln green (restored later), was connected with a legend that the regiment was descended from Robin Hood's band of outlaws, whose stronghold was in Sherwood Forest.

The patrol jacket, first worn in 1867, when it replaced the frock coat, had many regimental variations of the trimmings of fur, or astrakhan, and braid. In 1880 a new forage cap, with a peak and a noticeably French appearance, was authorized for officers, 'Royal' regiments wearing a scarlet band on it in accordance with tradition.

The Glengarry had been adopted as the forage cap for other ranks of infantry in 1874, and had ribbon tails, as in Scotland.

In 1872 officers' mess dress became the subject of regulations, and took the form of the shell jacket, worn open, and normally with a roll collar and lapels of the facing colour, with a waistcoat. Up to 1855 officers had dined in their full-dress coatees, and afterwards various unauthorized shell jackets and waistcoats had been worn, and expensive changes were liable to be made each time a new Commanding Officer was appointed.

The Queen's Own became a 'Royal' regiment in 1831, having previously had black facings. The regiment has the same motto as *The Royal Artillery*, and *The Royal Engineers*—'Quo fas et gloria ducunt.'

PLATE XVI (40) EGYPT. 1882

This was the last war in which the traditional red and blue uniforms were worn. Although khaki had been in use in India for over thirty years, it seems to have been practically confined to that country, and no stock of it was kept at home, so units were sent to Egypt in what was known as home field service dress. (The same procedure was followed for the Zulu War, 1879, and the first Boer War, 1881.) Almost the only concession to the climate was the topi, or tropical helmet. (Topi = a clump of trees. Hindustani.)

Owing to the heat, packs were often not carried on the march. Greatcoats would be unnecessary in the Egyptian summer, and many illustrations of the time show the infantryman wearing his equipment, with ammunition pouches, bayonet, haversack and water-bottle, and only a mess tin in a black cover on his back, strapped on where the braces crossed.

The artillery officer, taking advantage of active service conditions, which always result in a relaxation of the rigours of dress, has modernized himself considerably, by procuring khaki breeches, a khaki cover for his topi (as issued in India for the Afghan War in 1879), and puttees, and is consequently more comfortable and less conspicuous.

Both officers have modified tunics, with outside pockets and no gold lace, which were officially approved in 1878, and were known as 'frocks'.

PLATE XVI (41) SOUTH AFRICA. 1900

In 1900 khaki was described in the Dress Regulations as 'foreign service uniform', and was not worn except on active service. The jacket had a stand-up collar, of the pattern long known as 'Prussian', and cavalry wore chain shoulder-straps. Leggings with spiral straps were the regulation for mounted officers, and other ranks wore puttees. Officers had khaki helmets, but those issued to other ranks were white, with loose khaki covers.

Sam Browne belts were generally worn with two braces, and other ranks of light cavalry—hussars and lancers—wore no waistbelt. The sword was carried in a leather loop on the shoe case, attached to the saddle.

Trumpeters carried a trumpet and a bugle, and the strings shown are those of a 'Royal' regiment—red, yellow, and blue intertwined.

Cavalry went out armed with carbines, but they were found ineffective against the long-range shooting of the Boers, and were exchanged for Lee Metford rifles.

The *14th Hussars* arrived in South Africa early in 1900, and took part in many engagements, including Paardeberg, Kimberley, Relief of Ladysmith, and numerous minor actions. The horses had a great deal of hard work, covering enormous distances in Cape Colony, Orange River Colony and the Transvaal, often at exhausting speed.

PLATE XVI (42) SCOTTISH REGIMENTS. 1910

The blue frock, in use by all arms of the Service (Green patrol jacket for Rifles), was made with a special cut for Scottish regiments, having skirts shaped away from below the belt buckle and tartan trews were worn with it, as they had been with the frock coat from the early nineteenth century. The service dress jacket was made in the same style, and badges of rank were worn on the gauntlet cuffs.

The full-dress doublet, with its characteristic Inverness skirts, was worn by all ranks of Scottish regiments, either with the kilt or with trews, and field officers had a line of gold lace above the white piping on the flaps. White drill shell jackets had been worn for about sixty years.

The Glengarry cap, with or without the diced border, according to regimental custom, took the place of the round forage cap worn by non-Scottish regiments. *The Royal Scots* and *The King's Own Scottish Borderers* wore Kilmarnock bonnets in full dress from about 1902, having previously worn the universal spiked helmet. Both of these Scottish head-dresses have been worn as forage caps by regiments from other parts of Britain and Ireland. The Kilmarnock bonnet was in general use from about 1800 until it was replaced by the 'pork pie' cap, about 1840, and the Glengarry brought another reversion to Scottish style about 1874 and was worn by the line regiments until the field service cap replaced it in 1890.

The sash was worn over the left shoulder by officers of Scottish regiments only and the plaid, with large regimental brooch on the left shoulder, formed a part of the full dress of kilted regiments. Mounted officers and pipers wore a part of it round the body.

The old cross-belt, with breast-plate, survived as an interesting relic of the past and gold-laced waistbelts, different for each regiment, were worn. Mounted officers, however, wore a white waistbelt with sword slings and a regimental plate over the fastening.

The claymore (*claidheamh mor* = great sword), had a removable basket hilt, which was worn in full dress, but field officers carried the ordinary infantry sword.

Scottish officers carried a dirk, usually very ornate and set with semi-precious stones, in a frog on the right side, and those in kilts wore the 'skean dhu', a small dagger, in the top of the right hose.

With all these national characteristics and the many regimental differences, the uniforms of the Scottish regiments were among the most interesting and the most historic in the army, and their picturesque effect and the strange and stirring music of the pipes never failed to react on the English public, who were invariably thrilled at the sight of a highland regiment.

None of the above notes apply to *The Scots Guards* who, apart from their pipers, wore the normal Guards' uniform, the diced border on their forage caps and their badges being the most notable national features.

PLATE XVII

(43)
1889
The Royal Scots Greys
Mounted band

(44)
1890
The 14th Hussars
Trooper (stable jacket)
Officer (serge frock)
Officer (full dress)

(45)
1900
The 11th Hussars
Officer (patrol jacket)
Lieutenant-General (*frock coat*)
Field-Marshal (*full dress*)

The 17th Lancers
Officer (full dress)

The Scots Guards
Officer (state dress)

(46)
1904
The 11th Hussars
Sergeant and Troopers

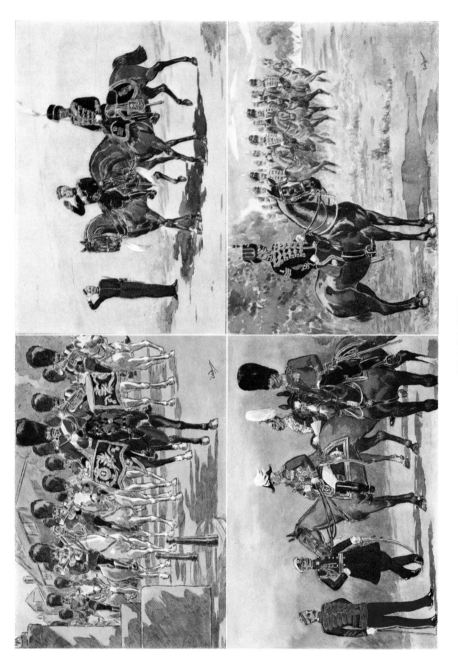

PLATE XVII

Figs. 43, 44, 45 & 46

PLATE XVII (43) ROYAL SCOTS GREYS. MOUNTED BAND. 1889

The mounted bands of the cavalry and *Royal Artillery* were one of the most picturesque features of the army, until mechanization dismounted them, and the glitter of dancing colours, the well-trained horses and the sound of their music seemed to carry the mind back through centuries of army history.

None was more pleasing than that of *The Greys*, the scarlet and gold blazing forth so strikingly against the white of the horses, the tall bearskins providing a foil for the bright colours and giving dignity and added height to the bandsmen.

Regimental drum-horses were generally of a different colour from the remainder and were fine animals, specially selected and trained and worthy of their richly embroidered banners and the silver drums which many of them carried.

Cavalry bandsmen had worn the same uniform as their regiments since 1836, but in the heavy regiments they wore a different-coloured plume from that of the troopers and an aiguilette.

The Greys were one of the last regiments to be mechanized, and with their horses went one of the most familiar and attractive sights of the old army.

PLATE XVII (44) THE 14TH HUSSARS. 1890

The full dress of Hussars was changed only in minor details, after 1855. (The 14th were Light Dragoons until 1861, and·their uniform up to that date is shown in Plate XIV (33).

There were, however, several changes in horse "furniture" and in the undress uniforms. Other ranks ceased to use shabracques (cavalry saddle-cloths) in 1872, and officers, except *The Household Cavalry*, the *Guards*, and General Officers, did likewise in 1897. (There is slight variation in the dates when the actual change was made in each regiment.) Drum horses also continued to wear shabracques and officers' lambskin, leopardskin, etc. saddle-rugs were in use until 1914. The steel collar chain was replaced by a head-rope in 1893, but is still used by *The Household Cavalry*. Sabretaches were abolished for other ranks in 1888 and for officers about 1902.

Serge frocks were issued about 1891 for drill and manœuvres, and the stable jacket (which was a shell jacket) was discontinued in 1899, except by *The Household Cavalry*.

The 'pill-box' cap was only worn for walking out after 1900, and the field service cap became the universal wear for drill and training. It then had a very narrow chinstrap.

A regimental peculiarity of the 14*th Hussars* was that the officers wore no cockade on the busby. (The circular gilt fitting below the plume was known as the cockade, and all ranks of *The Royal Horse Artillery* wear none.)

PLATE XVII (45). 1900

The full dress of General Officers had gone through changes similar to those of other officers—in 1829 the coatee with heavy fringed epaulettes, gold-laced sword-belt, gold and crimson striped sash over the right shoulder, and overalls with gold lace stripes—in 1855 the tunic, and a few years later a return to jacked boots and white leather breeches.

In 1900 some of the historic features still remained, such as the Field Marshal's baton, the cocked hat with red and white feathers, holster pipes and shabracque and the Mameluke scimitar. This dress remained unaltered, as long as full dress was worn.

Badges of rank for Generals (still unchanged except for Brigadiers, who now wear a crown and three stars and are no longer Generals) were:

Field Marshal—crossed batons within a wreath of laurel, surmounted by a crown.
General—crown, star, crossed baton and scimitar.
Lieutenant-General—crown, crossed baton and scimitar.
Major-General—star, crossed baton and scimitar.
Brigadier-General—crossed baton and scimitar.

Badges of rank were worn on the shabracque by Generals and Guard-officers. Browbands and rosettes were worn by all officers' chargers on full dress occasions and were of the regimental facing colour.

The frock coat shown was of the universal pattern, the only difference for Generals being that they had blue velvet facings. The patrol jacket was different, as regards its trimmings, for each cavalry regiment. They were also worn, in green, by Rifles officers.

There were three forage caps for officers—the overhanging, peaked one for Staff officers, the 'pill-box' type for cavalry, and the peaked one with vertical sides for infantry. Scottish regiments wore the Glengarry.

PLATE XVII (46) 11TH HUSSARS. SERGEANT AND TROOPERS. 1904

The 11*th Hussars'* badge is the crest and motto of the Prince Consort, who was Colonel of the regiment which formed his escort when he arrived at Dover, in 1840, for his marriage to Queen Victoria.

They were the only regiment in the army wearing crimson overalls as part of their full dress, from which they acquired the nickname of 'the cherry-pickers' or 'the cherubims'. (Early in the nineteenth century several cavalry regiments wore red overalls, including the 9*th Lancers* and the 10*th Hussars*. Officers of the 10th still wear scarlet ones in levèe dress.)

The 11th were raised, as dragoons, in 1715 and took part in nearly all the important campaigns to the end of the nineteenth century, including the famous charge at Balaclava.

They were among the earliest regiments to be mechanized, and in the recent war they took a prominent part in the North African campaigns and later in Europe, as a unit of the renowned 'Desert Rats' armoured division.

CHAPTER X · 1899-1913

'In a dense thicket every man is his own General, and subordination to orders, where combined movements are impossible of execution, becomes a vice rather than a virtue.' ('Sergeant Lamb of the 9th', 1775.)

THE TRANSITION PERIOD

The last stage of colourful warfare had passed. There was no more line-of-battle in solid ranks, no more volley-firing, and scarlet and gold and dense clouds of smoke had way given to drab-coloured clothes and smokeless propellants. The grim business of killing or being killed was stripped of its glamour and ritual. Precision weapons were employed in concealed positions, and as civilian life progressed more rapidly toward the machine age, each new discovery of science or more efficient production, which could have any use in war, was adapted to improve the methods of mutual destruction.

When a nation invented a better weapon, or a more powerful explosive, it held the advantage only for a short time, before it came into universal use, or an antidote was found, or a further improvement was made. Thus warfare became increasingly complicated.

It was the end of the era in which a commander could watch with his own eyes the progress of a battle, with his troops spread out in front of him, like a game of model soldiers. From now on he would often have to work in a distant headquarters, making his decisions from maps, reports, and fine calculations of time and space and all the other factors which enter into the winning of battles.

But, as always, there were some of the Generals and senior officers, brought up in the old tradition, who could not easily adjust their outlook. John Buchan wrote in *Memory Hold the Door*: 'The more competent and better trained a soldier was, the more averse he would be to alter his traditional creed till its failure had been proven with utter finality.' He was speaking of 1914, but his words apply equally to any period. Manœuvres at home were still carried out in full dress, or something very near it, and

o

some of the mock actions, which took place during training, looked suspiciously like old-time battles, so one could not say more than that the army was in the transition stage when the South African War began.

THE BOER WAR

To quote Lord Montgomery's famous expression, 'after removing the muckage', this is why the war was fought. It was another case, like the Sudan, of having to fight the same war again, after having failed to force the issue to a satisfactory conclusion the first time. After 1881, the Boers, having got the upper hand, made things quite intolerable for the British colonists, by means of legislation and generally acrimonious behaviour. The discovery of gold on the Rand in 1886, in addition to the diamond fields already being exploited round Kimberley, made the Boers more anxious to oust the British, and the latter more determined to stay, thus producing the inevitability of a clash, sooner or later. President Kruger began the war, by calling out 10,000 burghers and sending an ultimatum, in October 1899.

GUERRILLA V. TRAINED SOLDIER

It lasted until 1902 and, in all, it involved the use of about 450,000 troops—regulars, volunteers and Dominion forces, against which the Boers used between 80,000 and 90,000 men. We had not been concerned in a war approaching this scale since the Napoleonic period, but it was only a slight prelude to the world wars of the twentieth century.

The necessity for employing so many troops, with superior equipment and organization, against these comparatively small numbers, was due to the fact that their methods of campaigning consisted mainly of guerrilla warfare. They had, nearly all, learned the arts of game-tracking and stalking, and had become good rifle-shots during their ordinary farming life. They were very mobile—practically every man mounted, and knew the country and could live on it, thus being able to manage without vulnerable supply trains, lines of communication and all the paraphernalia of a European army. In addition they were quick-witted and cunning and often were not scrupulous about using any tricks which occurred to them. The topography of the country also helped them a great deal. In many parts, the 'kopjes' rise abruptly out of vast level expanses of veldt, giving excellent observation posts and, as the climate is often dry for many months, any movement of troops raises a dust cloud, which advertised their presence to lookout men twenty or thirty miles away.

The result was that our army, which at first was not accustomed to this type of warfare, could find nothing solid to hit at until, by long and laborious encircling movements, they could round up a body of the enemy and pin it down to action. Even then the Boers could often dodge the issue and disperse before the slow-moving troops could come up with them. The fact that they wore no uniform made it often possible for a Boer to ride off to his farm, conceal his rifle and ammunition, and masquerade as a peaceful citizen—a practice which ultimately necessitated the internment of thousands of people of doubtful loyalties.

MOUNTED INFANTRY

From our point of view it was obvious that greater mobility was required and therefore large numbers of cavalry had to be used. It was not cavalry work according to the drill book, but rather mounted infantry tactics which were wanted, as cavalry actions were becoming a thing of the past. The rifle had ousted the sword, and mounted men gave too good a target. The cavalry carbine, with its short range, soon had to be replaced by the infantry rifle and the men had to learn more about dismounted fighting and use their horses only for mobility, as the dragoons of the seventeenth and eighteenth centuries did. There was not, of course, sufficient regular cavalry for the job and many Yeomanry regiments were sent out, most of them being used as mounted infantry. The Colonials, too, from South Africa, Australia, New Zealand and Canada, were just the men to fill this gap and were thrilled at the idea of joining in. Names like *The Diamond Fields Light Horse, The New South Wales Bushmen, Kitchener's Fighting Scouts*, etc., etc., gave a colourful touch to the news bulletins.

In addition to the mounted regiments, each infantry battalion had had its M.I. detachment since about 1888, and these performed functions similar in many ways to those of the Bren carrier platoon in recent times—rapid reinforcing of threatened points, occupying positions for the rifle companies to take over, etc. In many instances, though, the M.I. detachments of a number of regiments were taken to form a battalion (as the grenadier companies were in the seventeenth and eighteenth centuries), which became part of the Divisional Troops, or were put into a cavalry brigade. Maxim and Nordenfeldt guns could accompany the M.I., as they were mounted on carriages with artillery wheels and drawn by horses. Each regiment of cavalry or infantry had a section of them. (There were also cyclist sections on the home establishments of infantry regiments, for purposes of reconnaissance, carrying messages, etc., but they were of little use in South

Africa, as there were very few roads on which a bicycle could be ridden.)

CARBINES

In the recent war the carbine came back, but this time as an infantry weapon, for close fighting, in the form of the Thompson sub-machine gun, the Sten machine carbine, and the shortened rifle, built on the lines of a sporting model, for jungle snap-shooting. The sub-machine gun appears to have originated among the Chicago gangsters, being later taken into use by the U.S. Police, and finally adapted for military purposes. America has been the home of nearly all automatic weapons.

THE PATTERN OF THE WAR

At the beginning of the war there were less than 5,000 British regular troops in the country, and the general pattern of events was similar to that of the Indian Mutiny. The first stages consisted of besieged garrisons holding out, in Ladysmith, Mafeking, Kimberley, etc., while relief columns were organized and fought their way, with many checks, towards them. Each was eventually relieved and the second stage involved the occupation of other important towns and the rounding-up of elusive Boer commandos.

THE ARMY'S WEAK POINTS

There were many reverses sustained by the relieving columns —e.g. those of Lord Methuen at Modder River and Magersfontein, of General Gatacre at Stormberg, and of Sir Redvers Buller at Colenso and Spion Kop, and the general impression, as regards generalship and Staff work, in the early part of the war, is little better than that of the first Boer War. It is true that the army's experience of this kind of warfare had been more or less limited to that of the first Boer War, in which only a small number of troops took part, and in the previous century, against the Americans; and that since 1856 it had fought mainly against savages in campaigns requiring quite a different technique. But the Tirah campaign of 1897—quite a large-scale affair—and other campaigns on the North-West Frontier of India should have taught many lessons which would have helped. However, we have always been slow to change our methods, and many of the Generals seemed to have reverted to a sort of Crimean mentality.

Most of them were personally very brave, and much too gentlemanly, but they seemed bull-headed and deficient in cunning (the latter trait was all too evident on the other side). They appeared to lack the necessary quality of mental agility and to be unable to improvise quickly in emergencies, or to have sufficient confidence in their original plans when they went wrong. Their reconnaissance work was frequently faulty and they worked on false deductions. In fact some of them seem to have been quite at sea under these new conditions.

MODDER RIVER

At Modder river Lord Methuen walked into a trap. He thought there was only a Boer rearguard, but found a heavily manned position, four miles long, sited invisibly in the river bed. (A more skilled version of the tactics used by the Indians at Meanee, 1843.) He sent troops to cross an unfordable part of the river and made other mistakes which, however, were compensated for by the spirited work of his troops and, in spite of all the difficulties, the Boers were forced to retreat.

MAGERSFONTEIN

At Magersfontein he allowed the enemy to entrench a position which he could have occupied himself, and then made a frontal attack against the strongest part of it, when he might have outflanked it. He ordered Wauchope's Highland brigade to make a night advance and attack at dawn—in the style of Tel-el-Kebir, but with very different results. They came within 400 yards of the Boer position while still in quarter-column, and met a blaze of rifle fire as they began to deploy, which seriously damaged the morale of some units. The brigade was then left more or less unsupported and under heavy and accurate fire for most of the day, and when ordered to retire, still under fire, they fell into confusion—almost panic. Thus a good brigade was reduced to disorder by bad generalship.

There were two interesting features in this battle. The Boers, whose position was about twelve miles long, used slit trenches, sited at the foot of the hills, instead of high up—an innovation which came fully up to expectations in protecting them from shrapnel and shell fire and in making their own fire more effective, as their bullets travelled parallel to the ground instead of plunging down into it. The second point of interest was that the kilt proved very unsuitable, as highlanders, lying in the sun for hours, had the backs of their legs so blistered that they could hardly walk.

COLENSO

Colenso provided another unpleasant example, one of its outstanding blunders being the advance of the 14th and 66th field batteries, without escort and without cover, to within 700 yards of the Boer riflemen. The gunners behaved admirably and did their drill as if on a field day, but were nearly all hit, and the remnants, after firing all their ammunition, were ordered to shelter in a nullah and leave the guns. Seven V.C.s (one of them awarded posthumously to Lord Roberts's only son) were won in efforts to retrieve the guns by riding out with the teams across open ground, in full daylight, but the net result was that Buller lost all except two. He might have recovered them if he had tried again after dark, but instead he retired his whole force and helioed a message to Sir George White in Ladysmith, telling him to surrender the town, as he could not relieve it in time. White refused and asked Buller (who was then C.-in-C.) to keep on trying.

At Colenso one brigadier did not believe in extended order and tried to keep his brigade in close formation. Some regiments, on the other hand, had become very skilled in fieldcraft.

METHODS OF COMMUNICATION

The heliograph—a controlled mirror, on a tripod, flashing the sun's reflection in Morse code, was useful in South Africa and could be read at a range of thirty miles or more, but in the damp climates of Britain and northern Europe it proved almost useless, as one could never rely on sunshine. Another fairly new method of communication was the 'pigeon post', used during the relief of Mafeking. Telephones and telegraphs were, by now, in common use, and the Royal Engineers had Telegraph Sections, which laid wires during operations. Another new feature was the use of a few observation balloons—a crude shadow of coming events.

SPION KOP

The battle of Spion Kop was one of the best examples of bad Staff work. The system broke down entirely and, when senior officers became casualties, others were put in command without those under them being informed, and no one knew who was doing what. Sir Charles Warren, in command, was busy collecting stores in the rear, while confusion reigned elsewhere, and the hill was surrendered while he was still making preparations to hold it. There were nearly 2,000 casualties during several days of most creditable fighting, but owing to bad organization the result was nil.

THE 'OTHER RANKS'

The behaviour of the men in the ranks was usually quite up to British army standard, but there were occasions—such as Magersfontein, Waggon Hill (Ladysmith), and one or two others, when they fell below it. When they did they could generally be rallied quite quickly, and it is only fair to attribute their failures partly to deficiencies in their training, which had not adequately prepared their minds for what they had to expect—and partly to lack of experience of this type of fighting on the part of the officers, which caused some tactical blunders. It is always the unknown which is most difficult to stand up against—hence the very realistic battle training during the 1939–45 war; and the feeling of being let down—e.g. being ordered to march in close formation, as at Magersfontein, until an apparently innocent piece of ground suddenly spouts thousands of bullets—puts a great strain on morale. All the same it does seem that the discipline of some units was not what it might have been. This, however, on occasions was due to the very heavy losses in officers, who besides being easily distinguishable by their swords, etc., had still the same disdain for taking cover as those of the 23rd Foot had at the battle of the Alma, 1854. Many a good officer ceased to be of further use owing to his walking about in the firing line, or standing up to give his orders.

MAFEKING

Fortunately it was not all so gloomy and there were many brilliant exploits and successful operations, among which Colonel Baden Powell's defence of Mafeking takes a high place. He had 700 men—nearly all volunteers and civilians—to man an undefended and straggling town, with a mixed population of Europeans and natives and held it for seven months against two or three thousand Boers with artillery. Food became very scarce and they ate horses and anything that came to hand, including a swarm of locusts.

It was the most active and enterprising defence among all the besieged garrisons and Baden Powell, who was called by the natives 'the wolf that never sleeps', lived up to his name, gave the enemy a very worrying time and kept the morale of the defenders at a high level right through the siege. They inflicted over a thousand casualties on the Boers.

ELANDSLAAGTE (THE GLEN OF ELANDS)

Elandslaagte, near Ladysmith, was the scene of a successful battle, up to a point, against about 2,000 Boers in position with guns, on two kopjes, divided by a wide kloof. There was first a reconnaissance by *The Imperial Light Horse*, and six guns of the *Natal Volunteer Artillery*, with an infantry escort of half a battalion of *The Manchester Regiment*.

For the main battle Colonel Ian Hamilton (later of Gallipoli fame) brought up the *Devons*, five companies of the *Gordons* and the other half of the *Manchesters*. There were two batteries of field guns which went into action at 4,400 yards and the infantry then advanced in small columns—probably half-companies (equal to a platoon), in fours, spread out so that a battalion had a front of about 500 yards and a depth of over 1,000 yards.

At about 900 yards, range they opened rifle fire (too soon to have any serious effect) and thereafter they advanced by short rushes in extended lines. Then came the escalade of the steep, boulder-strewn slope, up to the Boer position and, finally, a bayonet charge with bugles, pipes and cheering. But the Boers, having done their shooting, did not wait for the bayonets—except those who were tired of active service and wanted to surrender— and so the grand finale (as usual in this war) fell rather flat.

One squadron each of the *5th Dragoon Guards* and the *5th Lancers* made several charges over very rough ground and got among some retreating parties of Boers. Their laager was captured after one of those incidents, in contravention of the rules of war, in which they hoisted a white flag and then fired on unsuspecting men who had left their cover. They lost about 300 killed and wounded and some horses and gear, but the rest got clear away.

One can see plainly on the one side the careful and neat planning of a set-piece battle, almost in the style of the Crimea, but modernized—khaki, extended order and so forth; and on the other, crafty guerrillas who would do all the damage they could and then scatter across country when things became too much for them. A little more cunning on our side might have sent cavalry to block all the exits before attacking the position.

FRENCH'S RELIEF OF KIMBERLEY, 15TH FEBRUARY 1900

One of the most dramatic episodes of the war was the cavalry forced march from Enslin to the relief of Kimberley, in which General French used a division of cavalry and mounted infantry, 10,000 strong, with ten batteries of horse and field artillery, said to be the largest mounted force ever employed by the British Army.

Kimberley, with a population of over 30,000, had been besieged for four months, while blunders and disasters ruined the efforts of the various relief columns. Food supplies were very low and the inhabitants were severely harassed by a Boer 6-inch gun, which fired from beyond the range of the few small guns they had. Shelters were organized in the diamond mines and Cecil Rhodes was getting anxious about civilian morale and the outcome of the siege. (Compare this with London in 1944.)

Lord Roberts was then C.-in-C., with Kitchener as Chief of Staff, and his personality was speeding up the tempo of the war. He ordered French (with Colonel Douglas Haig as his A.A.G.) to move at once to the relief. This great force of cavalry swarmed over the country at such speed that strong Boer commandos, which had been expecting the usual foot-slogging advance, were flabbergasted and simply bolted from their outflanked positions without making any serious resistance.

For five days the cavalry division marched almost day and night, in very hot weather, with the meanest of rations, in order to increase their speed, and agonizing shortage of water. About 2,000 horses were ridden to death and the remainder arrived almost at the last gasp. It was a ruthless sacrifice of horses, but the object was achieved with very few human casualties and the siege was ended.

PAARDEBERG

The battle of Paardeberg, at which Lord Roberts was present, brought things nearer to the 1915 conditions of trench warfare. Cronje, with 4,000 men, had been rounded-up and headed-off by large forces and finally stood at bay in the bed of the Modder river.

There they dug weapon pits, about eighteen inches wide at the top and hollowed out underneath, with sangars built above them, so that each man fired through a loophole in the parapet, without exposing himself. They were cleverly sited to cover all the ground over which the British might advance and to give practically no target at which they could fire. The Boers could not move in daylight after the attack began and had to draw their rations and ammunition at night, but, owing to their cunning and industrious spade-work, they were able to withstand a bombardment from fifty guns, firing lyddite and shrapnel, for ten days with very moderate casualties. Their positions covered only about one square mile and this was probably the most intensive bombardment yet carried out.

Meanwhile the British troops were forced to entrench at a considerable distance and to move forward very cautiously, digging fresh cover as opportunity occurred. *The Royal Engineers'* job became even more dangerous from this period than it previously was, as they used to rush across the open with the infantry who would lie down and form a firing line a few feet in front of them, while they sited and started digging new trenches.

The Boers' weakest point was their waggon laager, for which they could provide no better cover than the river banks. Most of their oxen, horses, and supplies were destroyed by shellfire, and it was said that the stench of lyddite, rotting bodies, and the general filth of an undisciplined army penned into such a small area, drifted over to the British trenches, a hundred yards away or more, in nauseating and overpowering concentrations.

In fact one might truthfully say that bacteriological warfare was carried on at Paardeberg, as it was said to have caused numerous cases of typhoid and enteric fever.

In Cronje's force, as in many other commandos, there were Germans, French, Italians, Irish, and various other nationalities, besides the main element of Boers. They were an ill-assorted and ill-disciplined collection, many of them tough and brave and even chivalrous, but with considerable mixing of cowards and renegades. No doubt the Boers got the discredit for many acts perpetrated by the scum which had joined them. The Commandant had to be a man of tremendous force of character, as Cronje was, and to use the sjambok when necessary. There were sixty women in his entrenchment which, like other Boer concentrations, resembled a gipsies' camp, rather than that of a civilized army.

The Canadians, at their special and urgent request, made the final attack, which resulted in Cronje's surrender on the anniversary of Majuba, 27th February 1900.

BLOCKHOUSES

The final, long-drawn-out stage of the war involved the construction and manning of hundreds of 'blockhouses', or small redoubts, enclosing large tracts of country, inside which mobile columns hunted the Boer commandos. An infantry battalion had to garrison about thirty-five of these miniature forts, which was a dull though arduous duty, as the men were usually far from any civilization, had few amenities, and had to be on the alert twenty-four hours a day and especially at night. The system was elaborated by the use of searchlights, barbed wire and, where possible, by patrolling armoured trains. The Boers carried out demolitions, on a small scale, of railways, tunnels, etc. (One would think that this was the beginning of the 'pillbox' system of defences, now so familiar, but it seems that the idea did not develop with continuity. The Germans revived it late in the 1914–18 war, but only to make super-strong points in the already fully developed trench systems.

THE END OF THE WAR

The war ended on 30th May 1902, having lasted two and a half years and exacted a very strenuous effort from the whole Empire to defeat this guerrilla army. Our casualties had been heaviest in horses and worn-out boots, and deaths from sickness far outnumbered those from battle. The results were important—we had enriched the Empire and had extended the area of the world where tolerance and fair play make life more pleasant; also the Empire had had a rehearsal for the dimmer times ahead when all its members would have to fight together for their existence. Much had been learned, too, about the latest developments and probable further changes in warfare.

THE NAVY, GUNS, FILMS

The Navy had taken part in the land operations, as it had done in the Crimea and in the Indian Mutiny. Naval brigades were formed and Captain Percy Scott, of the cruiser *Terrible*, improvised home-made carriages for naval twelve-pounders and 4·7-inch guns, which were moved by very large teams of oxen, the usual form of transport in South Africa. They were hurried into Ladysmith just in time for the siege, and were able to compete with the Boers' 'Long Toms'. During the siege of Kimberley, the engineers of De Beers manufactured a gun, which they named 'Long Cecil' (after Rhodes), as the garrison was so ill-provided with long-range guns. Apart from these the operations mainly required mobile field guns—the twelve-pounders of *The Royal Horse Artillery*, the fifteen-pounders of *The Royal Field Artillery* and some field howitzers of about four-inch calibre. Some mountain or pack batteries from India, with their guns carried in sections on the backs of mules, were found very useful in the frequent hill fighting. Shrapnel was the predominating form of ammunition, lyddite (H.E. invented at Lydd, Kent), being used by the howitzers and the heavier guns. (The howitzer was a development of the mortar, used from ancient times, to lob missiles over the defences of fortified towns, so that they would fall inside, instead of hitting the walls. The type now in use was, of course, a breech-loader, and could drop shells into entrenchments.)

Some people will be surprised to hear that motion pictures— very bad ones, dark and streaky and flickering, were taken of battle scenes in South Africa. The cinematograph was in its very early stages and these films—poor as they were—gave it a great impetus, simply owing to the vital interest of the people in anything connected with the war.

BATTLE HONOURS

Battle honours were few in number and included 'Defence of Ladysmith', 'Relief of Ladysmith', 'Defence of Kimberley',

'Relief of Kimberley', 'Modder River', 'South Africa'. The *60th Rifles* and *The Rifle Brigade* have both 'Defence' and 'Relief' of Ladysmith. It had never been the custom to grant honours for unsuccessful actions, regardless of the fact that some of the highest achievements of discipline and devotion to duty have occurred in them, and in this war it must be admitted that defeats outnumbered victories. There are very few infantry regiments which did not have a battalion in South Africa during some part of the war and nearly all the cavalry regiments took part.

ARMY TRAINING

After every war, the unwarlike British relapse happily into peace and very soon give up serious consideration about being prepared for any possible future war; even the Services themselves do not appear to take things very seriously. The annual manœuvres certainly had a professional look about them, and it was obvious that one thing was being impressed on the men —the need for entrenching when they were held up by the concentrated fire of modern weapons. But still there were traces of Crimean mentality and it was taking time to assimilate thoroughly the lessons of South Africa. It was probably argued by many of the 'Blimps' that a European war, if it ever came, would not be at all like the Boer War, but would be fought more in the traditional style. The following incident is evidence that, in any case, training was not all it should have been.

'THE BATTLE OF ASHDOWN'

Some years after the Boer War manœuvres were being held on the White Horse downs in Berkshire. In those days the grand finale was always arranged to take place in view of a 'grandstand' (almost as in the early part of the last century when the King watched field days in Hyde Park), regardless of what might have happened if the battle had been left to work itself out. In this case Weathercock Hill was the 'grandstand' and on it were gathered all the 'brass hats', including Royalty and several well-known Generals.

A purple observation balloon was overhead and vendors of ice cream and ginger pop had installed themselves to supply the civilian spectators.

In a hollow on the Ashdown side of the hill was a large body of cavalry in khaki, dismounted and massed in a very small area, where a few shells would have made untold havoc.

Looking down the Vale of White Horse from the other side of the hill, dark masses of cavalry began to appear two or three miles away and as they came nearer one could see that they wore the blue service dress of *The Household Cavalry*. They eventually rode right up the hill, in closely packed squadrons which a few concealed machine-guns could have riddled, and one wondered what the 'enemy' were doing about it.

Next they broke into a gallop with trumpet calls and cheering and simultaneously counter-cheering and an added rumble of hoofs on the downland turf brought the 'enemy' from the reverse slope on to the top of the ridge.

Evidently both sides came into contact so suddenly and unexpectedly that they could not halt at the customary distance, and there followed the amazing sight of two large forces of British cavalry charging smash into each other. Their momentum carried them through one another and the chaotic mass of blue and khaki churned round in a circular movement in their efforts to halt or to avoid serious damage.

There were many empty saddles and runaway horses and numerous casualties strewed the ground. Orderlies were sent galloping for horsed ambulances, which arrived some time later, lurching at speed over the ruts and anthills.

Quite possibly this highly 'regrettable incident', enacted in public and before the 'big shots', actually did some good in bringing home obvious delinquencies in the matter of training. Or, it may have been a realization of Germany's intentions, which was slowly dawning on Europe. In any case there was a great improvement in training from about that time and in 1914 the regular army was very efficient and tough.

EDUCATION

Education was not outstanding then and the type of N.C.O. who was portrayed in a familiar periodical, teaching bayonet fighting, was still there. His words, accompanying his demonstration of stabbing a stuffed sack, were: '. . . 'avin' thrust the baynit 'ome, you gives it a sharp twist to the left, thus makin' the wound not only fatal, but himmortal.' But whatever they lacked, those N.C.O.s did know their stuff about leading men.

'THE SHAPE OF THINGS TO COME'

This was a period of accelerated evolution, during which the prototypes of many things which have brought far-reaching changes into our methods of life—always with their adaptation for war—were being tried out. In the first years of the century, apart from the railways, the horse and the bicycle were the only practicable methods of transport. Village doctors and parsons made their rounds on horseback or horse-drawn trap, and those who could afford it, kept a carriage and pair, while horse buses and hansom cabs formed the main elements of the London traffic. Life had changed but slowly through the past ages, but now a strange new era, comparable with nothing in the world's history, was on its way.

On 23rd April 1900 the first thousand-mile trial run for motor-cars was staged—from London to Edinburgh and return—and cars were expected to finish the course within three weeks, if they managed to do so at all! In 1902 there was a parade of private cars, which had been offered, with volunteer drivers, for army service. A photograph was taken showing Lord Roberts (who was then C.-in-C. at the War Office) and other Generals and Staff officers, seated up in high brass-bound 'horseless carriages', such as may still be seen at the 'old crocks" annual turnout.

In 1909 Hornsby's 'caterpillar engine' appeared—a traction engine running on endless tracks, which could cross quite wide ditches. From this came petrol tractors, looking like Heath Robinson's impressions of a gravel-washing plant, which were used, in small numbers, to haul heavy guns.

Wireless was fitted on the German trans-Atlantic liner, *Kaiser Wilhelm der Grosse*, in 1900, and in 1901 the first trans-Atlantic radio messages were transmitted by Marconi, from Poldhu, in Cornwall, to Newfoundland.

The first aeroplane flight was made by the Wright Brothers at Kitty Hawk, North Carolina, on 17th December 1903. The plane had a 12 h.p. engine, and the longest flight lasted 59 seconds, attaining a speed of 30 m.p.h. Bleriot made the first flight across the Channel on 25th July 1909, and soon afterwards Hendon aerodrome was opened. Experiments were made with army air-ships, but we were always behind other countries with these, and they were not nearly up to the standard of the Zeppelins, one of which made a 38-hours' flight in 1909.

All these inventions, intended, like the first bow and arrow probably were, to benefit human creatures, now had to be studied by the Staffs of all the important armies and navies, to see what their implications were as regards aggression and defence. Their early uses, so far, seem to have been largely for warlike purposes, but, conversely, wars have developed and improved them for civil purposes far more speedily than would have been the case in normal peace-time.

PEACE-TIME SOLDIERING

Some books about the army are inclined to give the impression that a soldier's life is spent almost entirely on active service but, as may be judged from the small number of medals being worn in normal times, this is far from correct. The soldier gets his good times as well as his tough ones and peace-time service has a character all its own. Instead of working as civilians do with a lot of people who take no interest in each other after five o'clock, a regiment lives together like a huge family, and all its successes, its tough luck, games, sorrows, and humorous incidents, are of personal interest to every man.

There was a period of hard training each year, reaching a climax in the autumn manœuvres, followed by plenty of leave. Soldiers had not much money, but things were cheap—cigarettes sixpence for twenty, whiskey twopence a glass and so on, and a smart man in a scarlet or blue uniform had an interest value for the other sex and would not have been so keen to be allowed to put on 'civvies' as the present wearers of battle dress.

Barrack rooms were not like a comfortably furnished home, kit had to be laid out exactly according to order, there were rigid rules and a lot of 'spit and polish', fatigues and 'jankers' for those who did not keep up to scratch, but they all 'mucked in' together, shared the pleasures of grousing, and subconsciously felt that it was a good life and that they had something to be proud of, more than ordinary stay-at-home people.

Ceremonial was often a bore—all the extra cleaning-up, standing on parade for an hour awaiting the General's arrival, doing guards and occasionally going to take part in some lengthy show like a coronation, a jubilee, or a durbar. But there is a humorous side to everything, which the army can appreciate better than most people.

There were, of course, less pleasant interludes, such as being sent on strike duty, and abroad to restore order during riots. These were among the most distasteful duties of all, specially to the officers, who could be wrong if they used force or ordered firing, and equally wrong if they did not; and all ranks had to exhibit exemplary patience while being a target for abuse, often supplemented by bottles, stones, and other missiles.

There were almost unlimited opportunities for sport, which was held to be an important part of a soldier's training and was encouraged accordingly in all stations. But the country which excelled in the facilities it offered was India. Every regiment spent a considerable part of its tour of foreign service there, in addition to spells at such other stations as Gibraltar, Malta, Cairo, Aden, Hong Kong, the West Indies, etc.

In India the private soldier lived a gentleman's life. He had native servants to do all the dirty work and could even get the 'nappy', with his little lamp and portable kit, to come and shave him whilst he lay in bed. The barracks were more spacious than at home and in the evenings there was a choice of hockey, cricket, football, or rugger. In addition, for sergeants and officers, there was tennis, squash, golf, polo, hunting, etc., and plenty of dances and social entertainments. The country itself was full of interest and fishing and shooting were there for all who desired it. British regiments went to hill stations in the 'hot weather' and, among other amenities, nearly every man had a dog, if not two or three.

Various other pets were kept; one regiment owning a bear, which was refused admission to a train en route for the hills. The station-master having protested: 'But, sirr, regulation is not,' the adjutant suggested that he should retire to his office and produce a regulation. He returned, after some delay, beaming with smiles at having solved the problem thus: 'Sirr, regulation is not, but I have made ticket for one double daag.'

Some of the Hindustani words which have acquired a place in army—and civil—language, will long live on even though the legions have been withdrawn. These are just a few. Cushy (Hind. *khush*) = contented; Blighty (Hind. *vilayat*) = a foreign country; chit (Hind. *chitthi*) = a letter; garry (Hind. *garhi*) = a carriage; pyjamas (Hind. *pajama*) = the loose trousers of a Mussulman; rooti gong (Hind. *roti*) = bread. The 'gong'—the Long Service and Good Conduct medal—is said to be the reward for eating army rations for eighteen years.

PLATE XVIII

(47)

1900

The Gloucestershire Regiment	The 7th Middlesex (London Scottish Rifle Volunteers)	The Irish Guards	The Cameronians	The Royal Welch Fusiliers
Corporal	*Lance-Corporal*	*Regimental Sergeant-Major*	*Sergeant Signaller*	*Pioneer*

(48)

1900

The 6th Dragoons	The Irish Guards	The Coldstream Guards	The Suffolk Regiment	The 2nd Life Guards
Trooper	*Drummer*	*Drum-Major*	*Drum-Major*	*Trooper*

(49)

1906

The 60th Rifles	The Seaforth Highlanders	The 2nd Life Guards	The Sherwood Foresters	The 6th Dragoon Guards
Bugler	*Bass Drummer*	*Trumpeter (state dress)*	*Drummer and the regimental ram*	*Bandsman*

PLATE XVIII
Figs. 47, 48 & 49

PLATE XVIII (47 AND 48). 1900

The magazine Lee Metford Rifle, the first with a bolt action, had been issued in 1888, and with it, a short bayonet.

Equipment had been slightly altered and the pouches now matched the remainder in colour and had lost their box-like appearance. From 1889 a new valise, shallower than the old one, was worn on the shoulders, with the great-coat rolled and strapped on to the belt.

Beards and whiskers had vanished some years before, but the 'walrus' moustache was still the fashion and it was forbidden to shave the upper lip. (Beards had another spell of popularity on service in South Africa, as they did again among the desert patrols and 'Chindits' of the 1939–45 war.)

The Irish Guards were raised in 1900, by order of Queen Victoria, in honour of the distinguished services of the Irish regiments against the Boers, and their first Colonel-in-Chief was Lord Roberts, who was an Irishman. The Sergeant-Major in the illustration is wearing the officers' forage cap of this period. In full dress the regiment wore a bearskin cap with a blue plume on the right. The drummer is shown wearing the Broderick cap—a new head-dress of German origin, which was first issued to *The Irish Guards* on their formation, and became the universal forage cap for other ranks, from 1902 to 1905. In the other Guards regiments the men's forage cap was the 'pill-box' (like that shown on the Dragoon) worn on the right side of the head, and the folding 'field' cap was the universal pattern for other units. (This was a stylized version of the woollen Balaclava helmet, and could be buttoned under the chin, covering the head and neck, except for the face.)

Guards Sergeant-Majors wore a large embroidered royal coat of arms on the right upper arm, while those of other regiments wore only a brass crown above the cuff.

The London Scottish were always one of the best known and smartest Volunteer (after 1907, Territorial) regiments, and they were the first T.F. regiment to land in France, in 1914.

The illustration shows the 'back number' worn by *The Gloucesters*, in memory of the battle of Alexandria, 1801 (see Chapter III). It was originally the number '28', but was changed to a small sphinx after badges replaced numbers in 1881.

The Cameronians were the only regiment besides *The Highland Light Infantry*, which still wore the shako.

The Royal Welch Fusiliers alone possessed the privilege of having their pioneers on ceremonial parades, with axes and white leather aprons. In the eighteenth century every regiment had its pioneers, as it does now, but at this period they were not much in evidence. The officers of R.W.F. also have a distinguishing mark in the 'flash'—a bunch of five black ribbon tails, sewn to the back of the collar. This was originally a bow of broad ribbon tied to the 'queue' or 'club', to keep the grease off the coat, and it disappeared with the 'pigtail', in 1808. As the R.W.F. returned from overseas service in 1834, still wearing flashes, permission was obtained to keep them as a unique regimental distinction.

The Dragoon is wearing the scarlet frock, then in use for drill and training, and the Life Guardsman is in modified full dress, minus plume and cuirass, with overalls and small gloves.

In 1902, for the first time, khaki service dress became the working rig for peace-time, as well as for active service, and full dress was reserved for ceremonial. After this anklets and cavalry pouch-belts and sabretaches were no longer worn, and equipment with full dress was generally reduced to the waistbelt and frog and one pouch for blanks, except in the Guards, who still wore the full set when on guard duty.

Officers' sashes were, once again, worn round the waist and the rank distinctions of lace were abolished, except in the Guards and Household Cavalry.

PLATE XVIII (49). 1906

All the Infantry bands wore wings (similar to those of grenadiers and light infantry up to the Crimean War) but only the drummers' wings had lace and fringe. (Drummers of highland regiments had lace but no fringe.) Their tunics still had a little of the lace, now only on the seams and round the facings which, in the eighteenth century, almost entirely covered the coat.. The Guards' drummers were the only ones who retained the laced buttonholes across the front, which infantrymen wore on their coatees up to 1855. The loops were spaced in ones, twos, etc., according to regimental custom, and the blue 'spots' were small fleurs-de-lis, said to be a relic of the days when England claimed sovereignty over France, and the French Arms were quartered in the Royal Standard. Drummers of the Guards, only, still had lace chevrons on the outside of the sleeve and, in state dress, their bandsmen wore gold lace buttonholes and chevrons. Regimental lace for the bands of line regiments was abolished in 1866 and was replaced by a universal pattern.

Plate XVIII (48) shows the difference between the dress of Drum-Majors of the Guards and those of line regiments. Those of the Guards carried a short staff (except in ceremonial dress), wore small gloves and retained the gold lace of earlier times. Incidentally, it is beneath their dignity to flourish and twirl their staves in the manner which is customary in other regiments. The shoulder-belt worn by Drum-Majors is of the regimental facing colour, with the Royal cypher, drum-sticks and regimental devices.

The bass drummers of many regiments wear leopardskin aprons, but the normal one is of plain white leather.

Bandsmen's white tunics were abolished in 1873 and from then they all wore the uniform of their regiments (with the additions mentioned) and their regimental head-dress. Exceptions were *The Royal Engineers'* band, who wore bearskin caps and *The Highland Light Infantry*, who wore feather bonnets.

Bandsmen of *The Household Cavalry*, when in state dress, wore the gold-laced coats of the seventeenth century and 'jockey' caps. In full dress the trumpeters had gold lace on the edges of their scarlet tunics, and different plumes from those of the troopers.

Otherwise, apart from Dragoon Guards and Dragoons, whose bands wore special plumes and aiguilettes, there was no marked difference between troopers and bandsmen. The 11th *Hussars*, whose band wore grey busbies, was an exception.

The bands of Infantry regiments consisted of side, tenor and bass drums, fifes, bugles, and brass and wood instruments, except in Rifle and light infantry regiments, which had no drums or fifes and Scottish regiments, which used pipes in place of fifes.

The bandsmen were trained soldiers and usually went on service as stretcher-bearers. Buglers took their bugles with them and were often used as company commanders' runners. They were not allowed to sound calls when near enough to the enemy for them to hear, as they would very probably know the meaning and might also imitate them to cause confusion, e.g. sounding the 'Cease Fire', or 'Retire'. Bugles, hunting horns, and pipes were, however, used to assemble airborne troops after their landings in France and Germany in the recent war.

Regimental pets, of which there were a number—e.g. the wolfhound of *The Irish Guards*, the antelope of *The Royal Warwickshires*, the goat of *The Royal Welch Fusiliers*, and the ram of Derbyshire—went on parade on special occasions and had to be trained to listen to martial music at close quarters, without showing fear or resentment.

The forage cap, illustrated, became the universal pattern in 1905.

In connection with bands, the word Tattoo, which became so familiar to the public after the 1914–18 war, may need explanation.

Its origin is somewhat confused with that of 'Retreat', as the two words seem to have been used rather indiscriminately in ancient documents, but the ceremony appears to have been a part of normal routine since the seventeenth century.

'Retreat' was originally a drum signal to retire during action, but the word was later used to describe the daily procedure at sunset, when watches were to be set and the gates of a fortress, camp, or walled town were about to be closed. The drummers beat their drums on the ramparts, or at the gates, for about fifteen minutes, to give everyone time to come in before the locking-up or placing of barriers.

'Tattoo' was originally 'Taptoo' (named from the sound of the drums) which was the bedtime and 'closing-time' signal, and was given usually at ten o'clock in summer and eight in winter. The Drum-Major and the drummers of the quarter guard and any other guards, marched round the lines, beating a warning for all troops to go into their quarters for the night.

These two old customs are still observed, but by means of bugle or trumpet calls. 'Retreat' is sounded about sunset and is the signal that the day's work is finished, except, of course, for those on guard, and 'Tattoo, 1st Post' corresponds to the beginning of the drummers' march from the main square (in the old days), and 'Last Post' to their return there, to be dismissed.

PLATE XIX

1904

The Army Ordnance Department	The 6oth Rifles	Aide-de-camp to the King	The Royal Engineers	The Army Veterinary Department	The 2nd Life Guards	The 10th Hussars
Colonel (Staff)	*Officer*		*Lieutenant-Colonel (Staff)*	*Colonel (Staff)*	*Officer (mess dress)*	*Officer (frock coat)*

PLATE XIX

PLATE XIX. 1904

Cocked hats were worn by Generals, Personal Staff, and Colonels holding Staff appointments. In *The Royal Engineers* all field officers, employed on staff duties, wore it. The feathers were ten inches long for Generals and eight for Staff Colonels, with variations in the gold lace loops. There were differences in dress laid down for the commander of each garrison, and for various other appointments which involve more detail than can be given here.

The aiguilette was worn, in 1904, on the right shoulder by Field Marshals, members of the Army Council, Personal Staff of the Royal Family, which included officers of *The Household Cavalry*, and Governors-General, and on the left by all Staff Officers. It was gold for Generals, and gold and scarlet, intertwined, for Staff officers.

Mess uniform consisted of a shell jacket, not intended to be buttoned-up, a waistcoat—in most cases scarlet or white—and the usual overalls or trousers. The universal mess jacket had turned-back lapels, but *The Household Cavalry* wore the type illustrated, and Scottish regiments had one with a stand-up collar and buttons all the way up.

In accordance with tradition, the full dress of officers of Rifle regiments was similar in style to that of Hussars. (From 1878 to 1890 the 60th wore the universal spiked helmet, with bronze fitings.)

CHAPTER XI · 1914-18

HUMAN NATURE

One psychological effect of the South African War was a demonstration of the satisfaction and animosity displayed by the other great powers when we went through our worst period of blunders and disasters, and had we not possessed the strongest navy in the world, it is quite probable that some of them would have seized the opportunity of attacking us. The Germans had, at this time, become sufficiently bold in their rivalry and jealousy of the British Empire, to provide gunners to man the Boers' heavy guns (some of them Creusot guns from France, and some Krupps), which were used in the sieges and the Kaiser even went so far as to telegraph his congratulations to President Kruger, after a British defeat.

The whole story of our wars in the nineteenth century, from the Napoleonic attempts to destroy us, up to and including the Boer War, is one of consolidating the Empire—adding an essential piece here, cleaning up a mess there, improving lines of communication and generally making things secure and tying in the loose ends. The Crimean War was the only one which did not, so obviously, come under this heading, but it also was fought to prevent the development of a menace to the Empire.

With the twentieth century came a second era of having to defend it against assaults on a gigantic scale, which were intended first to destroy the home country and then to seize the outlying dominions and colonies.

We had had further evidence of the jealousy of Germany and France many times in Africa, and of the latter in Indo-China. But as events turned out, our old enemy and ally of the Crimea, was to be on our side, as a co-victim of the great attempt.

The Boxer anti-foreign rising in China, in 1900, in which all the European powers were concerned, provided further proofs of German selfishness and greed, and more ominous incidents occurred during the Russo-Japanese War in 1904, in Tangier, 1905, and the Agadir episode in 1911.

But, as usual, until the last our official attitude seemed to consist of trying to imagine that, because we had no object in making an aggressive war, no other nation would be so uncivilized as to desire it and to blind ourselves to the envy and malice engendered by the possession of such a magnificent Empire. Consequently, our preparations were no more adequate than in previous wars.

1914—ENTHUSIASTIC RECEPTION OF THE CHALLENGE

When it finally came, in 1914, the challenge of Germany seemed to be accepted with enthusiasm by the people of the British Empire, as if they had known all along that a 'showdown' must come and were glad to end pretence and get on with the job. There was another aspect, too, which applied to nearly all the nations engaged. Very few had experienced anything of this nature and it appeared like a glamorous and dramatic escape from the too-settled routine of peace-time. That was what the young men thought.

There were scenes of tremendous excitement, and recruiting not being organized on the same lines as in the recent war, regimental depots were swamped by the inrush of eager recruits. There were many instances where hundreds of men slept out on the barrack squares and ate improvised meals, minus knives, forks and spoons, pending the provision of adequate arrangements. Every man was keen to get across the Channel and was afraid it would be all over if he was not sent quickly. Training and equipping these men was no simple matter with the absurdly small resources available and in the training areas one could have seen battalions dressed in a motley of red, white, khaki, civilian clothes, and an improvised blue uniform—like postmen wearing field service caps, with dummy rifles, or none at all.

COURSE OF THE WAR

Again 'removing the muckage' this, with extreme brevity, is what took place. Britain, France and Russia were allied in order to prevent German aggression and were joined later by the United States and Japan. Germany's satellites were Austria (to form a link with Italy, and too near to be left as a possible spring-board for the Allies) and Italy—thus completing a solid block across Europe from the Baltic to the Mediterranean; Bulgaria and Turkey—to menace the Middle East and Russia's southern flank and eventually to give access to Egypt and to India via Mesopotamia.

Their plan was first to overrun the Netherlands (which were neutral), take Paris and the Channel ports, knocking out France in the process, then to invade England and so put the British Empire out of action. Meanwhile Russia, whose forces were then thought to be of minor importance in fighting efficiency, would be held in check and later dealt with finally. This would leave no opposition in Europe. Next, an advance into Egypt would make it possible to overrun the whole of Africa by easy stages. When these moves had been consolidated, it should not be difficult to take India which, with Russia out, would leave the Germans free to seize any part, or eventually all of Asia and Australasia. America would then be all that remained and, being entirely isolated, would probably make terms. Germany's so-called allies would, in due course, be dealt with as conquered territories. In short, the scheme was no less than complete world domination by the *herrenvolk*, who would use the vanquished races as slaves or, if they were not amenable, exterminate them.

But, as often happens in grandiose plans, something went wrong. The first act was a failure, mainly owing to the efficiency, toughness and extreme determination of the 'contemptible little army' from across the Channel, aided by some good luck in the shape of blunders by one or two German generals. Paris was narrowly saved and the Germans were forced back to the Marne, where they had to dig in, and were held immobilized for four years. Fortescue describes the Mons retreat and the first battle of Ypres as 'the grandest work ever done, in every respect, by any British army'.

Russia, though badly knocked about, was not out, and Italy, having 'sat on the fence' until May 1915, joined the other side. Japan came in on the side of the Allies soon after the outbreak of war and the United States declared war on Germany on 6th April 1917.

Turkey joined forces with Germany in October 1914 and the eastern part of the scheme was then brought into play, to weaken the British in the west—we were now frankly regarded as the main obstacle—and to get footholds for future use, if success eventually came. This resulted in the fighting in Palestine and Mesopotamia.

Meanwhile the Navy had bottled-up the High Seas Fleet and mopped-up its raiders in distant parts of the world. The Germans, now involved in a death grip, had to think of every possibility of loosening the hold of the Allies and saving themselves.

Thus the U-boat campaign resulted, which came very near success in early 1917, raids by Zeppelins and later by planes— little more than nuisance value compared with those of the second war—tremendous 'pushes' on the western front, and a final attempt by their fleet, which ended with the battle of Jutland, 31st May 1916.

The blockade of Germany was very effective and the Allies became stronger as time went on. They were able to get thoroughly organized on a war footing, which Germany had, of course, done before the war began. As they did so the offensive passed to them and the 'squeeze' of Germany began. The Dardanelles, Balkan and Italian campaigns were a part of this process, as well as of a search for a less strongly defended point of entry to Germany. The war changed from a scene of invading hordes of Huns, first to a confinement of their activities, then gradually to a siege, on a vast scale, of the whole of Germany, Austria and the territories they had occupied.

The western front was always the vital one, while the other campaigns, despite their importance and the large force used, were subsidiary to this main attack. The greatest battles were fought in the west and the war ended there, when the Germans realized that their plans had failed, and that their best course would be to surrender and save what they could, rather than fight to the death.

TOTAL WAR

This war was on a different scale from any which had preceded it and, instead of its being fought by comparatively small forces in a distant country, every man, woman and child was in it. It was the Germans who had conceived the thought of 'total war' and had made arrangements to include every resource they possessed in one great all-embracing effort. They were supposed to have carried their inhuman thoroughness to the extent of extracting various chemical substances from the bodies of the victims for use in the manufacture of explosives and for other war purposes, and of organizing an abnormal increase in their population, to provide reinforcements for the time when they would rule the world, replacing the 'cannon fodder' expended in their conquests. This was said to have been done in much the same way as the Ministry of Agriculture might organize an increase in the national stock of pigs or sheep. Their cold-blooded subordination of all the decencies of life to one soul-less purpose has had a sinister effect on the whole world since that time.

In order to defeat them it became necessary for the Allies temporarily to abandon the normal rights of the individual also and subject him to a mass of rules and regulations. This included the conscription, in 1916, of all fit men who could be spared from essential civilian duties.

This regimentation was much easier than it would have been in

Napoleon's time, owing to the country's industrial development and the enormous increase in population which had resulted. This island was already getting so overcrowded that individuality was, in any case, gradually being lost in the vast cities and the enormous organizations which had grown up, leading to mass-production, standardization and queueing for jobs, for travelling, and for most of the things normal people required. Human life was being forced into an uninspired standard mould by the pressure of numbers, and Britain was like a bee colony where the swarms do not migrate, but stay to increase congestion in the hive. This excess of population had two other important effects. It gave man power and a high output of munitions, but on the other side it gave extreme vulnerability as regards starvation in the event of a successful blockade.

WOMEN'S WAR SERVICE

This was the first war in which women, apart from nurses, joined the army with official encouragement. Previously their service had been limited to canteen attendants, wives who went on active service in many wars, and a few who masqueraded as men (e.g. Phoebe Hassel, a celebrity of the 5th Foot, who was pensioned by George IV, and died at Hove).

They acquired the vote during 1918 and became responsible persons, in contra-distinction to the very secondary position they had occupied for so long, which culminated in the absurd tyranny of Victorian fathers and husbands. Now they were able to show their value and their spirit, by enlisting in thousands in *The Women's Army Auxiliary Corps* (revived later as the A.T.S.), *The First Aid Nursing Yeomanry*, and other military organizations. Millions of other women took over the duties of men who had joined-up, or worked in factories.

MONS AND THEN THE 'DURATION' ARMY

Lord Roberts had spent his last years in tireless efforts to warn the country of the impending catastrophe. Others had tried also, but without success. The regular army, though very efficient, was far too small to cope with our participation in a European war, but during 1914 it performed its greatest service to civilization, since its birth in 1660. It had to be sacrificed in the Mons retreat and in the battle of the Marne, in which its insignificant numbers broke the first great eruption of the Germans, disorganizing their whole plan and thus giving time for the Allies to equip themselves and move into battle. But for this magnificent effort the war might easily have been lost in the first few weeks and the world might now be enduring its fourth decade of German tyranny.

Afterwards there was only a remnant surviving, but this was enough to hand on the torch and to form the backbone of the enormous army which was built up from the Territorial Force (formed from the Volunteers by Lord Haldane in 1907) and civilians who, after the first rush, continued to enlist voluntarily under Lord Kitchener's scheme. This called for men in batches of 100,000, until conscription came into force in January 1916.

In 1914 the available forces, for an overseas expedition, consisted of one cavalry and six infantry divisions of regulars (a division was then approximately 20,000 strong), and twenty-seven garrison battalions (descendants of the 'invalid' companies of one hundred years before), which relieved regulars in overseas garrisons and eventually enabled two more divisions to be formed.

As a second line there were fourteen Territorial divisions and fourteen brigades of Yeomanry, but these needed a considerable amount of training before they could be sent overseas. 'Service' battalions were added to all the regiments, and Territorial battalions were duplicated and triplicated. This brought the average number of battalions per regiment up to about ten or twelve, but in some cases, e.g. *The Royal Fusiliers*, it was between thirty and forty.

AN IMPRESSION OF THE PRINCIPAL ARMIES

1. *The British*. In 1914 the armies on both sides entered the war in various stages of development, most of them still retaining many of the characteristics of the previous century.

The British Regular Army was undoubtedly the most modern and its standard of individual training was the highest. Apart from the Russians and the Japanese, who defeated them in the war of 1904, it was the only army which had fought a twentieth-century war on a large scale. It had had experience of modern precision weapons and of the necessity for giving as small a target as possible, which made command—from the section up to the army corps—such a very different matter from what it was in the old days. It alone had reached the stage where each man had been taught to think and act for himself, instead of merely carrying out a drill.

The British reputation for marksmanship and fire-power, going back as far as Crécy, was fully maintained by the men of 1914, who had been rearmed in 1908 with the Short Magazine Lee Enfield rifle, with a magazine holding ten rounds and with a charger guide for loading clips of five cartridges at a time. This was the handiest, best balanced and most accurate rifle for service purposes which had ever been produced and with it a long bayonet was used to compensate for the shortening of the barrel. Every trained man could, on occasion, fire fifteen to twenty aimed shots in a minute, and the Germans were so astonished at the rate of fire, that they at first believed that each man had an automatic rifle.

Every form of transport was used in the various theatres of war, from the recently invented caterpillar tractors, and cars, lorries, motor bicycles and London buses, to camels, elephants, donkeys, native porters, mules and, of course, horses. Various types of boats played their part and a special corps known as the Inland Water Transport, was formed, which made use of the highly developed canal systems of northern France and Belgium, for moving stores and evacuating wounded by hospital barges.

In those days regimental transport consisted of horse- or mule-drawn limbered waggons, the old four-wheeled g.s. waggons, and a Maltese cart for the mess stores. On the march the machine-guns were usually mounted on pack saddles carried by mules. Horse and field artillery moved in traditional style, with teams of six horses, each gun followed by its limbered ammunition waggons and, as late as 1916, Field-Marshal Sir Douglas Haig could be seen riding to various headquarters behind the lines, accompanied by an escort of his old regiment, the 17*th Lancers*, carrying lances with red and white pennons.

But things were changing fairly rapidly and cavalry, which went out in 1914, mounted, with swords and lances to use in charges, eventually suffered the indignity of being sent into the trenches as infantry, which was an acknowledgement that horsed cavalry was very near its end. (Later on, after the war, it took over its new role in the mechanized army and became cavalry once again, but armoured and petrol driven.) There were actually one or two successful cavalry charges in France in 1914 and, in Palestine, lances were used with considerable effect by the Indian cavalry. These were probably the last operations of their kind which will ever be carried out by civilized—and consequently mechanized armies.

Officers, who went to France in uniforms of distinctive cut, with their rank shown conspicuously in 'slashes' on their sleeves and with Sam Browne belts and swords, soon discarded the more obvious features, wore private soldier's equipment and placed their badges of rank less noticeably on their shoulder-straps. Brass buttons and 'spit and polish' almost disappeared, with the notable exception of the Guards division, whose units could be

seen during their rest periods behind the line, carrying out ceremonial drill, with everything scrubbed and polished, as if they
had been in London.

A few old customs persisted rather surprisingly against the
muddy background. The pipers of Scottish regiments, whose
wild and stirring music is even now indispensable in war, performed the same outstanding feats of personal gallantry as they
had in every previous war, and piped their men 'over the top'
with a zeal which ignored machine-guns and artillery barrages.
At Annequin, in the La Bassée sector, in 1916, some pipers
carried things a little too far by playing the relief troops up to the
remains of the village street, which was about 300 yards from
the front line, but out of sight. Up to then 200 or 300 men used
to form-up daily at eleven o'clock in the morning and move off to
the trenches without enemy interference, but the pipers changed
all this by bringing down such a storm of 'whizzbangs', 'coal-
boxes' and 'Jack Johnsons', that this peaceful and over-confident
parade was seen no more.

A few regiments took their pet animals with them on service,
among them *The Royal Welch Fusiliers*, whose goat died during
the Mons retreat and was given a funeral with full military
honours in the cemetery of a Belgian town. Very few foreigners
have ever understood the British temperament and the inhabitants thought the men must be raving mad, and could only see it
as an act of completely shocking levity, and a desecration of the
cemetery.

2. *The French.* The French, who had about 1,750,000 troops
available in 1914, were scarcely even in the transition stage and
put into the field dragoons in cuirasses and plumed helmets, and
both cavalry and infantry, armed with weapons of thirty or forty
years ago, in dark blue coats, red breeches and kepis. Their
casualties were so heavy, owing to this conspicuous attire, that
as soon as possible they changed to 'horizon blue'. The discipline
of their troops seemed much looser than that of the British and
their trench systems much more sketchy and less solid. They
wandered about in a casual way and seemed to do things more or
less as it pleased them, but they were cheerful and patriotic,
though perhaps too excitable. The average *Poilu* was a quick-
witted, brave and enduring little man, but it always caused amuse-
ment to see him taking a swig at the *vin ordinaire* in his water-
bottle as he guided our platoons into the line. His lack of stature
was shown by the fact that our troops had to keep their heads
down all the way along the *boyaus* (communicating trenches) to
avoid crashing their 'tin hats' on the overhead timber struts. The

French 75 millimetre field-gun earned the reputation of being one of the most efficient weapons in the war.

3. *The Germans.* The German army, about 2,500,000 strong on mobilization, was in 'field grey'. Their dress was modern, except for the *pikel-haube* (spiked helmet), with its brass eagle, which was worn with a cloth cover, and the fact that the officers still carried swords. Their 1914 army had a rigorous discipline of the old order of 'theirs but to do and die', and they moved in heavy formations and attacked in solid masses. Some of their peacetime full-dress uniforms had retained traditional features, discarded many years before by other armies, such as the mitre-shaped grenadier cap, the gorget, white trousers, etc., showing that the Prussian military tradition had long held a firm grip on the nation.

The patriotism and self-negation of the Germans was of an extremely high order, though misguided and, in a way, unimaginative, and as a purely militaristic state—of which Britain has always been the antithesis—they had reached the ultimate ideal of martial development. They were not all up to this standard, though, and a story has been recorded that one regiment erected a notice over its front line trench saying, 'We are Saxons, you are Anglo-Saxons. Do not fire and we will not,' or words to that effect.

The original men of the Prussian Guards were of unusually fine physique, and during the first battle of Ypres some seven-footers were killed.

4. *The Russians.* The Russian army was about 4,000,000 strong—the largest in the world. It had undergone a tremendous scheme of reorganization, but was still poorly equipped and ill-supplied with modern weapons and materials.

It was part of the Russia of the Czars—a colossal, isolated and backward country, with the minimum of education and a serf-like obedience and discipline. The men were very tough and long-suffering, but they were 'dumb' and not inclined to reason; the N.C.O's were mostly crude and illiterate, and the staff work was not brilliant.

They suffered enormous numbers of casualties, but slogged along, until the revolution of 1917 shattered the old regime and disorganized the country. After this all contracts with other nations were repudiated and a separate peace was made with Germany, to the detriment of Russia's allies.

DIVERSITY OF THE WAR

The army was engaged in campaigns in almost every type of climate and country, against enemies whose methods and natures were almost equally diverse. There were desert battles against the Turks in Palestine and Mesopotamia, minor engagements with the Arabs, operations in the German colonies in East and West Africa and others on the North-West Frontier of India. The seaborne invasion of the Dardanelles, with all its mistakes, involved heroic efforts during the landings and, finally, one of the most skilful evacuations in military history, which was ordered from Whitehall in December 1915, just when this expensive campaign had nearly succeeded. It must have provided a number of object-lessons for study in planning the landings on the Normandy beaches in 1944.

In Italy there was mountain warfare in which trenches were blasted out of the rock and guns were hauled up on to snow-covered peaks by aerial cables.

STATIC WARFARE

But the bulk of the fighting was in France. After the first great battles, when the Germans had been pushed back and the Allies were not strong enough to keep them on the move, a stalemate developed. 'When you can't advance any more, dig in and hold on', was the military motto of this period and both sides followed it with such effect that soon a solid maze of trenches and barbed wire extended from the North Sea to the borders of Switzerland. The distance between the front lines varied from as little as twenty or thirty yards, up to a mile or more, but the lines were continuous and linked up from end to end. Between them was 'no-man's-land', a strip of desolation, filled with shell craters, rusty barbed wire and the general debris of constant fighting, which by day was a wilderness inhabited only by gruesome remains, and at night became a hunting ground for patrols and raiders. In daylight the positions of the two lines could be traced for many miles in either direction by the large numbers of observation balloons anchored in rear of each, and in darkness by the constant streams of Verey lights and the flashes of bursting shells.

Here the armies lived and died from the end of 1914 until nearly the end of the war and the most terrific battles such as that of the Somme, in 1916, never moved the lines more than a few miles.

FLANDERS MUD

In winter this flat and rather depressing country became saturated and waterlogged, which added very seriously to the discomforts of life. The mud in the trenches was often well above the knees and sometimes progress up to the front line was reduced to about a hundred yards an hour. Men weighted down with rifle, bayonet, entrenching tool, large full pack, haversack, water-bottle, greatcoat, 200 rounds of ammunition or more, grenades, and often an additional burden—a sandbag full of something, or a roll of barbed wire—had to drag several times at each step to release the leg from the evil-smelling, squelching clay, and would arrive nearly exhausted. Thigh gum-boots were issued, but often the suction broke a strap and the boot, and probably the sock, disappeared in the mud, and had to be dug out by hand.

In the Festubert sector the trenches became full to the brim with greenish-grey foul water and the men lived in island breastworks, like large grouse butts, standing at intervals across the sodden wilderness. All reliefs and working parties had to come up at night and cross the abandoned trenches on slippery duckboard bridges, and sometimes a duck-board tilted, or a Boche machine-gun opened up and the last man fell in unnoticed by those in front. Embedded in a couple of feet of mud under the water, he had not much chance of calling for help, or of clambering up the slimy sides and a number of 'missing' casualties must have occurred in this way.

RATS—'AS BIG AS BLOOMING CATS'

Another minor unpleasantness was the plague of rats—many as large as rabbits, which thrived in the trenches and in 'no-man's-land'. They were everywhere in thousands, crawling over sleeping men, in their kit, in the rations and sticking their noses out between the sandbags, making a peculiar wheezing cough. Many were killed with sticks and entrenching tools and, as a pastime for dull moments, subalterns used to shoot them with rifles and revolvers. This sport, however, became so dangerous to inspecting G.O's, who sometimes rounded a corner to find themselves looking down the muzzle of a revolver, that an order was issued prohibiting it.

THE EVOLUTION OF FORTIFICATIONS

These static conditions amounted to siege warfare on a colossal scale, though the comparison with, say, the siege of Badajos (1812), is not at once obvious. To understand it, it is necessary to know a very little about the evolution of fortifications.

These had changed in accordance with the improvements in weapons. In the Middle Ages high stone walls, surrounded by a moat, could withstand the weapons of those days, were extremely difficult to assault and gave a good view, or 'command' for the bowmen or musketeers, while the moat made a night attack difficult. The object of all the various types of turrets, towers, bastions, ravelins, etc., was to keep the whole of the surroundings under observation and fire, so that the enemy could not hide themselves in a corner, while they mined or breached the walls. At that time a really good fortress, with stout defenders, could only be taken by starving out the inhabitants.

A change came with iron cannon-balls, about 1480. Guns could then seriously damage the walls and from that time fortresses began, metaphorically, to sink into the ground. The walls became lower and, later, earth ramparts were built against the front of them, to increase their resistance. This made them more vulnerable to escalade, so the obstacles in front had to be improved—ditches thirty feet deep, etc.

As the range of guns increased—in the year 1800 walls could be breached from about 800 yards—subsidiary outlying forts became necessary, to menace the enemy's batteries. Rifled cannon were introduced about 1850, and by 1870 their breaching range was up to 4,000 yards.

After this, with guns rapidly increasing in number and power, such a concentration of fire could be brought to bear on a fortress, that it became a death-trap and dispersion was essential. At first the girdle of outer forts was placed farther away—up to five or six miles from the main stronghold. But, as time went on, these only served to delay matters, as the enemy would concentrate on each in turn and destroy it, so the next stage consisted of numerous small concealed redoubts, forming a defended area and covering all lines of approach with crossfire and dispensing with the main fortress. The enemy could not concentrate his fire on more than a proportion of them at one time and, with smokeless propellants, could not locate many of them, if they were well sited and concealed, except by bringing his infantry under fire. Thus the fortress became, in effect, a series of trench redoubts of permanent and scientific construction.

Trenches were used as early as the Civil War, but in each period their plan conformed roughly to that of permanent fortifications, of which they were the improvised equivalent. In 1914, however, they began with armies in battle, digging-in just where they happened to be—not fortifying a prearranged battleground. As opportunity came, the trenches were improved to incorporate, as far as possible, all the recognized principles and were gradually elaborated in every possible way, the network of them being often a mile or more in depth, to include accommodation for supports and reserves, and in dangerous areas, where the enemy was likely to mount a big 'push', complete alternative systems were dug a few miles behind.

A further development, on the lines of the forts of those days, was the provision of deep 'dugouts' to house and shelter all the men and, much later, concrete machine-gun nests, to hold on if a trench were taken, menace its captors, and facilitate its recapture. (Before the 'dugout' stage it was astonishing how a single sheet of corrugated iron overhead gave a feeling of comfort and security.)

The German trenches were much more elaborate than ours, often containing dugouts two or three storeys deep, with nearly 'all modern conveniences'. They meant to hold them (apparently not expecting much more progress), while ours were considered as temporary shelter until the great advance we were always promising ourselves.

Things did not reach the stage of 'island' redoubts with all-round defence until late in the war, as there was a reversion to the idea of the 'curtain wall', as in ancient fortresses, i.e. continuous trench lines, with no gaps. (In prearranged battles in the nineteenth century, trench redoubts formed the strong points, while the curtain walls consisted of infantry in line.)

The construction of obstacles was also a skilled and laborious task, and no one will ever know how many hundred thousand miles of barbed wire were used. It took the place of the wooden pallisades used in medieval wars to prevent rushes or surprise attacks.

Regarding Germany, and the adjoining territories the Germans had overrun, as a huge fortress, the analogy can be traced in this way.

Their trench lines were their outer fortifications and those of the Allies, in France, the Netherlands, Russia, and later in the Balkans and Italy, were the investing lines of the besiegers, which they used for protection while they sapped nearer to the enemy and made preparations for the assault.

These lines also prevented egress or the entry of supplies and, where the sea formed the boundaries of the fortress, the Navy did similar work by means of the blockade, minefields and raids, such as the one on Zeebrugge.

The Royal Flying Corps acted as long-range artillery and their observation flights were, in effect, like the work of spies behind the enemy lines.

The great German 'pushes' on the western front, in Italy, and on other fronts, and the naval battle of Jutland, were efforts to break the siege and regain the offensive, while those of the Allies were assaults on the fortress.

The old type of permanent fortifications also played a part in the war, but they either failed to stop the Germans, as in Belgium, or the defenders' casualties, as at Verdun, were much heavier than they would have been in an equally effective trench system. Aerial bombing was in a crude and elementary stage at this period and did not have very serious effects until late in the war.

TRENCH WEAPONS

Efforts to put an end to static warfare resulted in tremendous ingenuity being exerted to find methods of blasting the enemy out of his 'rabbit warrens'. In the process every known weapon came under review and experts concentrated their efforts, first on improvising and then on improving and inventing.

The former included bombs made out of ration jam tins (followed later by the Mills grenade) and catapults, similar to the ancient Roman ballista, for hurling them (hence the word ballistics—the science of projectiles). Bomber sections (in effect a revival of the old grenadier companies) became a part of battalion headquarters. The mortar, nearly the most primitive form of cannon, was revived for dropping shells into trenches and was improved in the form of the 60-pounder, which fired 'toffee apples' (a round shell fixed on the end of a steel rod) and the Stokes gun (now the 3-inch mortar) for rapid firing. Later there was an 11-inch trench mortar, which fired a very powerful shell, with a long range.

In 1915 the Lewis gun—the first light machine-gun—designed in Canada, which fired with great rapidity, but jammed fairly frequently, was issued to battalions in small numbers. *The Machine-Gun Corps* (from which later *The Royal Tank Corps* was formed) took over the heavy machine-guns, which were handled by mobile companies, using motor cycle combinations.

Other trench weapons were—rifle grenades, daggers, homemade bludgeons and knuckle-dusters, and men going out on trench raids (to collect information, lower the enemy's morale, etc.) used to blacken their faces to prevent their showing up in the darkness.

Flame-throwers (*Flammenwerfer*) were invented by the Germans, and at Ypres in April 1915, they made an attack with chlorine gas, which came as such an incapacitating surprise, that it might have enabled them to break through had they followed it up immediately with strong forces. After this, gas became a recognized weapon and was used by both sides—released from cylinders when the wind was favourable, or sent over in shells. The early respirators were made from impregnated army 'grey-back' shirts, and consisted of a bag, enclosing the head and neck, with eyepieces and a rubber breathing valve which had to be held between the teeth. There was no 'anti-dim' compound and, after moving about for a few minutes a man was bathed in perspiration, nearly blinded and half suffocated.

Smoke came back to the battlefield during this war. Up to 1889, when cordite was invented, it had been a prominent feature of every battlefield, but now it was produced artificially and was proved to reduce the accuracy of enemy's fire very considerably when used in front of attacking infantry. They might feel sure there were men behind it but they could not estimate the range or see where they were thickest, and the psychological effect was such that it undermined their morale.

Mining under the trenches went on continuously and scenes were enacted like those at the siege of Tournai, in 1709. Vimy Ridge was one of the sectors noted for this kind of activity and on most evenings, during the late summer of 1916, at about 6 o'clock, one might see the familiar cloud of earth and smoke rising into the air; figures rushing from both sides and going to ground at the lips of the crater—the thud of grenades and the staccato cracks of machine-guns—finally flashes above and slow puffs of smoke from shrapnel, as one side, or both, called for artillery support; a few minutes later things would settle down to the normal intermittent shelling, mortaring and sniping.

Steel helmets came into use in 1915 (for the first time since the seventeenth century) to protect the head against shrapnel, which was used extensively. At first there were only enough for the front line infantry companies, who handed them over on being relieved, but when production increased they were issued to every man of all arms. Armour was tried out experimentally, but did not come into use.

THE GUNS

The most outstanding, and appalling, development was that of the guns. One difference from previous wars was the more rapid and accurate firing of the field-guns due, amongst other things, to the introduction after the Boer War of recoil buffers. Previously a gun ran backwards at each discharge, and then had to be re-laid, but the recoil mechanism allowed the barrel to recoil, without moving the carriage, afterwards quickly forcing it back to its original position. The combination of charge and shell in one unit, like a large rifle cartridge, had also greatly speeded-up the loading. Guns using this type of ammunition were known as 'quick firing' or Q.F., a description which did not apply to those of over about 6-inch calibre, whose missiles were too heavy for man-handling.

The artillery ranged from 13-pounders, 18-pounders and 4·5-inch howitzers, a short distance behind the lines, to 60-pounders and 6-inch guns, farther back 9·2 inch howitzers behind them, and in rear of all 15-inch howitzers and 12-inch guns on railway mountings.

At first ammunition was often in short supply, and one of the early signs of improvement was at midnight on Christmas Eve, 1915, when all the guns of the 2nd Division (and probably others) fired rapid for two minutes—by way of indicating that 'peace on earth' was an inappropriate sentiment and there was to be no repetition of the football matches and 'fratting' of Christmas 1914.

The longer the static warfare continued the more guns were packed into the line and the more efficient were the systems of observation, support, counter-battery work and retaliation. Infantry in the front line had only to take up a telephone and get artillery fire on to any point in a minute or so. The R.A. organized static barrages, creeping barrages—advancing in front of the infantry—and box barrages—cutting off sections of enemy trenches from rear and flanks, while they were being attacked, so that no help could reach them.

When fighting was in progress it became like a maniacal game of toy soldiers, each side trying to mow down the 'Poor Bloody Infantry' of the other. Concentrations of fire were so heavy that large woods were reduced to a few splintered stumps, villages reached the state where nothing was recognizable as the remains of a house, and large areas of ground were churned over and over into shapeless heaps of soil.

The continuous roar and rumble of the 'drum-fire', in the bombardments, was a sinister but satisfying sound (when it came from behind), and the upheaval and cascading of innumerable fountains of debris, overlapping and mingling, rising and falling without cessation, made it look impossible for anything to be alive in the enemy lines. But the deep concrete dugouts had surprising resistance. Though flung about in the ground, they held together like steel strong-boxes, and when the shelling lifted, as often as not, up came the Huns with their machine-guns ready to meet our infantry.

Some idea of the scale of fighting and the massive concentrations of men and guns can be obtained from the following very short notes about two of the largest battles.

THE SOMME

The Somme, 1st July to 18th November 1916, was probably the worst example in all history of the massacres of static warfare, exceeding the enormous losses at Paschendaele and Verdun. Preparations went on for weeks before, eliminating any element of surprise. Both sides massed their guns in the threatened area, collected immense quantities of stores and marshalled their troops for battle.

The British attacked on the 1st of July with fourteen divisions —about 140,000 infantry—on a front of 27,000 yards and lost 60,000 men in the first two days. By the end of July, after putting in many more divisions, they had advanced about two and a half miles on approximately half the battle front, and had suffered 170,000 casualties. The Germans had about 60,000 infantry on this front at the beginning of the offensive.

After July the battle continued with constant attacks by two or three divisions, on small sectors of the line, and counter-attacks by the enemy. Divisions from all parts of the front were moved, in turn, to the Somme, where they had two or three weeks of absolute hell, lost, on an average, half their men and two-thirds of their officers, and were then marched, by devious routes, to quieter sectors and went back into the line where, owing to lack of men, some of the regiments stayed in the trenches for five or six weeks without relief.

By the 19th of November, when the attempt to break through was abandoned, we had lost over 400,000 men against less than half that number of German casualties, and had gained nothing of importance.

The reasons for making this colossal effort cannot be discussed here for reasons of space, but the original plan was altered as a result of the French loss of about 370,000 men during the battle of Verdun (February to June 1916). They were to have provided the main forces, and the front was to have been seventy kilometres wide, but they were now only able to play a subsidiary part and the front had to be reduced to twenty-five kilometres. It was a simple bull-headed scheme for either driving straight through a densely fortified area by sheer weight of numbers, or, failing that, attracting the main forces of the enemy into this defined battle area and just fighting it out until they had to give way. There was little finesse about the whole thing—nothing new and nothing clever, just masses of guns and masses of men. The attacks were mostly made in daylight by about four or five 'waves' or loose lines of infantry, whose expectation that there would be little resistance after the ferocious bombardments they had seen, was usually found to be quite incorrect. (Actually some of the attacks were made after only a few minutes' bombardment.) Barbed wire was very difficult for guns to destroy, all the gaps were covered by machine-guns, and our infantry were deluged with bullets and shrapnel, while in the open with no cover except the shell craters. This explains why we lost twice as many as the Germans.

It was almost a total failure and its main result was to destroy a large proportion of our volunteer troops—the best men, who had rushed to enlist without selfish thoughts to delay them and were now fully trained and experienced. Churchill calls them 'a young army, but the finest we had ever marshalled', and he says, 'If two lives or ten lives were required by their commanders to kill one German, no word of complaint ever rose from the fighting troops'. —'No physical conditions, however severe, deprived their commanders of their obedience and loyalty.'

Though the material results were a dead loss their efforts were not in vain, as the Germans admitted that the morale of their men was never so good after this ordeal. The ceaseless artillery fire, the never-ending attacks and the unlimited sacrifices of our troops seem to have impressed them with the futility of hoping to win the war. There are numerous previous instances in the annals of the army—e.g. Minden, Waterloo, Balaclava, Maiwand, etc.— where stoical devotion to duty, in the face of terrific odds, has so impressed the enemy that his morale was shaken. He felt it was something almost uncanny which he could not hope to emulate and thus a moral ascendancy was gained, which contributed heavily towards his ultimate defeat.

TANKS

During the Somme battle we made a blunder similar to that of the Germans in their first gas attack, by exposing our secret weapon—the tanks, in small numbers. These were developed during the war by fitting an armoured body on to a caterpillar tractor and mounting small guns and machine-guns in it. The name was a 'security' one, suggested by the fact that the first trial model—'Little Willie' (which did not pass its tests), looked rather like a large water tank. The early type had a profile resembling a flattened diamond, with a gun casemate on each side and a pair of cart wheels trailing behind, which acted as a sort of rudder.

Their first action was on 15th September 1916, near Combles and Martinpuich, where they caused alarm and despondency among the enemy. In several cases, when our infantry were pinned to the ground by devastating machine-gun fire, with uncut wire in front of them, a single tank lumbered forward over the wire and over the enemy trench, and at once received the surrender of all its occupants. In one instance the bag was 300 and in another 370. The Germans never forgot their horror of these first apparitions and, when Hitler revived their army, they went in heavily for infantry anti-tank guns and then for Panzer divisions.

There were only about fifty tanks in France at this time, but later in the war over 400 were used in one action (Cambrai, November 1917). Had they made their first appearance in hundreds, there is little doubt that the German line could have been breached and then crumpled up, with a small fraction of the losses endured on the Somme.

AIRCRAFT

Four or five miles from the Somme front was a sight which seemed astonishing even in those days. The 'Happy Valley' near Bray sur Somme, was packed absolutely solid for about two miles with infantry in bivouac, transport lines, horse lines, ration dumps, R.E. dumps, etc., with traffic in and out all day. There were no gaps and one could not have crowded more on to the ground. It was like Epsom downs on Derby day.

And this was the stage reached in air warfare. The primary factor to take into account is that *The Royal Flying Corps* (still a part of the army) had almost unquestioned moral superiority. For days there was no shelling and nothing came over. Then, one morning, early, about half a dozen planes circled overhead, scattering little bombs, whose explosions were not much heavier than those of Mills grenades, and which did almost negligible damage. There were no anti-aircraft guns, but men fired at them futilely with rifles. In a few minutes they cleared off and no more came.

Later that year a grand air attack, consisting of nearly two hundred planes of all sizes and shapes, roused enthusiasm among the men in the line as it passed over to the east. The new arm was growing up.

THE GERMAN PUSH OF 21ST MARCH 1918

The last great offensive of the Germans again illustrates the colossal scale of these battles. They employed thirty-seven divisions, with another thirty in support, and 6,000 guns, on a front of forty miles. This amounted to three-quarters of a million Germans, which were opposed by about 300,000 British, and the enemy's guns averaged 150 to a mile, or one to every twelve yards. The Germans, since the Russian collapse, had great superiority in numbers, and in some of these attacks the frontage of a whole division was only 1,000 yards = nine or ten infantry-men per yard.

The British, partly owing to shortage of men (American troops were not yet in the line, and we and the French had suffered stupendous losses), now used the system of isolated redoubts and 'pillboxes' with, of course, a co-ordinated system of fire. In the first attack, against General Gough's 5th Army, which began in early morning mist (like the battle of Inkerman, 1854), these small forts were quickly submerged and by-passed, but most of them held out, until eventually reduced by mortars and point-blank fire from field-guns, causing delay and embarrassment to enemy columns of up to about thirty-six hours.

There followed five days of stubborn retreats, gaps being filled by cavalry, parties of shoemakers, storemen, cooks, A.S.C., A.O.C., Staffs of training schools, and any 'odds and sods' who could be scraped together, while *The Royal Air Force* (now a separate service) worked strenuously at low-flying machine-gun attacks. During this anxious period a bulge, over thirty miles deep, had been made but at this point the 5th Army accumulated sufficient reinforcements to make a stand, and the Germans reached their limit, having exhausted themselves and outrun their supplies.

Their second attack, against the 3rd Army—twenty divisions against eight—was made in clear weather, allowed our machine-guns full play, and did not get through the forward zone. The Germans used choking gas and contaminated certain areas with mustard gas shells, but apparently did not appreciate the value of smoke.

General Byng had also rather messed-up their plans by his very successful trick of evacuating the front trench system and occupying another in the rear. Bombarding the empty trenches and then moving their stores and guns forward delayed them four days, so the concerted effect of the two attacks was much diminished.

The net result of the great push was no more important than ours on the Somme, though they had been much nearer to success than we had. As on the Somme the attackers lost about two to one, our casualties being in the region of 100,000, and 500 guns.

'Infiltration' tactics were used by the Germans in this battle. They advanced with no set formation and mortar and machine-gun sections would, as quickly as possible, select and occupy positions from which they could bring fire on to the defenders of pillboxes, etc., while the rifle sections attacked or by-passed them. The main difference was that sections had their orders before, instead of during an advance, and were trained to use their initiative without being tied down by too much detail.

BEHIND THE LINES

During the quiet periods of trench warfare an infantry battalion did about nine days in trenches and then three days in brigade reserve a mile or two back, and a week or so, about once a month, in divisional reserve farther behind. At uncertain intervals of several months a whole division would be moved right away for two or three weeks' rest and training.

The short spell in reserve might be spent in ruined houses or Nissen huts with, quite possibly, a bit of shelling, and some alarms. Otherwise they were occupied in resting and getting the mud off, and nothing much besides, except letter-writing, and perhaps a rat-hunt, to while away an afternoon.

The longer spells might be in quite reasonable billets. A small amount of training was done then to keep the men fit and prevent them forgetting what they had learned about open warfare. They could also have scratch games of football, visit the N.A.C.B. (equivalent of the N.A.A.F.I.), do a little shopping, or attend a concert or a picture show and live more normal lives by making friends with the inhabitants. Towns within four or five miles of the line like, for instance, Béthune, were fully inhabited and civilian life went on as usual, subject to occasional long-range shelling. There were many things to buy, wine was plentiful and cheap, there was good champagne for about twenty francs a bottle, and any French woman could always provide a first-class omelette and coffee, to make a change from the rations (which were, nearly always, very good). Baths, often those of the French miners, at a pit-head, field laundries, and the de-lousing engine were also important items in the rest programme.

A slightly less appealing feature of these rest periods was the fact that on almost any evening, about dusk, a man might find himself in a drab-coloured London bus, en route for a digging party in the front line, returning (if all went well) through shattered villages looking grotesque in the dawn twilight.

On the rare occasions of divisional rests, training and entertainments were more ambitious and there were parties and even one or two quite good race meetings, complete with bookmakers and a band.

Seven days' leave to 'Blighty' came every few months except when all leave was stopped owing to anticipated large-scale operations. Travelling up in the boat train England looked a picture of all that the heart desired. London was still full of lights and glamour and romance—not the poor, shabby, impoverished shell it was after the 1939–45 war; life was safe and comparatively luxurious, and everyone was surprisingly attentive and kind. But very quickly one was again at Victoria, among the good-byes of mothers and best girls, crowds of fully armed and equipped soldiers, raucous jests and snatches of 'Tipperary' and 'Keep the Home Fires Burning'. The guard's whistle blew, and it was back to that queer life of mud and terrors and thrills, which seemed like another world, cut off from normal life and penned into a narrow space by dark clouds of uncertainty, barbed wire and great flashes in the night.

At one time the average anticipation of life of an infantry subaltern, in the line, was reckoned at three weeks, but all kinds of exciting changes could happen, such as being sent to the Mediterranean, or to some other romantic goal of the travel-minded. Anyhow, no young man thought he would be a candidate for a wooden cross—numerous as they were—at least not until he had been in the line a long time.

'L' BATTERY R.H.A. AT NÉRY, SEPTEMBER 1914

Just one very well-known incident, seen from the 'worm's-eye view' of a soldier in action, must be included, to give an idea of the spirit of the army in those years. It is an outstanding one, but none the less typical of thousands of instances where individual soldiers just would not give in, though everything was against them and they seemed to be alone in a shambles of destruction.

This was during the Mons retreat. 'L' battery, which formed part of the rearguard, had been fighting covering actions for ten days and had bivouacked at Néry, near Compiègne, on 31st August 1914. They were then not in contact with the enemy and had reason to expect a short spell free from molestation.

At dawn on 1st September the battery was preparing to march off and continue the retirement when, quite unexpectedly, a shell burst among them. It was fired from a ridge only about 600 yards away, which was thought to be held by French cavalry but, in the early morning mist, no one had seen them withdraw and no message had reached the battery.

It was a ranging shot which found the target straight away and, next minute, before they could move off the ground or get the guns into action, there were ten German field-guns and two machine-guns doing their utmost to exterminate them.

Horses and men were flung to the ground in all directions, many of them blown to pieces. Guns were overturned, ammunition waggons blew up, and there was a chaos of shattering din, smoke, screaming splinters and showers of earth.

But the battery went into action in the midst of this holocaust, with the enemy fire increasing. In a very few minutes only No. 6 gun remained serviceable and out of the whole personnel of the battery who had been present, only four men were still unwounded. These were B.S.M. Dorrell and Sgt. Nelson (both afterwards awarded V.Cs. and commissions), Gunner Derbyshire and Driver Osborne (both given the Médaille Militaire—the highest French military decoration).

Soon Sgt. Nelson was wounded, next Derbyshire, then Osborne had a rib broken. But they kept No. 6 gun in action for an hour, the whole time under this incessant close-range fire, and did serious damage to the enemy.

At last, when they were almost exhausted (this would have been a heavy task for unwounded men not under fire), 'I' battery, which had driven at speed to their rescue, came into action and the scream of their shells was the most comforting sound these weary men could have heard.

At about the same time *The Queen's Bays*, who had also been surprised and badly shot-up, occupied a position in a sunken road in front of the battery, and opened a destructive machine-gun and rifle fire, and with these combined efforts the enemy had to withdraw, having suffered pretty heavily.

These four men, in simply sticking to their job, as if it had been their whole world, had carried out the best traditions of the army and had frustrated the enemy's intention of destroying the rearguard and catching up with the main body of the retreating B.E.F.

THE ARMISTICE—ARMIES OF OCCUPATION

The war ended with an armistice, signed at 11 a.m. on the eleventh day of the eleventh month of 1918, and those who study portents may have seen an omen in these figures. They look like something well advanced, yet not completed.

The war and the armies of occupation must have considerably broadened the outlook of the nation, as it took men, who otherwise would not have left this country, to the oddest and most unfamiliar parts of the world. Some went to the north of Russia, where the sun scarcely sets in the summer, and the Mussulmans among the Indian troops could hardly be dissuaded from starving themselves. They had to obtain a special dispensation to allow them to eat before sunset during their annual forty days' fast.

Others visited the Black Sea and the Caspian where a British line, across the forests and mountains, from Batum to Baku, held the Bolsheviks off from vital oil supplies. There the inhabitants of the coastal towns spent the summer evenings bathing in the warm and placid waters with a nonchalant contempt for the western custom of dressing for a swim.

The streets of these towns of multi-coloured wooden houses were often enlivened by volleys of rifle shots, fired just in good spirits by Cossack youths riding in for a week-end party. They were almost too authentic to believe—astrakhan caps, long coats with cartridge pleats where the breast pockets would be and workman-like daggers, which they used when the mood, or the vodka, took them.

Many men from quiet English villages smelt the ancient and glamorous cities of Stamboul, Damascus, Cairo, Baghdad and Delhi, and thousands enjoyed the peerless and never-tiring hospitality of Durban, with its palm-bordered Ocean Beach and its sugar estates.

A MILLION DEAD

From 1914 to 1918 a million of the Empire's men were killed —mostly of the best types, the young and adventurous and physically perfect—the first to join up and the first 'over the top'. Thus, inevitably, the vitality and enterprise, and the general standards of the nation suffered in the following years. This, combined with the natural reaction after a war of such unprecedented magnitude, may to some degree have accounted for our pusillanimous foreign policy which led up to the second war, and the more self-indulgent outlook which developed among the people. Unfortunately, the torch was not held high, and retribution was to follow.

ANIMALS' MEMORIAL

The Scottish National War Memorial in Edinburgh Castle includes monuments to all the various species of animals which were made to help and suffer in 'total' warfare, including several which were then unfamiliar—dogs, reindeer, carrier pigeons, canaries and white mice.

PLATE XX

(50)

1914

The 3rd Dragoon Guards	The 4th Hussars	The 1st Life Guards	The Berkshire Yeomanry	The 21st Lancers
Sergeant	*Trooper*	*Trooper*	*Sergeant*	*Trooper*

(51)

1914

The Northumberland Fusiliers. (Now 'Royal')	The Rifle Brigade	The Coldstream Guards	The Worcestershire Regiment	The Gordon Highlanders
Fusilier	*Rifleman*	*Guardsman*	*Private*	*Private*

(52)

1914

The Royal Engineers	The Royal Flying Corps	The Royal Horse Artillery	The Royal Marine Artillery	The Army Ordnance Corps. (Now 'Royal')
Sapper	*Sergeant*	*Bombardier*	*Bombardier*	*Private*

PLATE XX

Figs. 50, 51 & 52

PLATE XX (50). CAVALRY. 1914

Cavalry full dress, which had not changed greatly since 1855, except for the reintroduction of knee boots in 1871, was more decorative than that of the infantry, but it also had lost many of its traditional features. For instance, compare the hussar of 1914 with those of 1815 and 1833, in the previous illustrations.

The explanation is that up to the last alterations the same uniforms were intended for ceremonial and, with only slight modifications, for active service. Consequently, as more attention had to be given to their suitability for war conditions, they were simplified and made more comfortable and less showy and expensive. But after the Boer War, when it was finally realized that they had become purely a traditional dress, for purposes of ceremony and pageantry, one would have thought they might have been redesigned to include some of the features which have figured in the highlights of history.

In 1914 Dragoons wore white metal helmets, similar to those of *The Household Cavalry*, but with shorter plume sockets, and Dragoon Guards the same pattern, but made of brass. Only the heavy cavalry wore waistbelts, this difference being maintained in service dress.

Lancers had striped girdles, like those worn by all cavalry except hussars, in 1815, and they and hussars wore their sword belts under their tunics. The top part of the lancer cap and the tunic front, or 'plastron', were both of the facing colour, except in the case of the 9th, whose caps were dark blue.

Heavy cavalry wore a single broad stripe of yellow or buff on the overalls and light cavalry two narrow ones. *The Household Cavalry* did not follow this rule and the 1st and 2nd *Life Guards* wore two narrow scarlet stripes with piping between and *The Royal Horse Guards* one broad one. In full dress they wore pipeclayed buff leather breeches and for 'walking out' they, alone, still wore the shell jacket. The farriers of *The Life Guards* wore blue tunics and black plumes, and carried axes.

There was one regiment in each of the four types of cavalry which was an exception to the rules—*The Carabiniers* wore blue tunics, *The Greys* wore bearskin caps, the 11th *Hussars* crimson overalls and the 16th *Lancers* scarlet tunics. Officers of the 11th and of the 5th *Royal Inniskilling Dragoon Guards* now wear crimson and green trousers, respectively, with service dress jackets. Some of the reasons for these peculiarities are: About 1860 *The Carabiniers* were made into light cavalry and wore light dragoon tunics with their own brass helmets. *The Greys* won their grenadier caps at Ramilies, and the 16th *Lancers* did not revert to blue when all the other light cavalry did so, in 1841.

The sergeant of *The Berkshire Yeomanry* is shown wearing the normal cavalry undress uniform with the addition of a bandolier and facings, which took the place of full dress and was worn by the Yeomanry for church parades, etc. The Badge of the regiment was the ancient white horse, carved in prehistoric times on a chalk hill near Lambourn, and immortalized by G. K. Chesterton in the 'Ballad of the White Horse'.

The sergeant of the 3rd D.G. is in 'walking out' dress and the hussar is in dismounted full dress. Sergeants of cavalry regiments wore special regimental arm badges above their chevrons.

PLATE XX (51). INFANTRY. 1914

After khaki service dress came into use for general purposes (1902), full dress was only worn on guard duties and ceremonial parades. (The General Staff and *The Household Cavalry* wore blue undress uniform on manœuvres until 1912.)

'Walking out' dress consisted of the full dress tunic and trousers, round forage cap, belt and swagger cane. Sergeants carried bayonets, this distinction evidently being a relic of the days when they wore swords (up to 1855). This dress had to be worn when off duty out of barracks. There was also a blue frock for undress purposes.

The last year in which the whole army wore full dress was 1914, as after the war it was confined to *The Household Cavalry*, the Guards, regimental bands, and officers attending levees. Other troops only wore it on special occasions such as the Command Tattoos, the Royal Tournament at Olympia, etc.

But in the full dress of 1914 there was not a great deal that remained of the old uniforms, apart from the traditional colours, and the head-dresses of the Guards, Fusiliers and Scottish regiments. The Guards had kept the old slash cuffs and the lace on their tunic skirts. Riflemen still had their green jackets and black equipment and the Scottish regiments their national costume, with the gauntlet cuffs of Waterloo days. But the ordinary line regiments had little to remind them of the feats of their ancestors, excepting the old customs which were still kept up, such as the celebrations of anniversaries like Minden, Albuhera, etc., and many other regimental observances, which were not seen outside the barracks.

But, in spite of the pressure of standardization, many regiments had managed to preserve some relic of ancient deeds as, for instance, the red and white hackle of *The Northumberland Fusiliers*, which commemorates the defeat by this regiment of nine times its own numbers of French, at St. Lucia, 1778. *The Wiltshire Regiment* at one time had a dent on their buttons in memory of the defence of Carrick Fergus, by the 62nd, against the French in the eighteenth century. They carried on when all their ammunition had been expended, using bricks and stones, and those who had a little powder ramming their buttons into their muskets in place of bullets. There were, and still are, numerous similar relics, unknown to the public, but important to the continuity of the regimental spirit and traditions.

In 1914 Territorial Army infantry battalions, when in full dress, wore scarlet tunics with brown leather belts, and forage caps instead of helmets. Their officers had silver lace and all ranks silver buttons, whereas those of regular units had gold lace and brass buttons.

PLATE XX (52). 1914

The Uniform of *The Royal Engineers* had changed little since 1868, Plate XIII (31), except that the busby had been replaced by the spiked helmet in 1878. It was revived in 1929, but as full dress was so little worn then, few people saw it.

Tho Royal Flying Corps originated from the Balloon Company of the R.Es. which, in 1911, became part of the Air Battalion, and was made into a separate corps on 13th April 1913. The double-breasted jacket, with no visible buttons, was a distinctive feature of their dress, which gave an early suggestion of the smart effect of stream-lining.

The Royal Horse Artillery were the only corps still wearing the shell jacket in full dress, and their appearance had not altered much since they had exchanged the bell-shaped shako for the hussar's busby, in 1837. Bombardier is a word of very ancient origin, connected with the bombards of Crécy, and is a rank corresponding to that of corporal. The R.H.A. full dress can still be seen on days when Royal salutes are fired in Hyde Park, as the Riding Troop, which was their headquarters of equitation from 1803 to 1938, has been re-formed for this purpose and is now known as the King's Troop. They are the only gunners who have horses and wear full dress, and their weapons are 13-pounders—the guns which used to gallop into action. (Field Artillery were not supposed to move faster than at a trot.)

The Royal Marine Artillery (later merged with the Royal Marine Light Infantry, to form *The Royal Marines*), used to man the guns of warships. They were dressed similarly to *The Royal Garrison Artillery*, except that they wore white topees in full dress. Both branches of *The Royal Marines* wore the Broderick cap (abolished for other troops in 1905), which gave a silhouette view like a German and it was discontinued during the 1914–18 war. *The Royal Marines* wear a blue service dress, except when on land expeditions, or in tropical climates, when they wear khaki. Their work now includes service in ships of the Royal Navy, and being in charge of landing craft during operations. The Commandos are now entirely formed of Marines and are their special responsibility.

The Army Ordnance Corps (now *Royal*) can trace its origin, through a complicated ancestry, connected with R.A., R.E. and civilians, back to 1418. In 1445 its headquarters was established in the Tower of London, where it remained for about four hundred years, and among the appointments held by its officers during its early history, were those of Master Bowyer, and Master Fletcher.

PLATE XXI

1914

The 5th Lancers

Trooper

PLATE XXI

PLATE XXI. LANCERS—TROOPER. 1914

In 1914 the lancer cap was still worn and had changed little from the original one of 1816. The 'plastron' front was another characteristic feature peculiar to lancers, who were also the only cavalry still wearing the striped girdle, which dates back to 1811. 'Plastron' is a word of ancient origin, which was used to describe the metal breastplate of a suit of armour. The cloth version of it was first worn in 1883 and was reversible, having one side dark blue.

Lancers went to France and other theatres of war, in 1914, with their lances and swords, and in the early stages they made one or two charges in the old style. But, with the rapid development of mechanization and accurate long-range weapons, horsed cavalry were approaching their end, and as the war progressed they did more and more dismounted work.

For a long time the Cavalry Corps was kept in readiness for the expected break-through when, it was thought, the trenches would be left behind and open warfare would begin again. On one or two occasions they were brought up close to the front line, mounted and ready for the advance, but as this prospect receded, many of them had to leave their horses far behind and go into the line as infantry.

They did come into their own again for a short period right at the end of the war.

CHAPTER XII · 1919-38

In the interval between the two German wars human nature followed its normal rather unsatisfactory course, and jealousy, suspicion, greed, and resentment resulted in the usual complications. There was trouble in Ireland, Egypt, Turkey, India, Iraq, Palestine, Burma, Cyprus and China. Several of these disturbances produced minor wars and others were patched-up, generally by 'appeasing' the malcontents, which meant conceding all their demands.

After a period of civil war, murders and atrocities, Ireland (except Ulster, which had no such desires) was given independence in 1922, one regrettable result being the disbanding of five famous old regiments: *The Royal Irish Regiment, The Connaught Rangers, The Prince of Wales's Leinster Regiment, (Royal Canadians) The Royal Munster Fusiliers*, and *The Royal Dublin Fusiliers. The Royal Irish Rifles* continued to exist under the new name of *The Royal Ulster Rifles*, and *The Royal Irish Fusiliers* and *The Royal Inniskilling Fusiliers* were amalgamated into one regiment, but both contrived to preserve their identity. The cavalry regiments with Irish titles were not affected. A further serious consequence was the abandonment of some most important naval bases in the south of Ireland.

The case of Egypt was similar, but we did not go so far as to abandon the defence of the vital Canal zone.

The Arab revolt in Iraq (then Mesopotamia) in 1920, assumed serious proportions and, in one encounter the 2nd battalion of *The Manchester Regiment* had nearly 400 casualties.

AIR TRANSPORT

In 1932 the 1st battalion of *The Northamptonshire Regiment* was transported by air from Ismailia, on the Suez Canal, to various stations in Iraq. This was an early instance of using this mode of rapid transport of reinforcements, thus preventing the outbreak from spreading dangerously, which would have happened if it had been necessary to use the old methods and allow several weeks to elapse before the troops arrived.

In India considerable military operations had to be undertaken —in Waziristan in 1919, against the Moplahs on the Malabar coast in 1921, at Peshawar against invading Afghans in 1930, in Burma, 1930–2, and again in Waziristan shortly before the second German war.

THE NORTH-WEST FRONTIER

People may wonder why it is that the North-West Frontier was such a constant source of trouble during our occupation of India and why it was necessary to use such large numbers of regular troops against ill-equipped tribesmen. A typical example of a frontier district is Waziristan, which lies between Afghanistan and the Indus, for there live some of the most war-like and primitive tribes. It has been a frequent scene of operations and was the home of the infamous Fakir of Ipi.

This country is almost entirely composed of rocky hills and precipitous nullahs which form the only lines of communication. In the highest parts there are trees and a few patches of cultivation near the rivers, but otherwise nothing grows except an occasional thorn bush. The summer temperature is anything up to 130 degrees in the shade and in winter much of it is covered in snow.

The Mahsud Wazirs, who live under distinctly primitive conditions, have few peaceful occupations to chose from and so have to exist mainly on the proceeds of armed robberies. But for the presence of the British they might have found raiding over the border much more profitable but, with this obstacle, it was a mystery how they collected sufficient loot to keep them going. They were helped out by a considerable amount of work—road-building, etc., provided by the hated Sirkar in the hope of teaching them to live in a more civilized way. Each man brought his weapons to his job—quite often they marched up in platoons. They have an ingenious method of shovelling, one man guiding the shovel while two others pull on strings attached to it, thus enabling three to do the work of one quite comfortably.

The Mahsud children are brought up to lie and steal and fight, and the essential preliminary to manhood is to acquire a rifle, and in most cases this will necessitate knifing its previous owner, or watching for a chance to steal one at night from a sipahi who is momentarily off his guard—not at all easy with good troops, but it does happen.

NOSELESS WOMEN

The women are as barbarous as the men and are said to take a prominent part in the torturing of prisoners and obscene mutilations of the dead. The punishment for wifely infidelity, if treated leniently, is to have the nose cut off, and women maimed in this way are not an uncommon sight. They are not attractive by European standards when whole, but one can easily understand that this operation destroys the last vestige of glamour, even in the eyes of a hairy odoriferous hill-man.

DOMESTIC WARFARE

Family feuds are a part of normal life and it is not unusual to see two watch-towers at opposite ends of the same village, from which the opposing snipers keep permanent observation and gloatingly record the score of victims.

In addition there are frequent skirmishes between neighbouring tribes and, living under these conditions, the men either become adepts at mountain warfare or do not enjoy long lives. Near the Malakhand Pass—a more northerly part of the frontier—there used to be an annual tribal battle immediately after the harvest. The British fort, high up in the pass, commanded an excellent view and, as the fighting always took place in the same area, it became a seasonal event like the Royal Tournament at Olympia, the mess roof being used as a grandstand.

NATIVE MOBILITY

Nearly all the attributes of the Boers apply to these Pathans, with the added advantage of callous barbarity. They have some horses and camels, but these are so valuable that they generally leave them at home when fighting, and they can easily cover forty miles a day on foot. Their methods of descending a *khad* (steep declivity) is to run at top speed with arms outstretched for balance, and with the aid of gravity they attain a velocity which must be somewhere about thirty miles an hour, and look almost as if they are flying. The result is that when troops have fought their way to the summit of a hill there is not an enemy in sight.

FIELD-CRAFT AND CAT BURGLARS

Their tactics, too, are rather similar to those of the Boers, but in addition they have studied our methods, as a certain number served for a few years in the Militia or the regular Indian Army, and then went home to instruct the others. They are experts in field-craft and, in this rocky terrain, with their dirty grey clothes, it is often quite possible for them to advance to within 100 yards without exposing a single movement or giving any reason for suspicion. Their night exploits in robbing camps and stores would be the envy of the most highly trained cat-burglar, and every sentry had to have his rifle chained to his wrist. They can even steal the blankets a man is sleeping on by skilfully tickling him with a feather to make him turn over, and while performing these evolutions they wear no clothes and have their bodies oiled so that they are as slippery as a wet cake of soap and almost impossible to hold.

HOME-MADE RIFLES

Besides the rifles they steal or inherit, the frontier tribes produce some from factories hidden away in the hills, where they try to copy the service weapons in every detail, even to the ordnance marks and the crown and royal cypher, but they have always found great difficulty in making a bolt which will not jam or blow back, so that many of them stick to the old Martini model. Besides his rifle every man has a knife, or two, shorter than those of the Afghans, but of the same characteristic shape, with home-made Damascene patterns on the blade and artificial blood at the hilt end. One has to admire their single-minded devotion to the arts of war, but apart from this they are not very lovable.

A REALISTIC TRAINING GROUND

The Pathans are crafty as well as adaptable and intelligent, and were always out to imitate or invent new tricks of warfare, such as surrounding a damaged armoured car, waiting for darkness, and then creeping up to set fire to it in the hope of either roasting the crew inside or knifing them as they came out. The local inhabitants were always on the prowl, waiting for a mistake or a little slackness, regardless of whether there was an official war on or not, and if a picquet or a small party of troops relaxed its precautions, even for a few minutes, it was more than likely that only naked bodies would be found.

There was a touch of reality in all training, and in ordinary camp life, as there was always a sporting chance of being shot-up during a game of tennis, or of being knifed in one's tent, and it was never safe to leave the camp with less than about twenty armed men.

KEEPING ORDER

The British method of keeping order was to have stone-walled, tented camps along the main routes, at intervals of a day's march for camels; and store convoys, several miles long, had to be protected all the way by hawk-eyed picquets—mostly Indian troops—who marched out from the camps at daybreak. The awakening from a sultry night (sleeping in the open for coolness) was generally occasioned by the roaring and bubbling of unwilling *unts* (camels) and the sad and discordant braying of mules, being loaded. Now and then there was a rattle of chains, crashing of boxes and stampeding of hoofs, interspersed with high-pitched and picturesque curses from the drivers. Life was normally rather dull, but at any moment, with the suddenness of most tragedies in the East, a quite unexpected battle was in progress.

Good roads were built along the old goat tracks and after this convoys consisted mainly of mechanical transport with armoured fighting vehicles as escort. This aided the mobility of troops and reduced the picqueting, but still it was an arduous business to keep the peace.

Aircraft could help in the punitive expeditions which are necessary from time to time, but the main part of the job, as always, devolved on the infantry, as it was almost impossible for planes either to discover or strafe a prowling 'lashkar'. All they had to do was to lie absolutely still among the rocks and they were invisible. But the R.A.F. could inflict a punishment which annoyed them intensely by bombing selected villages (always after dropping 'notices to quit'). It just meant that the mud houses had to be built again, but they did not like it.

THE ARMY 'CUT TO THE BONE'

Between 1918 and 1936 the army at home, in common with the other services, went through the usual starvation process, which used to be repeated after every large war. It was accentuated this time as there was much talk about European wars being a thing of the past, just as there was after 1815.

Service was unpopular and recruiting was extremely bad, and in the 1930s one could have seen battalions at home with a strength of two hundred or less, carrying out manœuvres with wooden machine-guns and flags representing non-existent troops. Sometimes there seemed to be as many flags as men.

BELATED ATTEMPTS AT RECOVERY

Nevertheless, those responsible did what was possible, with the means available, to modernize and keep up to date, at least in theory, so that they would have knowledge to put into practice, if a large army should be required again. In 1936 there was the beginning of an effort to prepare on a more adequate scale, but things had not gone very far, and the process of mechanization was far from complete when the war came in September 1939. It had been more or less confined to experimental formations, and the whole system of waging war was, in fact, still in the process of being overhauled at this very critical time.

In 1937 the Bren light machine-gun became the standard automatic weapon, replacing the Lewis and, for infantry, it was to be the main source of fire-power, rifles and bayonets being then considered as secondary weapons, intended mainly for the protection of the machine-gunners—a view which soon had to be revised.

Many other changes were made, such as the reduction in the strength of brigades, companies and platoons from four sub-units to three in each case, marching in threes instead of fours, and great simplification of drill. A new Militia system was introduced in an attempt to fill some of the gaps. The cavalry regiments had nearly all been mechanized and, in many cases, were amalgamated in pairs, and nearly all the artillery horses had gone. Practically all the Yeomanry had been converted to field artillery, but now there was need for a large expansion of the anti-aircraft artillery and of the searchlight companies, and much of this had to be done by converting Territorial units.

Added to all this Hore-Belisha, during his short term of office as War Minister, caused many upheavals in high places and introduced a number of changes in the conditions of life in the army—some undoubtedly good, others viewed with distrust, as it was thought that they would lead to a slackening of discipline. So many things were in the melting-pot when the army was once more ordered to battle stations.

PLATE XXII

(53)

1914

OFFICERS AND COLOURS

The Coldstream Guards	The South Wales Borderers	The Welsh Regiment	The Cameron Highlanders	The Royal Dublin Fusiliers
King's Colour, 1st Battalion	*Regimental Colour (pre-1881)*	*Regimental Colour*	*Regimental Colour*	*King's Colour*

(54)

1914

The Army Service Corps. Now 'Royal'	The Royal Army Medical Corps	The Royal Field Artillery	The Military Foot Police. Now Corps of Royal Military Police	The Army Pay Corps. Now 'Royal'
Sergeant	*Warrant Officer*	*Driver*	*Sergeant*	*Sergeant*

(55)

1914–39

The Coldstream Guards	The Grenadier Guards	The Scots Guards	The Irish Guards	The Welsh Guards
Officer (frock coat)	*White drill order*	*Officer (Service dress)*	*Officer (full dress with greatcoat)*	*Guardsman (guard order)*

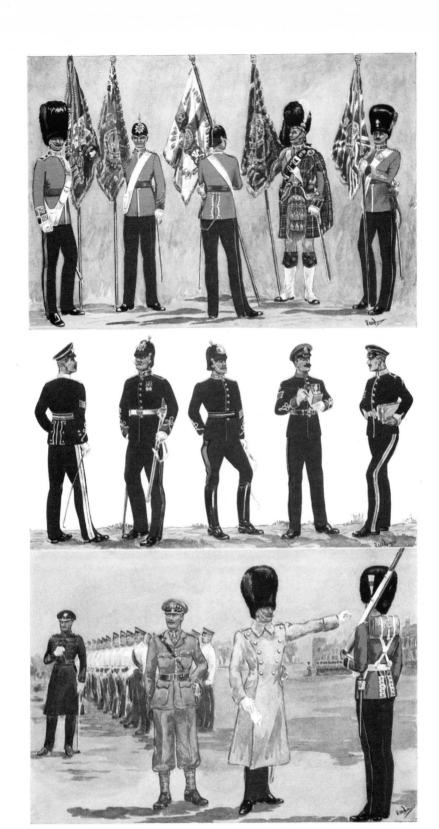

PLATE XXII

Figs. 53, 54 & 55

PLATE XXII (53) OFFICERS AND COLOURS. 1914

Officers' full dress had not changed since 1902. The following regiments had a black line at the top and bottom of the officers' lace and in the shoulder cords in memory of former distinguished commanding officers: *The Norfolk, Somerset Light Infantry, East Yorkshire, Leicestershire, East Surrey, Loyal North Lancashire, York and Lancaster,* and *The Connaught Rangers.* After 1902 the Guards retained lace distinctions of officers' ranks, those above the rank of Lieutenant having lace borders on the cuff slashes, and a very narrow line of lace on the skirts. Lieutenants had one band of lace on the cuffs and higher ranks two.

In 1858 Colours had been reduced from 6 ft. by 6 ft. 6 in., to 3 ft deep by 3 ft. 9 in. long—a much more manageable size, especially in a strong wind. At the same time the ornamental spearhead on Colour pike was replaced by the lion and crown—the crest of England. All Standards, Guidons, and Colours were supervised by the Garter King of Arms, who was the Inspector of Regimental Colours.

As in the past, each battalion (except Rifle regiments, which had no Colours) had a King's Colour, which was the Union flag, and a regimental Colour of the same tincture as the facings. The regimental Colour of a regiment with white facings had the red cross of St. George covering the whole flag.

The small Union Jack in the corner of regimental Colours was abolished in 1881 and a pre-1881 Colour of *The South Wales Borderers* is illustrated. The wreath of silver laurels in memory of Isandlwana and Rorke's Drift, is borne on the King's Colour.

Battle honours were embroidered on the regimental Colours, but later, owing to lack of space, those of the 1914–18 War, which were limited to ten, were placed on the King's Colour.

The Brigade of Guards did not conform to these rules, but followed a more antique system, by having the Union flag as the regimental Colour, and a crimson King's Colour. They also have a different procedure as regards Battle honours, placing them all on both Colours. Each company still retains its ancient badge, and these are attached in rotation to the centre of the regimental Colour. *The Welsh Guards* are unique in that they carry small swallow-tailed company Colours.

The Colours of the various battalions of a regiment are 'differenced' by the addition of Roman numerals, but the Guards have their old system. For instance, those of the *2nd Coldstream Guards* have the Union in the dexter canton (top left corner) and the 3rd battalion has the Union, with a 'pile wavy, or' descending from its lower right corner.

The Queen's and *The Seaforth Highlanders* each possess a third Colour.

In the case of *The Seaforths,* both the Colour and the elephant badge, worn beside the ordinary collar badge, a unique distinction, commemorate the battle of Assaye, 1803. They and *The Highland Light Infantry,* who also possess a third colour, and the 19*th Hussars* (then Light Dragoons), greatly distinguished themselves in this battle in which Wellesley, with about 4,500 men, defeated 47,000 Marathas with 115 guns. All these regiments have the elephant on their colours (drum banners in the case of the 19*th Hussars*).

The Royal Northumberland Fusiliers also have a third Colour, which is carried by a drummer only on St. George's Day, in memory of the battle of Wilhelmstahl, 1762. The *2nd Duke of Wellington's* have a special pair of Colours, in addition to the normal two, which were presented to the 76th Foot by the Honourable East India Company to commemorate their distinguished service in India.

PLATE XXII (54). 1914

Except for *The Royal Field Artillery* these corps date their existence under their present titles from comparatively recent times. Most of them, however, have had several reincarnations, and their predecessors served in nearly every war since 1660, but under varying designations and often as civilians attached to the army.

The R.A.S.C. is descended from the 'Waggon Trains', which were formed at various periods and were usually disbanded at the end of each war. Its dual role of supply and transport has become more complicated with each war, and its organization has to be something like that of a gigantic world-wide department store, specially designed for the conditions of war service in every imaginable type of country and climate.

The R.A.M.C., as such, dates from 1898, but it also has a previous history filled with vicissitudes. It appears that, until the Peninsular War, no medical officers were permanently attached to regiments, and the whole system of dealing with the sick and wounded and preserving the health of the army was never adequately dealt with until after the Crimean War.

The Army Veterinary Corps (not illustrated) dates from 1881 as a department, but it was also during the Napoleonic wars that veterinary surgeons were first attached to mounted units. Their uniform in 1914 was similar to that of *The R.A.M.C.,* except that the facings were maroon (no cuff facings), yellow piping round base of collar and on skirts and cuffs, and two narrow maroon stripes on the breeches and overalls. Mechanization has now removed the greater part of their work, but amongst other duties they provide dog-handlers for patrol and other war dogs.

The only notable change in the uniform of *The R.F.A.* since 1881, Plate XV (38), was the striped girdle. This and *The R.A.S.C.* one were like the cavalry girdles of Napoleonic times, but narrower. *The Royal Garrison Artillery* (not illustrated) were similarly dressed, but were a dismounted corps and wore trousers and infantry belts and pouches. In service dress they wore the old leather anklets. They were amalgamated with *The R.F.A.* in 1925.

The Military Police, Mounted and Foot, now *The Corps of Royal Mili-*

tary Police, and *The R.A.P.C.* were both recruited by selection from other corps. The former are familiar as the 'red caps', from wearing red covers on their service dress caps. Their unpopularity, which is superficial, is a tribute to their efficiency, and on service they have many arduous duties in addition to those of dealing with crime. The Military Provost Staff Corps, which wore a similar uniform except for the cap, is a separate corps which provides Staff for military prisons and detention barracks and camps.

All these corps wore the universal cap and, in full dress, the helmet, surmounted by a ball, except in the case of the C.M.P. and the A.P.C. who wore spiked helmets.

PLATE XXII (55). 1914–39

This illustration shows the five regiments of *The Brigade of Guards* in five different uniforms. White drill order was not worn after 1914, but the remaining ones were worn by all the regiments until 1939. *The Welsh Guards* are depicted in 1936 to show the new guard order, introduced by King Edward VIII—cape folded and worn on the shoulders in place of the greatcoat, which was previously carried in this position, the cape then being rolled and strapped on to the belt.

The outstanding differences between the uniforms of the five regiments are described in Appendix III.

Other ranks in the Guards have long worn their caps cocked in a characteristic manner (by the regimental tailors) with the peaks coming steeply down over the eyes. This gives a smart and distinctive appearance and compels a man to hold his head up. When not on service or training they wore coloured forage caps with service dress. The peaks had a brass binding and the badges were placed mainly above the band.

Officers, except those of *The Scots Guards*, all have forage caps with black bands and broad gold binding on the peak, and wear them with khaki covers when in service dress under the above conditions. Their bearskin caps are higher and differently shaped from those of the other ranks. The frock coat, with loops across the chest, is worn as well as the blue frock, and the Guards were the first to introduce khaki 'plus four' knickerbockers.

Other peculiarities of the officers' service dress are: buttons grouped as in full dress, plain breast pockets and flat side pockets with slash flaps (the former without the pleat and the latter not pouched), and buttons on the cuffs.

In full dress the Guards' slash cuffs, lacing on the skirts, and Atholl grey greatcoats and capes, are peculiar to them and are survivals from 1868, when they were discontinued by other regiments. Quartermasters wear cocked hats.

Guards officers wear Garter stars as badges of rank, except the Scots and Irish, who wear, respectively, the stars of the orders of the Thistle and of Saint Patrick. Those worn by all other officers (except *The Household Cavalry*, who wear the Garter star) are the same as the star of a Knight of the Military order of the Grand Cross of the Bath, but there are a number of regimental variations in colour and size.

PLATE XXIII

(56)
1939

The Scots Guards
Piper

The Grenadier Guards
Drum Major (State dress)

(57)
1911

Staff Officer (blue frock)

Cavalry Officer (Service dress)

The Royal Dragoons
Squadron-Sergeant-Major (with guidon)

(58)
1937

The Honourable Corps of Gentlemen-at-Arms

The Military Knights of Windsor

Pensioner of the Royal Hospital, Chelsea

The Yeomen of the Guard

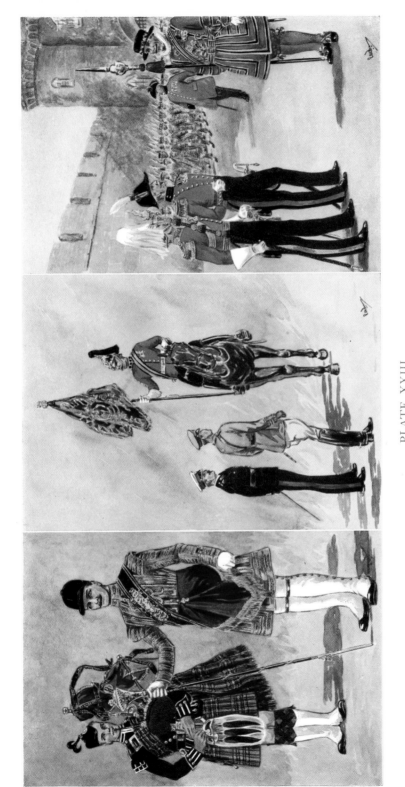

PLATE XXIII
Figs. 56, 57 & 58

PLATE XXIII (56). 1939

The heavily laced crimson coat dates from the seventeenth century and is worn in state dress by the Drum-Majors of the Foot Guards. The long white spatterdashes date back two hundred years, and the 'jockey' cap is similar to the old English cap of three hundred years ago. (See Plate V (12).) These features are in keeping with the many old customs and privileges, which are retained by the Guards.

One or two instances of these are the large embroidered Royal coat of arms worn above the right elbow by Regimental Sergeant-Majors, and the fact that Staff Sergeants wear no chevrons in undress uniform. The senior company of *The Grenadier Guards* is known as the King's Company, and has a special crimson silk Colour of its own, and that of *The Welsh Guards* is called the Prince of Wales's Company. Both of these, like the old grenadier companies, are composed of picked men who, besides being selected for their smartness, must be over six feet tall.

The Scots Guards are the only Scottish Regiment in the regular army which has drum and fife bands, and the Sergeant-Pipers of this regiment wear a crown over inverted silver chevrons, while those of other regiments wear four gold inverted chevrons without a crown.

Royal Stewart tartan is worn by the pipers only, of *The Scots Guards, The Royal Scots, The King's Own Scottish Borderers, The Black Watch,* and in 1943 the King conferred this honour on *The Cameron Highlanders,* on attaining their 150th anniversary and in recognition of their services in the recent war. The pipers of all Scottish regiments, with the exceptions of those of *The Scots Guards* and *The Black Watch,* who have feather bonnets in full dress, wear a Glengarry cap, in most cases adorned with an eagle's or a blackcock's feather.

The bandsmen, but not the pipers, of *The Highland Light Infantry* wear feather bonnets, although the regimental head-dress is a shako.

PLATE XXIII (57). 1911

In 1911 both the service dress jacket and the blue frock were altered in cut, the collars being made with lapels similar to those of a civilian suit, but after 1918 the Prussian collar was restored to the frock. In service dress the badges of rank were placed on an imitation slash on the cuff, and to distinguish rank from behind, bands were put on the sleeve: Subalterns—one, Captains—two, Majors—three with tracing braid between, Lieutenant-Colonels—three with four rows of tracing braid, Colonels—four with five rows of tracing braid. (For a short time, in 1902, a curious system of showing rank, ironically known as the 'asparagus bed', was used. It consisted of varying numbers of strips of braid, of different lengths, 'growing' upwards from the cuff. Apparently it was not a success.)

Crimson standards were carried by Dragoon Guards and Guidons by dragoons. Lancers and Hussars had had no Colours since 1834. Formerly the Colours were borne by Cornets, but in 1822 this became the duty of the Troop-Sergeant-Majors.

Gorget patches were worn on the blue frock and on service dress, by Generals and all Staff officers.

Gorget tabs and coloured cap bands are now only worn by staff officers of the rank of colonel and above, so the 'gilded staff' is not so much in evidence as in 1914–18, when all staff officers, down to 2nd Lieutenants, wore them. The colours are:

General Staff—Scarlet.	R.A.V.C.—Maroon.
R.A.M.C.—Dull cherry.	A.E.C.—Cambridge blue.
R.A.P.C.—Yellow.	A.D.C.—Emerald green.
R.A.O.C.—Blue.	Army Chaplains Dept.—Purple.

Colonels and Brigadiers have cords down the centre of the gorget patches of the same colour as the cloth. Higher ranks have a line of gold oakleaf embroidery.

In 1914 the following colours were worn on the officers' greatcoat shoulder-straps:

Cavalry	Yellow braid $\frac{1}{8}$ in. wide, round the edges.
Royal Artillery	Blue; scarlet loop from button down centre.
Royal Engineers	Scarlet; blue loop.
Infantry	Scarlet.
Army Service Corps	White.
Royal Army Medical Corps	White; dull cherry loop.
Army Veterinary Corps	White; maroon loop.
Army Ordnance Corps	White; scarlet loop.
Army Pay Department	White; yellow loop.

They went out of use during the 1914–18 war, together with the slash cuffs and badges of rank on the sleeves, as officers could no longer afford to wear anything which displayed their rank to enemy snipers using telescopic sights. In 1939 officers were dressed the same as the men, except for worsted crowns and stars on the shoulders. As has often happened, one regiment retained the thing which was abolished, and the Royal Northumberland Fusiliers continued to wear scarlet piping on the greatcoat shoulder-straps.

PLATE XXIII (58). 1937

This illustration shows some interesting survivals of old uniforms, worn by corps composed of retired officers and soldiers. They are not, of course, fighting troops, but come on duty for certain ceremonies, and on State occasions, such as the Coronation of King George VI, in 1937.

The Honourable Corps of Gentlemen-at-Arms was formed by Henry VIII, as a personal bodyguard, in 1509. Its present uniform is very much like that of a Dragoon Guard officer in 1854, except for the very high plume of swan's feathers and the peculiar partisan or halberd. In the coronation procession in the Abbey there were ten Gentlemen-at-Arms on each side of the King, marching in single file.

The old coatee also forms part of the full dress of the Military Knights of Windsor (founded by Edward III, in 1348), which they wear when attending service in St. George's Chapel, Windsor Castle, and on State occasions. The distinction of being one of the knights is conferred on a small number of retired officers (13), who have given exceptional service, and they and their families become part of the royal household, and are provided with quarters in the Castle. D.S.O.'s, M.C.'s, etc., with numerous bars, are quite commonplace among these veterans. (The normal sword is straight-bladed, with a cross hilt, and is now carried by a white shoulder-belt.)

The Royal Hospital was built by Sir Christopher Wren about 1692 to provide accommodation for 550 old and disabled soldiers, who had no families or homes. The Pensioners wear, in full dress, a tricorne hat with the Hanoverian cockade, and at other times a high-crowned cap shaped rather like a shako, with the letters R.H. on the front.

The Yeomen of the Guard, popularly known as 'the Beafeaters' (buffetier — sideboard man), date from 1485 and are said to be the oldest military corps in the world. (See Plate II [1].) Their establishment includes a Captain, Lieutenant, Ensign, Clerk of the Cheque, four Exons (Corporals) and ninety-two Yeomen, the last being retired N.C.O.s, and the higher ranks retired officers. The bodyguard is on duty at most of the Court ceremonies attended by the King. The officers do not wear the Tudor style of dress, but have scarlet coatees, cocked hats with drooping feathers and blue trousers.

The Yeomen Warders of the Tower are a separate corps, but are similarly dressed except that they do not wear the carbine belt.

Other interesting but less familiar figures are the officers of the Royal Hospitals, and the King's Marshalmen. The latter wear scarlet coatees and shakos and carry ebony batons. They were instituted as the king's personal police and are present at Courts and levees, and one always used to attend the Guard-mounting parade at the Horse Guards.

CHAPTER XIII : 1939-45

1939

The second campaign of the German War was the result of timid foreign policy, throwing away all that had been so bitterly won. We were not alone to be blamed, but we led the way—in gullibility and disarmament. Now it had all to be gone through again—a second edition of the same war, with every additional complication and improved and multiplied weapons which could be devised in the intervening years and with more concentrated efforts during the actual period of war.

In 1918 things had progressed as far as partial mechanization, 'infiltration' tactics, 'forward defended localities', i.e. glorified picquet systems with island redoubts built for all-round defence; tank battles, scientific use of gas and smoke, and highly organized gunnery. The *R.A.F.* had become a separate service and was a vital factor in land and sea fighting.

In the early part of the second war there was nothing really new excepting paratroops, but all the features of 1918 had been excessively developed and more were added later, with the perhaps unexpected result that, though the expense and the destruction of property were enormously increased, the casualties (anyhow as far as we were concerned) were nowhere near as heavy, and the war lasted nearly two years longer than the first one.

The whole thing was vain and futile repetition, and the psychological effect on the army was a visible effort to forget the first war and to try to imagine that nothing was the same, even avoiding as far as possible using quite the same names and expressions, the motive being, no doubt, the dread of the static warfare mentality. This was to be a war of movement and there was to be no re-enactment of battles like the Somme or Verdun, and trench 'lines' were not to be spoken of.

CATASTROPHIC RESULTS OF BEING UNPREPARED

The second war came as a great disappointment to the people (many of whom had remained in wishful blindness) just when trade conditions were completing their recovery from the last upheaval, and life was getting less expensive and more pleasant.

There was little enthusiasm this time and the spirit was very different from that of 1914. The challenge was accepted as a matter of course, but with grimness and reluctance.

Through not having prepared on any scale comparable with the enemy's thorough organization of mind, body, and material, we went through our usual series of disasters, magnified to a degree never before experienced. Outstanding among these were —the evacuations of France, Norway, British Somaliland, Malaya, Burma, Greece and Crete—all of them due to lack of men or weapons or air support, and not reflecting in any way on the troops engaged, but exceedingly damaging nevertheless. The falls of Singapore and Tobruk, with very large garrisons, were even worse shocks owing to their unexpectedness, and appeared, at a distance, to involve less creditable performances. In addition to all this the German invasion of nearly all Europe, the prolonged threat to England and to Egypt, the closing of the Mediterranean and Japanese threats to India and Australia, plus the submarine and air menace, made up the gloomiest scene in all our history. It seems that this country only puts forth her best efforts when faced with defeats and imminent dangers. However, people never doubted that things would come right in the end and, regardless of what other countries might do, there was no thought of quitting. It was far too near a thing for comfort, though, and it might be our last lesson if we have not learned it this time.

DUNKIRK

In 1940, after the collapse of France and the Dunkirk episode, we carried on alone against the most efficient military power ever seen in the world, and we were prepared to meet an invasion optimistically with practically no regular troops (actually only about one division was fully equipped) and *The Home Guard*, armed with pikes (old bayonets fixed on poles), truncheons, and incendiary bottles to throw at German tanks.

The Royal Air Force, by its wonderful success with shamefully inadequate numbers and equipment against the German air invasion, undoubtedly prevented a seaborne attempt and, aided by the high morale of everyone—not least the civilians of both sexes, we kept going somehow.

CHANGES IN THE ARMY

The changes in the army have been so far-reaching and so varied, and it is still passing through so many modifications and further stages of evolution, that it is not possible yet to give any detailed picture.

One can only mention a few of the obvious innovations, such as airborne forces, and the vast increase in the paraphernalia of war, which lengthens the periods of training and preparation and makes every expedition more costly and more heavily encumbered.

Enormous expansions were necessary to enable the old branches of the service to take over their new duties on a much larger scale—e.g. *The Royal Artillery* to deal with anti-aircraft and anti-tank gunnery, searchlights, etc., *The Royal Engineers* and *The Royal Army Ordnance Corps* to cope with the problems of mechanization. This necessitated the formation of a new corps—*The Royal Electrical and Mechanical Engineers*. (*The Royal Corps of Signals* was another of the earlier offspring of *The Royal Engineers*, like *The Royal Flying Corps*, which in turn gave birth to *The Royal Air Force*.) *Reconnaissance units* (mechanized and armoured) and combined operation troops are other logical developments, comparable with the light dragoons and light infantry which were formed to increase mobility in the eighteenth century. Other corps which are either of comparatively recent origin, or were formed during the war, are: *The Royal Armoured Corps*, which includes mechanized cavalry, *The Reconnaissance Corps* and *The Royal Tank Regiment*; *The Army Air Corps*, comprising *The Glider Pilot Regiment*, *The Parachute Regiment* and *The Special Air Service Regiment*; *The Intelligence Corps*, *The Army Catering Corps*, *The Royal Army Dental Corps*, *The Royal Army Educational Corps*, *The Army Physical Training Corps*, *The Small Arms School Corps*, *The Royal Pioneer Corps*, and *The Non-Combatant Corps*. These names give some slight idea of the various aspects of war, which have had to be modernized and dealt with on a more scientific basis, but the process of forming technical corps to concentrate on subjects which assume fresh importance goes on continuously. They come out of the old corps and start on their own, or the process is reversed and they begin independently and are later absorbed to form part of one of the original corps. To show that the mechanized cavalry are still regarded definitely as cavalry, five new regiments formed during the war were given the titles of Dragoons (22nd and 25th), Hussars (23rd) and Lancers (24th and 27th).

From 1939 to 1945 war was the main preoccupation of every person in the Empire and all the best brains of industry and science, and of professions and trades even remotely connected with the services, concentrated on victory. But, until the atomic bomb, they produced little that was radically new. The alterations consisted of improvements—multifarious and far-reaching—in existing weapons and methods, including guns, missiles, bombs, aeroplanes, wireless (of which radar is an outstanding development), fighting vehicles, transport, improved methods of packing and supplying all the various needs of active service, and so forth. The army itself had to deal with increased mechanization, the new airborne technique, a general overhaul of training, better methods of recruiting and selection of men for particular jobs, selection of officers, modernizing all the ancillary services, and hundreds of other problems in addition to the normal ones of strategy and all its requirements. It was nearly all the natural, but accelerated development to be expected from 'total' war, and it followed the train of evolution from previous centuries without diverging much from it. We were doing just the same thing—trying to kill the enemy, but in a far more difficult and complicated way, which was the result of mechanization in civilian life.

THE MEN

As regards the men themselves a superficial difference was noticeable between the recruits of 1914 and those of 1939. The latter smoked cigarettes instead of pipes, or did not smoke, drank lemonade and ate sweets and buns, swore very little and did not grumble. In the old days if there was no grousing it probably meant that something was wrong with morale! These men were soft at first, but were physically better than the last generation, and they soon toughened up.

The following minor instance bears this out. A company of three-weeks-old recruits, with no senior N.C.O's, were in wooden huts on a cliff overlooking the sea when one night a gale tore several of the roofs off. Next morning the company commander, before making his usual inspection, went to view the condition of the roofless huts. It was raining heavily but inside he found each man standing to his kit, which was all laid out in perfect order for inspection as if nothing had been wrong. At such an early stage of training this little incident showed clearly that they would soon become good soldiers.

Another noticeable change was that the men of 1939 were much quieter than their predecessors—a characteristic which was strikingly demonstrated when two sections of a convoy of troopships passed within twenty-five yards of each other at the entrance to the Suez Canal—one going to the Far East, the other, which had come out with them, landing troops in Egypt. The decks were packed with men, all watching the other ships, but there was dead silence as they passed. This was in 1944, but had it been in 1914–18 the air would have been shattered with shouts and cat-calls from every ship.

One other short anecdote shows that the British soldier had not changed much under the surface. A sentry, guarding one end of a very long bridge in the Middle East, saw two natives approaching beating a small emaciated and cruelly overloaded donkey. When they wished to cross the bridge they first had to unload the unhappy animal and give it a rest. Then they had to carry the donkey over the bridge, leave it with the guard at the far end and return for its load—a good-humoured way of teaching a badly needed lesson.

CHANGED CONDITIONS OF ACTIVE SERVICE

There are several important differences in the conditions of life on service which mostly had their origin in 1914–18, and have now become basic factors in war. One great difference from previous wars is that, as the result of aerial bombing, flying bombs, rockets, etc., a man can no longer feel sure that his family at home will have remained intact when he returns, or that he alone is enduring the hardships of war. He may even be sent to a perfectly safe area himself where the old order is reversed and he experiences the anxiety which used to afflict only the women.

Against this the air mail is a great comfort and enables him to keep in close touch. In previous wars letters often took as many weeks to reach a theatre of war as they now take days.

Another big change is the conscription of women, which never happened before, and means that a soldier's wife may be called up and perhaps have to close down the home, or even go overseas. This, though, is only one indication of the 'totality' of modern wars, which makes every individual a small part of the machine and leaves nothing outside its scope. A man's inclinations no longer matter. He wants to be a soldier—and has to remain in a factory. He thinks he could be much more useful as a civilian, but is conscripted into the army. This has become necessary, but it does not encourage enthusiasm or adventurous spirits, and another effect is that the civilian often thinks he has done just as good a job as the soldier and faced as much danger. Not infrequently he has, but he is inclined to omit the fact that the soldier has to go deliberately into battle, fight with his weapons and endure many other things, whereas his own reaction is normally passive and he lives at home and gets more pay.

The conditions of service in the ranks have greatly improved as regards supplies of personal requirements, welfare, entertainments, news services and, not least, pay, and when things settle down soldiering ought to be a job which compares favourably with most civilian occupations.

In contrast with former days the soldier is now taken into the confidence of the authorities to a considerable extent, by means of innumerable pamphlets, lectures and discussions, dealing with every aspect of war and of life in general, and he is consequently expected to have a better grasp of the reasons for the jobs he has to do.

TOUGHNESS

The rigorous conditions of modern war have reached a pitch requiring far greater average physical fitness, toughness and mental alertness than ever before; but on the other hand there is a far higher proportion of technical and other personnel which have to work in the rear. There are probably about a dozen of these to one fighting man. (Actually factory workers and many others on whom the war machine is dependent, should come under this heading, and it might have been expected that they would all have been conscripted on similar terms to those of the men in the Forces.)

On the subject of battle training here is a quotation from a letter written by an officer in Italy. 'During training you must induce utter weariness. When you've got everybody thoroughly worn out, keep them going for another forty-eight hours. Get them so used to foul conditions, short commons and no sleep, that action and reaction become completely automatic.'

You still find 'Nobby' Clarke, 'Ginger' Brown, 'Dusty' Miller, 'Pincher' Martin, and the rest in the modern army as in the old days, but their fathers, who served with 'Old Bill', would have needed a lot of practice before they could have gone over the battle obstacle courses which these young soldiers take in their stride, or have stuck the intensive training, which was on a scale never before conceived.

An important change in this was the introduction of reality— all kinds of weapons firing live ammunition, which effectively reproduced the deafening racket and confusion and a good part of the danger of a real battlefield. It was considered worth the risk of some casualties, and it certainly did give a man a far better realization of what he would be up against, than the old perfectly safe manœuvres, which could be taken seriously or not, according to the mood of the moment, and in any case called for a powerful imagination.

SECURITY

The imperative need for fooling the enemy's intelligence and spy system, proved by bitter experiences in the previous war, affected the lives of everyone, including civilians, and made a grim and repressive atmosphere.

A soldier had always to guard his tongue whenever he was away from his unit. His letters (as in the previous war) were censored and he must never mention the place he was in or give any interesting details of his work.

When troops went overseas they departed obscurely at dead of night for unknown destinations, arriving at dismal dockyards where not even a coffee-stall woman was admitted. There could be none of the old-fashioned stuff—bands playing, relations on the dockside, etc., and if the ship called at a port—even, for instance, in the Clyde, not a soul could go ashore. Sometimes ships waited a week for a convoy to assemble, and after this the destination remained a matter for much wild speculation, until disembarkation orders were issued, a few hours before landing. The fact that tropical kit was given out, told the men something, but still it might be the Middle East, the Far East, the Mediterranean or East Africa. Probably even the ship's captain did not know until he heard it over the radio.

Before 'D' day the troops taking part were entirely segregated in sort of internment camps, to prevent the possibility of telling the little they might know or surmise, and officers concerned in the planning suffered agonies of anxiety lest they might, inadvertently, drop some infinitesimal hint about the vital secrets entrusted to them.

The huge 'iron curtain', or wet blanket, hung heavily over everything, until one got used to it and this, plus the air menace, prevented any scenes of enthusiasm, like those in the first war, when whole villages used to turn out to welcome long columns of troops, and bands played drafts to the stations. War had become a hole and corner affair and glamour had very nearly made its exit.

THE MODERN 'FORLORN HOPE'

In the Forces there was no lack of opportunity for hair-raising exploits rivalling any in past wars—especially in the Commandos, the Airborne forces, the 'Chindits' in Burma, the long distance patrols in North Africa (which would often travel a thousand miles through enemy-infested desert, with no opportunity for replacing supplies or ammunition, or getting help for casualties to men or vehicles), or in fact in any unit in a theatre of war. Even Generals had a full share of hectic moments. Many were involved in close fighting and quite a number were killed.

An entirely new technique has developed from the large-scale use of parachutes and gliders, the former requiring men to accustom themselves to conditions which were outside all human experience of the past. An airborne force of all arms, including infantry, guns, light tanks, Royal Engineers, workshops, hospitals, etc., gliding or floating down from a dusky sky into enemy territory, must be an amazing sight. It certainly brings back a touch of the dramatic and spectacular side of war and, in keeping with this aspect, the operations for which these troops are used are necessarily often of a hazardous nature, with possibilities of a brilliant success at an appropriate moment, coupled with a definite risk of complete failure.

The Germans, under Goering, began to form airborne units in 1936 and the Russians in the same year had reached the stage of being able to drop simultaneously a force of 1,200 men, with 150 machine-guns, and 18 light field-guns, much to the astonishment of General Wavell, who was present at a demonstration. It was mainly the German parachutists who so quickly disorganized the Dutch defences in 1940, by appearing at unexpected places and causing confusion in the rear.

Our activities in this sphere did not begin seriously until 1940, and the first small operations began in 1941 with a raid on an aqueduct at Monte Vulture, in Italy, followed in 1942 by a successful attack on a radio-location station at Bruneval, in France. From then on the force grew and both parachutes and gliders were used in actions of increasing scale, in North Africa, Sicily, Italy, the invasion of France, Arnhem and the advance into Germany.

Besides volunteers, who were never lacking, though many could not pass the strenuous tests, a number of the old line regiments were made 'airborne' and have become the super light troops of the twentieth century. Some of these were battalions of *The Border Regiment, King's Own Scottish Borderers, Oxford and Bucks Light Infantry, South Staffordshire Regiment* and units of *R.A., R.A.S.C., R.C.S., R.A.M.C.* and *R.E.M.E.*

The men had to know all that the soldier of an ordinary unit learns, reaching the highest possible standard in weapon training, field-craft, map-reading and, not least, toughness. Besides this they had to do special air training and had to develop their self-reliance, initiative and determination to an outstanding degree. Napier would have called them 'unsurpassable soldiers'—so highly trained and individually formidable, that ordinary German troops (who named them the 'Red Devils', from their berets), would sometimes throw up the sponge on discovering their identity, though they had been fighting well up to that moment.

The battle of Arnhem, so well portrayed in the film and described in the official account 'By Air to Battle', was one instance of their high morale and 'genial ferocity'. The 1st Airborne Division, which started out 10,095 strong, lost in those few hectic days 7,605. They did their part magnificently in seizing bridges and holding on against hopeless odds, without reinforcements and almost without food, for far longer than could have been expected and added an epic honour to those they already had, dating back to Blenheim, Minden and Waterloo. The pity was that the 2nd Army could not advance quickly enough to reinforce them, but there is no doubt that their willing and generous sacrifice shortened the war by several months.

Airborne operations usually involve a type of fighting which is filled with lurid and personal adventure, spectacular coups, incongruous scenes and much 'cloak and dagger' work. The parachutists and glider teams drop behind the enemy front in order to create confusion, often having many vicissitudes en route, and their assembly after landing is frequently a complicated operation. (In the attack on Syracuse, 9th July 1943, the weather was bad and, out of 108 gliders, 50 fell into the sea and 25 were missing.) On the ground they fight with P.I.A.Ts. and 'gammon' bombs against giant tanks, their companies are attacked by regiments, they surprise enemy Generals at dinner and occasionally are entertained with champagne in the cellars of 'underground resisters'.

THE INFANTRY STILL BEARS THE BRUNT

At one period it looked as if the infantry was no longer to be 'the Queen of battles', but that things would develop into a struggle of tank *v.* tank and gun *v.* tanks and defences, the infantry only being needed for 'mopping-up', fighting in ground where tanks could not go, and for more or less static garrison duties. This may have sounded all right when thinking of Martin-puich (1916) but, with both sides strong in armour it did not work out, and infantry—airborne or otherwise, still has to form a high proportion of any main force, takes the lion's share of the bashing, and is expected to perform even more difficult tasks than before.

Field-Marshal Lord Wavell said about them, 'All battles and all wars are won in the end by the infantryman.'—'The infantryman always bears the brunt. His casualties are heavier, he suffers greater extremes of discomfort and fatigue than the other arms. . . .' Another quotation, from Lord Montgomery, says, 'In spite of predictions to the contrary, the infantry has lost none of its importance on the battlefield'. —'It has again been the infantry who suffered the heaviest casualties. I cannot praise too highly the stamina and persistence which the infantry displayed. . . .'

In 1914–15 it took about eight or nine months to train an infantry battalion, from the initial stage as civilian recruits until they were considered fit to go overseas. But, owing to the more varied assortment of weapons, the time required to obtain them and the increased individual skill and knowledge of many subjects which had become essential, it required about double this length of time in the second war.

MASSIVE SUPPLIES

In the old days the main armies, which were comparatively small, were concentrated in compact masses, and simply battered each other at short range and with a minimum of movement until one side was beaten. They needed little besides muskets, bayonets and ammunition to carry out their purpose (even rations were mostly obtained locally), whereas now an army cannot risk a full-scale action without massive supplies and vast quantities of scientific and mechanical equipment. To land an invading army about half a million items of equipment are needed, ranging from buttons to Bailey bridges. On 'D' Day, 6th June 1944, in operation 'Overlord', 287,000 men and 37,000 vehicles were landed in Normandy, and during the first month the totals reached 1,100,000 British and American troops, 200,000 vehicles and 750,000 tons of stores and ammunition.

The fact that a shortage of any one of these supplies might have disastrous effects, gives some impression of the colossal magnitude of the work of organization which goes on in the background, and explains the long delays which precede major offensives.

CO-OPERATION WITH THE R.A.F. AND THE ROYAL NAVY

One of the most important lessons of the war was that these large operations could not be carried out unless the three services worked so closely together that they almost became one. This might be described as the trinity of battle, but the simple fact is that no landing can be carried out in force unless the Army is there to do it, the Navy has control of the sea, and the R.A.F. has at least temporary air supremacy, and all their movements must be exactly co-ordinated.

The air factor attained such proportions that all troops had to be air-conscious in every movement, even when stationed in the south of England. Infantry must move by platoons using the cover of hedgerows, vehicles must travel with large intervals between them and must be parked under cover, or camouflaged. Camps had to be concealed and dispersed. No tell-tale footpaths must be made.

Much of the work of movement, transport, and bridge-building, etc., had to be done at night and an antidote to this difficulty was found by introducing 'artificial moonlight', provided by batteries of shaded searchlights. This was a marked difference from the first German war, when whole divisions paraded for inspection, complete with all their guns, transport, ambulances, etc., and covering many acres of ground. There was nothing like the four- or five-mile long columns seen then on the roads of France, except when battle conditions had forced the crowding of roads. Then the unwillingly massed transport or troops were generally very unlucky. Air bombardment, too, when it reached the stage of bombs weighing tons, and bombers were numbered in thousands, could destroy whole cities, which had taken centuries to build, in a matter of hours.

MODERN EQUIPMENT

The heavy equipment used on 'D' Day included some most interesting developments. To begin with, prefabricated docks, which went under the security name of MULBERRY, were towed across, after the landing, and placed in position for the unloading of stores. Later came PLUTO (pipe line under the ocean) which saved a tremendous amount of labour and tanker space in transporting petrol.

For use in the landing and after, there were several new adaptations of the tank—mine-sweeping tanks, R.E. tanks, with petards to fire heavy demolition charges, flail tanks to explode anti-personnel mines, mat-layers to help infantry to cross boggy patches. There were bridge-carriers for crossing anti-tank ditches, turretless tanks to form ramps against the sea walls over which other tanks could climb, flame-thrower tanks to burn out pillboxes, etc., and more turretless tanks which carried infantry inside their armoured hulls. Most of these and other vehicles were waterproofed so that they could leave the landing craft if they grounded in the water, and there were the now familiar DUKS—amphibious trucks with boat bodies.

Bailey bridges were another heavy and important item. They were like 'Meccano' sets and could be erected very quickly. About two thousand were used to replace demolished bridges over the rivers in France and Germany, and hundreds were also used in Italy and other countries.

GUNS AND 'V' WEAPONS

The ancient contest of guns *v.* armour continued with greater intensity and diversity than ever before, as the velocity of shells and their smashing and penetrating powers were constantly increased, to combat the heavier armour of tanks and the more massive concrete of field fortifications. It is not possible even to mention all the varieties of anti-tank, anti-aircraft, tank, and self-propelled guns, which made their appearance. Early in the war our tank and anti-tank guns were both too light, but the 25-pounder field-gun justified itself, and is likely to remain about that size for two reasons. One is mobility and ammunition supplies, and the other the fact that the psychological and moral effect on an enemy depends more on the number of explosions than on their size. Twelve 25-pounder shells will affect a man's nerves more than three 100-pounder ones from a 6-inch gun if he is not actually hit.

The rocket, which was used by the R.H.A. in the early nineteenth century, was revived and enormously developed, so that it threatens to outdo the gun for many purposes. By this convenient method a shell which, if discharged in the normal manner, would require an outsize gun to fire it, can be attached to a tube containing a slow-burning explosive which propels the whole missile by blast, and fired from a set of guide rails of comparatively simple construction. Various smaller types can be released from aircraft, from a tube held by a man, such as the American 'Bazooka', or from a light mounting like those of the 'Z' anti-aircraft batteries.

The maximum size and explosive content of this weapon had already reached the proportions of the German 'V2', which carried a ton warhead, during the war, and various nations have carried on with experiments since then. The Americans are reported to have a fourteen tonner which, in ordinary earth, makes a crater about 36 feet deep and 75 feet across. The rocket principle seems to have superseded the flying bomb with an engine, and the further possibilities of range and destructiveness appear to be almost unlimited.

FREAKISH GUNS WHICH LED UP TO THE 'V' WEAPONS

The idea of using enormous projectiles to blot out cities behind the battle front and thus destroy an army's bases or demoralize the civil population in its rear, originated far back in history, but until the advent of aircraft and giant rockets, it took the form of immense guns. These, however, were never really successful and did not justify the efforts and the material and man-power expended on them. So they remained in the category of freaks.

An example of these was the 25-inch gun used in the siege of Stamboul in 1453, which had to be moved by a team of 60 oxen, with 200 men marching alongside to prevent it toppling over and a working-party of 250 going in advance to prepare the road for its passage. When at last in position its daily output was about half a dozen of its 600-pound stone balls, and its range was about 1,800 yards.

'Mons Meg', still preserved in Edinburgh castle, was a contemporary European effort, built at Mons, and had a bore of 20 inches. It fired stone or iron balls, the latter giving a longer range, up to nearly 3,000 yards.

In recent times the Germans pursued the idea with greater persistence than other nations and produced 'Big Bertha' (named after Bertha Krupp) in the first great war, which shelled Paris from a range of about 70 miles, without any really serious effect. In the second great war they built a pair of 1,500-ton guns of 31-inch calibre, firing 7½-ton shells up to 28 miles, for use on the Russian front. It was reported that each gun employed 1,500 men under the command of a Major-General.

In the end this obsession helped towards their defeat, as they concentrated their efforts on 'V' weapons at the expense of their air force, but in doing so they added one more unpleasant factor to the future of warfare.

MINES AND CONCRETE

Mines and fortifications are both inventions of great antiquity but they were, like everything else, exploited to their fullest potentialities. They are the defence against armoured fighting vehicles and the antidote to mobility in general, and both were made use of to such an extent that progress was frequently slowed down to to the level of 1915–18.

The job of clearing a minefield on a cold, wet, muddy night, with frequent enemy shell or mortar fire, was among the most unpleasant in the war, but it was so frequently required that it became necessary for all front-line troops to learn the procedure. The men never knew when they might come upon a new type of mine or a new firing device, which would make their careful technique suddenly useless, as well as ending their personal careers.

Another branch of mining in which the Hun was specially ingenious, was the laying of booby traps. They would even go so far as to attach them to bodies, so that the burial party would be blown up and the simplest action, like hanging a hat on a peg or kicking away an empty tin, could result in instant obliteration.

THE ATOM BOMB

In August 1945 Hiroshima and Nagasaki each disintegrated under the effects of one bomb. About 113,000 Japanese were killed, probably twice as many were injured, and the centres of these two important towns were reduced to dust and small rubble. Within a very short time Japan surrendered.

This was the outcome of a race between Germany and the Allies to discover and adapt for war purposes that dream of many decades—the splitting of the atom, or more correctly, in scientific terms, nuclear fission.

It was cold-blooded murder. So was the ordinary bombing of London, Berlin, Prague, and many other British and European towns. But the enemy had asked for it, and had they been the first to perfect the bomb they would no doubt have used it on as large a scale as they could. It probably saved many more than 113,000 lives, which would have been lost in winning the war by more conventional methods.

Since then experiments have been made in spraying radioactive material from the air, and this is said to be an even more potent weapon, as it can destroy all forms of life—vegetable as well as animal—over wide areas.

No doubt both methods of destruction will be improved and probably atomic war-heads will be fitted to rocket projectiles, with a range far in excess of that of the V2.

Thus began a new era, in which science's greatest discovery made its début in a role of devastation. Its effects on the three services and on world affairs in general are incalculable as they have not yet fully developed.

MODERN BARBARISM

The totality of this war, besides involving the conscription of whole nations, both in the forces and behind them, and the wholesale and deliberate bombing of civilians also produced exhibitions of primeval barbarism in cruder and more personal forms, on a scale never previously known.

Throughout history there have been atrocities and massacres but these, with exceptions in Oriental countries, were nearly always committed in the heat of the moment by inflamed or drunken crowds of undisciplined troops or civilians. But never has there been anything like the cold-blooded, calculated, sadistic butchery perpetrated by the Germans in their extermination camps at Belsen, Dachau, Auchwitz, etc. This was all a part of a carefully thought-out plan. They first enslaved millions of conquered civilians, choosing nationalities from which they feared no retribution, and then deliberately worked them as near to death as they could, to help Germany to win the war, giving them starvation rations and the foulest conditions imaginable. Many of them were used as human guinea-pigs, to test the effects of war gases, bacteriological warfare, exceptional stresses, exposure, and privations of air and sea war, etc. Those who did not succumb to the experiments, as well as those who had become too weak for further forced labour, and many whom the Germans wished to exterminate for political reasons, such as Jews, anti-Nazis, etc., were then destroyed. Shooting was the least unpleasant method, but most of them were starved to death or herded into gas chambers, and the numbers ran into millions.

Their treatment of prisoners of war was a little better, (though extremely bad) as they were not certain they would win, and the Allies had a great number of German prisoners.

The whole system was the outcome of the German doctrines of waging war, developed through a century, and aided by their soul-less, inhuman thoroughness, and the unrestrained instincts of a savage bully who has the upper hand.

The Japs did not do these things scientifically, but simply reverted to medieval savagery which is nearer to the surface in Asiatic races, and tortured, starved, bullied and murdered their prisoners by many foul sadistic methods. One of these was to use Chinese prisoners in the same way as we use stuffed sacks for bayonet training.

Neither of these nations should ever be permitted to regain sufficient power to have any chance of repeating their loathsome crimes, nor should they be forgotten.

'FIFTH COLUMNS'

Such methods of warfare do not, at first, seem to be very closely connected with the subject of this book—the British Army, but the treatment of prisoners and the 'fifth column', or infiltration method do have an effect on every man in the Forces and cannot be left out.

In this war the Germans, following their highly developed technique of war without hindrance from scruples or feelings of decency, practised the method of bribing traitors and planting their agents all over the countries they intended to invade. For instance, they would have in their pay Staff officers in the forces of their future enemies, government officials, leaders of trade unions, managers of transport services, etc., plus a host of petty spies (some to spy on other spies), saboteurs and spreaders of sedition. These would keep them supplied with information but otherwise carry on as normal citizens until the appointed day.

Then, when the invasion began, quite probably without a declaration of war, vital bridges would be left intact and unguarded, aircraft would be found unserviceable, troop trains and supply trains mysteriously lost, other vital services disorganized, and doubt, suspicion and alarm spread among the population.

How successful they were was shown by the fall of France and of the other countries they overran.

This system of undermining or rotting the resistance of a country before attacking it, is a technique which is likely to precede future wars, or it may be so highly developed as to make a nation incapable of fighting at all, and it is even now going on in this country and in most parts of the world.

It is another of those things that every officer and soldier has to watch for. It involves not only the most stringent security precautions, but every man has to have his mind trained to be always on the look-out for the smallest suspicious occurrence, and to know what immediate action he should take.

THE DEFENCE OF CALAIS, MAY 1940

It is impossible in this small space to describe battles or the course of the war, nor is it necessary, as so much literature is available and is still being written. But one incident, out of hundreds, gives an idea of what the men had to endure and how well they faced up to it.

To quote Lord Montgomery once more, 'It is the human element which is the major factor,' and 'I call morale the greatest single factor in war'. The following is a very bald outline of what happened at Calais, and shows that the army was as rich in these qualities as ever before; and that, despite the general impression that everything has changed, the experiences of regiments were not so unlike those of previous wars.

The B.E.F., with both its flanks uncovered and no further possibility of taking the offensive, was retreating on the Channel ports. It was already nearly cut off by fast-moving panzer divisions, when a small force was sent from England to hold Calais for use as an evacuation port.

This arrived on the 22nd May and consisted of battalions of *The King's Royal Rifle Corps, The Rifle Brigade*, and *The Queen Victoria's Rifles*, one battalion of *The Royal Tank Regiment*, and one anti-tank battery under Brigadier Claude Nicholson. It was after-

291

wards joined by an anti-aircraft battery, whose guns had had to be destroyed in the retreat, some *Marines* and detachments of other units, and about 800 Fighting French—approximately 3,000 men in all.

As these troops reached Calais it was already in a state of confusion—roads blocked solid with refugees and French soldiers who had given up fighting, fifth column spies active, German batteries shelling the harbour, and fires burning in the town. The population was nervy and nearly all the dock workers had gone to ground. Hospital trains full of wounded were arriving in the docks for shipment to England.

The tank battalion had left their station at four hours' notice, with incomplete mobilization stores and, in the difficult conditions at the harbour, someone blundered and sent out a ship which still had on board most of *The Rifle Brigade's* stores, ammunition and vehicles. The Germans had reconnaissance aircraft overhead all the time, but the British had none until two days later. So, on the whole, it was not a specially encouraging start.

The tanks were promptly ordered by G.H.Q. to proceed to St. Omer and went out, only to find all roads strongly held by panzers, with whom they had an inconclusive engagement and were forced to withdraw. Later they made another unsuccessful attempt, accompanied by lorried infantry, to get through to Dunkirk, and when they returned to Calais they had only a small number of tanks remaining serviceable.

Infantry patrols, sent out on the first day, never returned, but the troops hastily formed an outer and inner perimeter defence and occupied positions round the town. The permanent defences were almost useless, as their guns could only fire out to sea.

On the second day 200 German tanks were reported to be approaching. The shelling increased and the outer perimeter was heavily attacked and was broken in one or two places by nightfall. It was sweltering weather and, as the water mains were broken by shell-fire, it became increasingly difficult to get water to the scattered troops. Ammunition was short and during the day all except two of the anti-tank guns were knocked out.

The next day was much the same, but German reinforcements were arriving constantly and the shelling increased greatly in intensity. There was a proposal to send reinforcements from England but, as it was now known that the B.E.F. could no longer hope to reach Calais, this was cancelled. Two destroyers gave all the help they could throughout the defence and small boats were still entering the harbour.

On the Sunday conditions were much worse. Dive-bombers

continually attacked the town. Ammunition was almost exhausted. Two complete panzer divisions were attacking, enemy tanks and mortar sections were in the streets, the quays were being machine-gunned, and half the town was on fire. Fifth column snipers were busy and it became impossible to distribute orders or rations to the men who, after being forced back from the perimeters, were in small isolated groups, cut off from one another by burning ruins and streets covered by enemy fire.

The War Office ordered Nicholson to hold on at all cost, until the evacuation of the B.E.F. was completed and, though the men could never have known this, they fought on with sheer hopeless determination, just as if the order had been given and they had realized that everything depended on them.

The enemy sent a demand to surrender, but Nicholson's terse reply was, 'The answer is NO'. Later that day they forced an entry to the citadel and captured him and the remains of his headquarters.

A new small perimeter was somehow formed round the harbour, but now it became clear that further resistance was hopeless for more than a few hours, as there was practically no ammunition, the men were nearly starving and without water, and had had no sleep for about four days, while the Germans continued to bring up masses of fresh troops. So, as many as possible were told to escape through the enemy lines at night, and make for Dunkirk.

But at night the numerous fires made the town as light as day, so this became impossible and instead, each group held out until its last round had gone and it was surrounded and either exterminated or captured.

About fifty men were all who got away by hiding under the pier, on slimy pillars down near the water until, in answer to the flashing of a pocket torch, the Navy managed to get them off.

The defence of Calais had, in itself, been useless, but it was a defeat which deserved more credit than many a victory, and it enabled 300,000 British and French troops to be taken off at Dunkirk, while for four days it occupied a large force of Huns which would otherwise have prevented this.

PLATE XXIV

(59)

1879–1914

FOREIGN SERVICE DRESS

The 17th Lancers	The 10th Hussars	The Camel Corps	The Royal Field Artillery	The 5th Dragoon Guards
Zululand, 1879	*Afghanistan,* 1879	*Sudan,* 1885	*'Hot weather' full dress, India,* 1914	*France,* 1914
Trooper	*Lance-Corporal*	*Trooper*	*Sergeant*	*Trooper*

(60)

1898–1937

SERVICE DRESS

The Royal Warwickshire Regiment	The Argyll and Sutherland Highlanders	The South Staffordshire Regiment	The Durham Light Infantry	The Somerset Light Infantry
Sudan, 1898	*South Africa,* 1900	*Service dress,* 1906	*Drill service dress India,* 1918	*Home ceremonial dress.* 1937
Private	*Sergeant*	*Lance-Corporal*	*Private*	*Sergeant*

(61)

1944

BATTLE DRESS

The Royal Artillery	Airborne Infantry	Commando	Royal Armoured Corps	Line Regiment
Staff-Sergeant	*Corporal*	*Private*	*Squadron-Sergeant-Major*	*Private*

Flash of
H.Q. 21st
Army Group

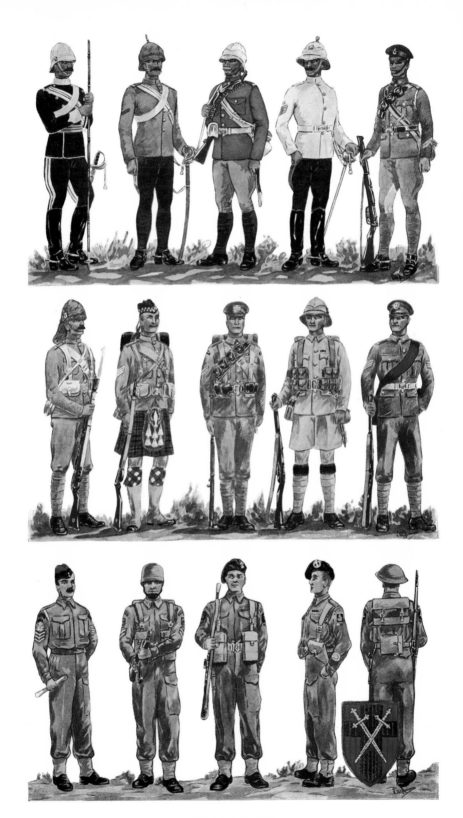

PLATE XXIV

Figs. 59, 60 & 61

PLATE XXIV (59) FOREIGN SERVICE DRESS. 1879–1914

This illustration shows some of the rather odd mixtures of dress which were in use by mounted troops, during the period when the contest, between utility for service conditions and the traditional garb of the army, was in full blast.

In the Afghan War khaki jackets and helmet covers were worn, partly as camouflage and partly for coolness, and the remaining items, except for knee-boots, which were replaced by puttees, were the same as in full dress. Brass spikes and chin chains were worn on the helmets, but the steel scabbards were blackened, as they made such conspicuous flashes in the sunlight that they would have attracted attention at a distance of many miles.

In the Zulu War, in the same year, such laxness was not permitted as the troops were equipped at home, and practically the only difference from home service dress was the topi. The brass spike, however, was not worn, and there was no puggaree.

In the Gordon relief expedition, in the Sudan, camel regiments were formed, as horses could not cover long distances over loose sand so well as camels, with their broad, cushioned feet, and their ability to travel without water or feed for long periods. Utility was then gaining ground in the matter of dress, as the men wore grey 'frocks' and khaki breeches. Their equipment was a cross between cavalry and infantry—bandoliers and infantry ammunition pouches, carbines and bayonets.

White drill was worn in India for training in the 'hot weather', from before the Mutiny, and later it came into use as summer full dress. Infantry wore white trousers, but mounted troops kept to their full dress pantaloons. The stages in the development of the helmet are noticeable.

In 1914 cavalry wore the bandolier with pouches for charger-loading ammunition (as used by the infantry before the 1908 webbing equipment), and a spare bandolier was often carried round the horse's neck. Light cavalry hussars, and lancers, wore no waistbelts, and the short magazine Lee Enfield rifle was used by all arms.

Breeches had acquired a smart appearance, but the 'flare' was less pronounced on those issued to other ranks than on those of the officers. Mounted troops wound their puttees downwards, as the reverse method was not satisfactory for riding, and wore their haversacks and water-bottles on the same side, so that when the water-bottle rose and fell with the motion of the horse, it hit the haversack instead of the man's hip.

A new sword was issued in 1912 which had a long straight blade, a solid hilt, and curved grip.

PLATE XXIV (60) SERVICE DRESS, 1898–1937

The Royal Warwickshire Regiment has the battle honours, 'Atbara' and 'Khartoum', and the dress shown is the Indian khaki drill of that period. The helmet is an improved pattern, named after Sir Garnet Wolsley, who was Commander-in-Chief in the Egyptian War of 1882. In the Sudan War, 1897–8, a large neck-flap was attached to it and at this time it still had a rather narrow brim and was similar in shape to the home service spiked helmet. Khaki drill has varied in colour from almost orange to pale greenish grey. Khaki is an unstable colour and even in cloth or whipcord it fades with many differences of tone.

The Durham man is wearing a later pattern of the Wolsley helmet, which gave much more protection from the sun. The wearing of puttees (Hindustani word, meaning bandages) had spread from India during the first Sudan War, and from that time they were worn on service, with red or blue uniforms, and with khaki service dress until 1938, when the doctors decided that they were not as hygienic as they had previously thought.

With the introduction of khaki, the highlanders held on to as much as possible of their national costume. *The Argyll and Sutherland Highlanders* gained battle honours for 'Modder River', 'Paardeberg', 'South Africa, 1899–1902', and the illustration shows their winter dress—Glengarry cap and khaki serge of a brownish colour. They were still too conspicuous and a khaki apron had to be worn over the front of the kilt, instead of the sporran. (Early methods of camouflage in that war included rubbing mud into the straps of the equipment.) In 1915 the highlander's apron extended all round, the Glengarry was replaced by a khaki Balmoral, and khaki hosetops and short puttees were worn. The final stage came in the Second German War, when battledress superseded the kilt for active service.

The South Stafford man is wearing the bandolier equipment which was designed for the charger-loading ammunition of the long Lee Enfield rifle, which had a magazine holding ten rounds and was the first weapon fitted with the bridge charger guide. The colour of service dress had been changed to a more greenish shade (now that it might be worn in greener countries) which is correctly described as drab, but continues to be known as khaki. The round cap had come in and the old black greatcoat was replaced by a khaki one in 1902.

In 1908 the short rifle, long bayonet, and webbing equipment were introduced (shown on the Durham man). The pouches each held three chargers —150 rounds in all, the invention of magazines having made it necessary to carry much larger quantities of ammunition, owing to the rapid rate of fire. (With muzzle-loaders in the old days a man normally only carried about twenty-four rounds.) A new entrenching tool, shaped like a small pick, was carried and the equipment assembled all in one piece was much more scientifically arranged than any of the previous ones.

The sergeant of *The Somerset Light Infantry* is wearing the nearest approach to full dress which was permitted between the two great wars (except for *The Household Cavalry* and the Guards, who retained their full dress). This consisted of service dress with white belts and the sergeants wearing their sashes. It will be noticed that he wears it on the left shoulder (see Chapter V). Full dress was not, however, abolished and was described in King's Regulations up to 1940, as if it were still in use.

During the 1914-18 War many 'civilian soldiers', who had no desire to grow moustaches, made them as small as possible, thus producing what was called 'an unsoldierly appearance', so an instruction was issued making it 'all or nothing'. Since then a large proportion of the army has been clean-shaven.

PLATE XXIV (61) BATTLE DRESS. 1944

The battle suit was introduced in 1937 and was the result of experiments lasting over several years, which included 'deerstalker' hats, bush jackets, etc. It is the nearest thing to a mechanic's overall and, as such, is symbolic of the mechanized era. All idea of 'spit and polish' had at last been abandoned and it seemed doubtful if men could feel like soldiers in it, or even take a reasonable pride in their appearance. As a working suit, though, it is comfortable and has many good points.

At first there were no identifying marks, for security reasons, but as the war went on it was embellished more and more with little coloured bits and pieces. Another effort to overcome its anonymity showed itself in the variety of colours used by the different units for their jack-knife and whistle and revolver lanyards. Arm of service strips were worn, e.g. red-blue for R.A., red for Infantry, etc., and Formation Badges, such as the battle-axe of the *78th Division* and Dick Whittington's cat for *The London Division*, and in some cases regimental flashes, like the tartan one of *The Cameron Highlanders*, were again in use, as in 1914-18. An unusual one is that of the 6th battalion of *The Black Watch*—a strip of the ribbon of the Croix de Guerre, which distinction was conferred on the battalion in the first great war, when it was cited in French Army Orders for distinguished service with the French.

Airborne troops are provided with a special steel helmet which has no brim to catch the wind, and a head-harness instead of a chinstrap. and dispatch riders have crash helmets with leather neck shields. The ordinary helmet is the same as in the 1914-18 war, except for having rubber shock absorbers and an easily detachable lining.

There was a change of equipment in 1937, when new pouches were fitted which each hold three Bren magazines, or a cotton bandolier of fifty rounds. The braces were shaped on the shoulders, the belt was narrowed and the fastenings for the small pack were improved so that it could be removed and put on without disturbing the remainder. There is one disadvantage— the belt cannot be adjusted easily or quickly. The difficulty arises if a greatcoat is put on, etc.

The Infantryman on the right is in 'battle order', with the new very snort bayonet, and the Mark IV rifle—a mass-produced edition of the Mark III, with alterations such as an aperture sight, only three rifling groves, no nosecap, and a general simplifying of the details. He is shown without webbing braces, as a number of units adopted the method of wearing the small pack hooked on to the pouches. The Airborne man has a Thompson sub-machine gun, and the Commando man a Bren light machine-gun.

The khaki field service cap, worn until 1943, was unsatisfactory. It was difficult to get war-time soldiers to wear it at the correct angle, their hair-grease soaked through and blackened it; it blew off in a light breeze or fell off during drill and gave no protection from sun, wind, or rain. It was replaced by the beret—maroon for airborne and parachute troops, black for the Royal Armoured Corps (handed on by the Royal Tank Regiment), green for commandos, and khaki for the rest.

The 1939–45 war produced an unprecedented number of medals, but the principal decorations for personal acts of bravery remained as in the 1914–18 war:

The Victoria Cross. Instituted in 1856, for 'conspicuous bravery or devotion to the country in the presence of the enemy'. It can be awarded to all ranks and, up to 1920, a total of 1,101 had been won. When only the crimson ribbon is worn it is easily distinguishable by having a miniature bronze cross attached to it. An additional bronze cross = a bar, which is extremely rare.

The Distinguished Service Order. 1886. For officers. Recipients must have been mentioned in dispatches for distinguished service, and the Royal Warrant of 5th March 1931 further specifies 'distinguished services under fire or under conditions equivalent to service in actual combat with the enemy.' Ribbon—red with blue edges.

The Distinguished Conduct Medal. 1854. For 'other ranks'. This replaced the Meritorious Service Medal of 1845, and is given for 'Distinguished conduct in the field'. Ribbon—red, blue, red.

The Military Cross. 31st December 1914. For Captains, Subalterns and Warrant Officers. In 1931 it was made available to officers not above the substantive rank of Major, for 'gallant and distinguished services in action'. Ribbon—white, purple, white.

The Military Medal. March 1916. For other ranks. For individual or associated acts of bravery. Ribbon—dark blue. In centre three white and two crimson stripes alternating.

A silver rosette worn on the ribbon of any of the above, except the V.C., denotes that the decoration has been twice awarded.

The George Cross. Instituted in 1940 for acts of the greatest heroism or of the most conspicuous courage in circumstances of extreme danger.

The George Medal. Awarded for similar acts, but slightly less meritorious.

WOMEN'S SERVICES

Women have served with the army from its earliest days, but not in uniform, and without any official recognition, until the Crimean War, the last in which soldiers' wives accompanied them on active service, and the first in which women received official recognition as nurses.

From the earliest times they always took a full share in the hardships of campaigning and made themselves helpful by doing the cooking, washing, first-aid, and various other jobs with their regiments, sometimes carrying ammunition or water to the men while in action and occasionally handling a musket.

A number of them became casualties from wounds and sickness, and they probably had some of their worst ordeals in North America, in the eighteenth century, where massacres and scalpings by Indians occurred when small isolated posts were overwhelmed. In the Indian Mutiny they suffered great privations in Cawnpore, Lucknow, Jhansi and other besieged garrisons, and in the end many of them fell into the enemy's hands and were murdered. In the Crimea a number of women were frozen to death.

Of the existing women's services the N.A.A.F.I. (Navy, Army, and Air Force Institutes) can trace the longest (strictly unofficial) pedigree, which goes back to Queen Anne's time when 'sutleresses' were attached to regiments and had a tent in the lines, where they provided wet and dry refreshments for the men.

Nursing became a branch of the army when Florence Nightingale took a staff of nuns and volunteers to the Crimea to combat the appalling chaos of the so-called hospitals there, which they did with great success, earning the lasting gratitude of the sick and wounded men.

But after that war there was again no nursing organization until the Army Nursing Service was formed in 1881, which grew into the Queen Alexandra's Imperial Military Nursing Service. A reserve was also formed later, and when the Volunteers were reorganized and became the Territorial Force in 1907, the nursing service was represented there by the T.F.N.S. (Territorial Force Nursing Service), the V.A.D.'s (Voluntary Aid Detachments) and the F.A.N.Y. (First Aid Nursing Yeomanry). The latter began their career in 1909 as mounted medical orderlies, whose job was to ride on to a battlefield, give first-aid to the wounded, and then bring them back for treatment in hospital. Their full dress, until 1910, was a scarlet tunic with hussar loops and braid, a dark blue riding skirt (they rode side-saddle), and a scarlet forage cap. In 1914 their role was changed and they became ambulance drivers or hospital nurses, and were given the new title of The First Aid Nursing Yeomanry (Ambulance Car Corps) in 1927. This was changed again in 1933 to The Women's Transport Service (F.A.N.Y.), and they are now more or less a part of the A.T.S., having lost their connection with nursing, but they still wear 'F.A.N.Y.' on their shoulder designations.

As regards the present nursing services, the Q.A.I.M.N.S. are the regulars and serve permanently at home and abroad, the T.A.N.S. are their counterpart in the Territorial Army. The V.A.D.'s of the British Red Cross Society and St. John Ambulance Brigade correspond to the 'duration' soldiers of the total wars of this century and expand their numbers enormously in wartime. They can trace their history back to 1882, as some of them served in the Egyptian War, and detachments also took part in the Boer War of 1899–1902. They were officially associated with the Territorial Force in 1908.

The other Women's Services, which perform duties not connected with nursing, date from 1915, when the Women's Legion was formed. The W.A.A.C. (Women's Army Auxiliary Corps) came on the scene in 1917, and the A.T.S. (The Auxiliary Territorial Service, now the Women's Royal

Army Corps) dating from 1938, are in effect a revival of this corps. They act as clerks, cooks, drivers, etc., besides performing many other skilled technical duties at home and abroad, and serve with the anti-aircraft batteries and searchlight companies, where they go into action with the men. N.A.A.F.I. dates from 1921 and E.N.S.A.—a department of N.A.A.F.I., from 1939.

In addition to the officially recognized army services, mention should be made of a number of semi-military or civilian organizations such as the Women's Voluntary Service, the Home Guard Auxiliaries, S.S.A.F.A. (the Soldiers', Sailors' and Airmen's Families Association), etc., in which women have been most helpful to the army, often living and travelling in great discomfort and danger in the war areas.

The M.T.C. (Mechanized Transport Corps) was formed in 1939 and is composed of drivers who work for innumerable government departments besides the army, and many of them brought their own cars into the service when they joined up. They have served in many war areas and some of them were captured in North Africa.

As regards uniforms an interesting point is that those of the women who took over men's work are simply adaptations of the dress of soldiers, while those who do nursing are allowed rather more femininity in their attire. There is not space to describe all the details of the badges, and small items, but the following are some of the main characteristics.

Q.A.I.M.N.S. Service dress and battle dress are worn on active service, with the shoulder title 'Q.A.I.M.N.S.' in white on dull cherry (the R.A.M.C. colours).

Ordinary outdoor uniform. Grey cap, jacket, skirt and greatcoat, collars edged with scarlet, badges worn on collars of both jacket and greatcoat and. on the cap. White is worn in tropical climates, both out of doors and in. Indoor uniform—grey with white apron and kerchief. Corridor cape— scarlet.

T.A.N.S. Blue-grey uniform, darker than Q.A.I.M.N.S.

V.A.D.'s—S.J.A.B. Outdoor uniform—black, double-breasted jacket, white or grey shirt with black tie, cap with white piping, or black felt hat with black ribbon edged white. St. John's badge in cap or hat.

B.R.C.S. Outdoor uniform—Blue. Single-breasted jacket, white or blue shirt with black tie. Cap or straw hat, with blue band edged with white and red.

V.A.D. indoor uniforms have several variations, S.J.A.B. members wearing black and white check or striped dresses, or grey, according to rank, with St. John's cross outlined in black on the apron. B.R.C.S. members wear dresses of a lightish blue with the red cross on kerchief and apron. Corridor capes of S.J.A.B. are dark grey and those of B.R.C.S. are dark blue, both with scarlet linings.

V.A.D. members wear the V.A.D. Council's badge on the left sleeve of the jacket or greatcoat, and on a brassard with indoor uniform.

Since 1941 nursing sisters are commissioned officers, and wear the ordinary badges of rank. V.A.D.'s also have the non-commissioned ranks of Section Leader—two chevrons, and Senior Section Leader—three chevrons.

A.T.S. The service dress uniform is simply a feminine version of ordinary service dress, but the jackets of all ranks are cut similarly to those of officers and are worn with a collar and tie and a cloth belt. Officers wear Sam Browne belts without braces, and they and the O.R.'s wear the normal badges of rank, and shoulder titles and flashes. Lanyards of brown and green are worn and the badge of the regiment or corps to which a member is attached is worn on the left front of the jacket. Battle-dress blouses are worn with skirts, and trousers are issued for special duties. The F.S. cap is of two shades of brown, the lighter known as 'beech' brown, with green piping, and is only worn on duty by the band.

F.A.N.Y. A.T.S. uniform with F.A.N.Y. shoulder titles. Chinstraps are worn over the top of the cap.

N.A.A.F.I. Khaki uniform. Leather buttons. Felt hat or beret. When overseas they wear A.T.S. uniform.

E.N.S.A. This is a branch of N.A.A.F.I. and contains men and women. The latter wear a uniform similar to that of the A.T.S., but with their own special cap, or a beret.

CHAPTER XIV · RE-CAPITULATION

THE NATURE OF WAR

War had its origin in the most primitive and automatic instincts of man, which coincided with those of a herd of pigs guzzling from a trough which is too short to accommodate them all at once—the primeval law of the 'survival of the fittest'. He, who will not fight to fill his belly, must fade away and die. Civilization and Christianity are the dead opposites of these instincts, but men are still born selfish and their 'original sin' is often stronger than the better ideas acquired during their evolution. Hence jungle law still breaks in on the gentler ideals of co-operation.

Being a more intelligent animal than the pig, man soon learned to hurt his enemy more when he got angry. He discovered how to use a club to hit him with, and stones to throw at him while still out of reach of his club. He also quickly realized the value of mobility and of the kinetic force, first of men and then of heavier animals, in a charge, and accordingly trained the horse to take part in his wars.

Unlike most animals, he had the desire to organize which led to tribal wars and invasions, increasing in size and destructiveness as populations multiplied and the knowledge of weapons advanced.

War being a vital aspect of survival, primitive men gave constant attention to improving their weapons and tactics and every new discovery, whatever had been its original purpose, was considered in this light. The early use of metals soon gave the idea of using metal sticks with sharp edges or pointed heads, which were countered by shields and armour. The bow was a tremendous brain-wave, probably intended at first for easier hunting. Then some early scientist in the Far East, doubtless after generations of meditation and experiment, produced an effect calculated to awe any enemy, by setting fire to a carefully planned combination of saltpetre, sulphur and charcoal. (The use of gunpowder spread to the backward continent of Europe in the twelfth century, and the English used cannon of sorts at Crécy, 1346.)

After much consideration it was found that this explosive mixture, besides its frightening display of fire and smoke and its thunderous roar, could be used to propel a heavy round stone out of a metal vessel, which could be pointed at an enemy. With luck it would shatter his body and, later, it was found that it could also seriously damage the walls he built to protect himself against attack.

After centuries of careful thought and research, mostly by people who did not do the fighting themselves, modern weapons are still the stick and stone, glorified out of recognition by human cleverness and ingenuity, urged on by man's primordial jealousy and fear of his neighbours, and his desire to interfere with other people's lives.

The discoveries of how to use wind and water power, then steam, electricity and finally petrol, were all quickly turned to account for war purposes, and ultimately made it possible to produce marvellously accurate weapons by the million. Then the stage was reached when, instead of throwing one stone at one man, it was possible to satisfy the barbarous instincts of humanity to such an extent that thousands of 'stones', each weighing several tons, could be carried by air at terrific speed and dropped accurately on the homes of the enemy, bursting with such force that one alone might kill hundreds of them. Gas was another ingenious thought, but was not such a success as to merit concentrated effort at the expense of other weapons.

A little beyond this came a really sensational improvement, comparable with the discovery of gunpowder—the atomic bomb, and about the same time 'guided missiles' and radio-active spray came into the picture, with bacteriological warfare still in the offing. What sane individual, knowing the potentialities of these weapons, could seriously say, 'I want another war?' Yet such is the subservience of masses of people to motives of greed or fear or hatred, that a nation can still do what scarcely any individual in it would even consider, if he were left to his own devices.

STRATEGY

Strategy is the collective use, taking a long view, and utilizing all available resources, of the tactics of a primitive man. Put very simply it consists of getting into position for a knock-out blow. This involves preparation and training, then manœuvring—footwork, to get the enemy off his balance, feinting to make him protect some less-important part of his body and, in doing so, uncover his heart. Finally, great strength must be held in reserve and concentrated quickly at the right moment to make the blow decisive.

Multiply this by the millions engaged in a war, take into account all the potentialities of modern weapons and their antidotes, the productivity of the factories, the morale of the nation, the food situation, the mobility and sea, land, and air strength in men and weapons of the forces engaged, and their efficiency and geographical situation. Then examine all these questions and a hundred others, in regard to the enemy and any potential enemies or allies, and some faint conception of the problems of a supreme commander may be visualized.

War has become increasingly complicated, exactly in the same way as civilian life has become more and more involved as the result of ever-increasing masses of people, mechanization and scientific invention—most of it in the last century and a half.

As regards our own army (and applying to those of all the civilized powers) the following are some of the important points in its development from 1660 onwards.

EIGHTEENTH CENTURY—FIRST HALF

The pike went out of use and cannon and muskets, previously used largely for their nuisance or moral value, were improved and better handled. Battles were still fought in masses as in the days of the Greeks and Romans, with much pomp and circumstance, brilliant uniforms, ponderous drill and rigid discipline. Cavalry was thought to be superior to infantry, but this was disproved in the case of British infantry at Dettingen, 1743 (and again, more conclusively, at Minden, 1769). Wars were fought in a leisurely and often a gentlemanly manner, armies were not expected to fight during the winter and mobility was often not of vital importance. Except in the comparatively small areas where the fighting took place, civilian life went on more or less undisturbed.

EIGHTEENTH CENTURY—SECOND HALF

In North America, against the Indians, supporting the French, and later against the colonists, who had learned from the Indians, the long-established tactics were found unsuitable. Slow-moving masses of men, who could only act on words of command, could not deal adequately with guerrillas, so the first reaction was the formation of light infantry. They were specialist troops, like the modern commandos, and the close-formed battalions were still the line of battle. The system of light troops was applied to the other arms in the form of light dragoons and, in 1793, horse artillery. At the end of the century rifle corps were formed, wearing camouflage uniforms, armed with more accurate weapons with a longer range, but slower to load than the smooth-bore musket. These worked on the light infantry system of individual training, rather on the lines of big-game hunting, but, like them, were trained also to fight in line or squares if required.

The Napoleonic wars began the era of 'total' war. The country was threatened with invasion. There was conscription and the army was brought up to a strength of over half a million. Fighting went on in many parts of the world, and disorganized the economy of nations, producing famine and great hardships for many years afterwards.

NINETEENTH CENTURY—UP TO THE CRIMEAN WAR

Waterloo demonstrated with still greater force the fact that cavalry could not defeat good steady infantry, who were ready to receive them. They must be used only at opportune moments, such as when the infantry were in vulnerable formation, or after their morale had been shaken by artillery fire or successful infantry attack, or both. After 1815 many regiments were made into light cavalry, as it was seen that the function of cavalry was developing more into one of reconnaissance, protection of a main body, and pursuit of a beaten enemy. The proportion of field-guns used at this period was roughly two guns per 1,000 men, and their range and destructiveness were increasing. Shrapnel was invented in 1802 and was a more serious menace to troops, at ranges up to about 1,200 yards, than roundshot or shells.

The principles of 'total' war were elaborated in documents left by Von Clausewitz, director of the Prussian War School, who died in 1830. His theory was that 'War is an act of violence pursued to the utmost', and that any restrictions on the use of weapons, resources or methods, of whatever sort, were merely foolish and did nothing more than give an unnecessary advantage to the enemy, or at the least, prolong the war.

The effectiveness of musketry increased with the replacement of flints by percussion caps, in 1839, and still more by the general issue of rifles, in 1854, with an accurate range of 300 yards. Rifled cannon came into use about 1855.

But there was no great difference in the tactics employed in the Crimea from those used in the Peninsular and earlier wars.

NINETEENTH CENTURY—AFTER THE CRIMEAN WAR

During the Crimean War the rule of wearing ceremonial dress for battle began to be relaxed and in the Mutiny this process was accelerated, some regiments wearing khaki.

The success of Moltke, a pupil of Clausewitz, and Bismarck in the Franco-Prussia War, 1870, led to acceptance of the principles of 'total' war by most of the military experts of Europe, and resulted in conscription becoming a permanent factor in nearly all important armies, that of Great Britain being a notable exception. (We relied on the Navy to give us time to prepare for a land war, after it had begun.) This meant that subsequent European wars began with the mobilization of armies containing millions of men, and that the destruction of lives and property was on a far greater scale than previously.

The next important change was the breech-loading Martini-Henry rifle, 1871, with a range of 1,000 yards, followed in 1883 by the Maxim—the first efficient machine-gun—in 1888 by magazine rifles, and in 1889 by the invention of cordite. By 1900 these weapons, plus corresponding improvements in artillery, had eliminated colour and ceremonial from the battlefield, as well as smoke, and produced conditions of semi-underground warfare at times. They also complicated the supply problem by using up enormous quantities of ammunition.

THE TWENTIETH CENTURY

The first few years of this century produced motor cars, aeroplanes and wireless, and the improved mechanization of factories and rapid advances in science generally, added to the build-up of teeming populations, made standardization and mass organization essential. These factors gave a sense of unlimited power to such autocrats as the Kaiser, Hitler, etc., which led to the construction of vast war machines to exploit it, and to heady dreams of world domination, resulting in the most gigantic wars in history.

Important features of these wars were, first, an enormous increase in artillery and automatic weapons—owing to the size of the armies, which prevented outflanking moves and made it necessary to blast a way through their entrenchments; secondly, the very rapid development of aerial bombing, which made it easy to wage war on civilians in the hope of breaking the wills of whole nations, and thirdly the rapid advance of mechanization and development of armoured fighting vehicles. Finally the atomic bomb, if used in large numbers, seems likely to reduce the whole thing to the absurd.

One paradox demonstrated by these wars was that though the main defences were unable to keep out invading forces—the Hindenburg Line, the Maginot Line, the Atlantic Wall, the East Wall, etc., yet broadly speaking aggression has not been a success. Germany, Italy and Japan, starting with all the advantages, ended up far worse off than they began.

Even world wars have not been able to solve the problem of over-population, which is their principal cause, either by the acquisition of territory or the slaughter of millions but, pending better international co-operation, the atom bomb seems likely to provide the answer.

These 'total' wars changed the character of the army very much. Up to the Boer War, expeditionary forces were found by the regular army—often augmented by the Militia and hastily trained recruits, but still composed of regular units. The Volunteers' duty had been home defence, but a change came when regiments of them, at their own request, formed a large proportion of the forces in South Africa. An equally significant event was the important contributions of the Dominions, now grown into self-reliant nations with their own forces.

In the two great wars conscription brought a great change. Professional soldiers had to bear the first shock and then be used to train and stiffen huge armies of civilians. Although they formed only a very small minority of the troops in the field in the later stages, their presence was absolutely essential. Without their experience and traditions, the task of training enormous forces, in the time available, and of organizing and controlling them when trained, would have been quite impossible. Even so, in these temporary armies things had to be done in a less professional manner, to save time, and also because they included men of all types from every imaginable mode of life, instead of, as in previous small wars, only men whose job was soldiering. One result of this was to make the army more broad-minded and more a part of the nation as a whole, rather than an exclusive caste. Another was the automatic abolition of the old system under which only men with private incomes were able to hold commissions. It seems likely, though, that under the new conditions of warfare these armies of millions may not be seen again.

Another great change which has developed very rapidly during this century is the growth of the impersonal cold-blooded side of war.

Men had always fought in organized bodies, which were drilled into human machines, but in the previous centuries they were able to see their enemies and the effects of their fire, and fighting nearly always ended in a bayonet charge. They thus experienced all the natural emotions, of anger, fear, horror, ferocity, determination, compassion for the wounded, and the rest. They fired in volleys, it is true, so that individual marksmanship was not so apparent, but in this century a great part of the fighting is done by 'machine-servers'—men who fire heavy shells at long range, or drop bombs from high altitudes, and may never set eyes on the enemy or on the results of their work. Unless they are fairly imaginative, they need feel no emotions about it. This tendency increased with the use of long-range rocket projectiles, fired by men who never even saw the enemy's country, and with atomic bombs it is possible for an aircraft crew to massacre the inhabitants of a whole city without seeing a drop of blood, and then take their evening meal in comfort, back in their home station.

Even more impersonal is the war-work of the millions who cannot join the forces at all, and a fact which is not fully realized is that in modern wars probably as many as twenty-nine out of every thirty men must either serve in non-combatant occupations in the forces, or as civilians producing equipment and supplies.

CHAPTER XV · THE ARMY'S FUTURE

The expansion of the Empire practically ended with the Boer War of 1899–1902, and since then the two world wars have produced a changed outlook regarding systems of government. This means that it has become a recognized principle—among most of the great powers—that every nation, as soon as it is sufficiently experienced, must be allowed to manage its own affairs. In most cases socialist enthusiasm brings this into action with dangerous haste, but the result, as far as it concerns the army, is that its duties will continue to be confined to those of military police and defensive wars. The first of these jobs is already much reduced, as garrisons will no longer be required in India, Burma, the greater part of Egypt, and Palestine. Armies of occupation, in Germany, Japan, etc., must go on for many years, but eventually they will end with a further large reduction of overseas garrisons.

The world, however, is more unsafe than ever, and we and the Dominions and the remaining Colonies must be able to defend ourselves if we are to survive and if modern barbarism is to be prevented from wrecking the progress so far made in the world's civilization. There are still nations whose outlook is back in the eighteenth century, to whom the latest weapons are very tempting and we often overlook the fact that the civilization of the British Empire is centuries ahead of that of most other nations. There is no doubt at all that if it gave up its position it would be definitely helping the subversive elements to gain control of the world, and thereby proving itself unworthy of its inheritance. For the good of the whole human race it ought to remain strong.

U.N.O.

U.N.O., like the old League of Nations, is a high ideal born of base parentage—the devastation of world wars and the fear of its recurrence. But the point has not been reached where international agreements are of any great value without armed forces ready to ensure that they are carried out, and until U.N.O. is provided with unchallengable forces, it cannot be much more than an ideal and its life must remain in jeopardy. The army's future is likely to be closely connected with U.N.O., and probably a large part of it will eventually form a section of a world police force. Whether it will be stationed in foreign countries it is not possible to forecast, but this seems unlikely, as the Empire has suitable bases in most parts of the world.

ATOMIC WARFARE

The newest weapons—atomic bombs, radio-active spray, and guided missiles, being the most revolutionary inventions in the whole history of warfare, must be expected to cause radical changes.

In the past, predictions about new weapons have always exceeded the results, but there is less doubt about these, now that their destructiveness has been proved. Their possibilities are almost beyond the wildest imagination of fiction writers. For instance, without a declaration of war (e.g. Pearl Harbour), out of the blue and all in an hour or so, our great cities and ports, railways and roads could be reduced to a state of chaos by atomic missiles, and large areas could be made uninhabitable owing to radio-activity. Crops could be destroyed by spray and casualties would be on an unheard-of scale and impossible to cope with.

There could be no answer unless we were prepared to give instant retaliation, which could only be done by having similar weapons ready to put into action at a moment's notice and produce similar destruction in the enemy's country. (This precaution would almost certainly prevent another war.)

Antidotes to these weapons may develop, possibly from some adaptation of radar. It is also possible that, like gas and bacteria in the 1939–45 war, they might be kept in reserve and never come into action at all, as both sides might fear the devastation they would cause. Their most likely use is either in the opening phase, for surprise effect, or when one side is losing and is so desperate that it will risk any amount of destruction to prevent defeat. In any case their use cannot be ruled out in any large war of the future.

As one atom bomb could destroy practically the whole of a centre like Aldershot (London would, as usual, be the 'Bull'), the forces will have to be scattered in small self-contained stations, with adequate supplies of everything they will need for at least several months of active service. These groups of units will probably be mechanized and armoured, able to be completely mobilized at extremely short notice, and capable of being as self-reliant as the desert patrols in North Africa were in the last war. Each would have to work on its own, against an invasion, using dispersal and invisibility as its defence, and being kept in touch with the general plan by wireless orders. Airborne divisions and air transport would be of vital importance.

There would have to be secret 'Mulberry' docks ready to be erected very quickly, and replaced if necessary, and if the normal ports were destroyed ships would be diverted to them, for bringing in food and materials, or embarking troops.

After the first shock would begin the process, terribly hampered by the destruction, of invading the enemy's country, to seize and destroy, or use, his air bases, rocket bases, war factories, etc. Meanwhile, air and guided missile attacks would be made on all such known targets. His armies would be more difficult to locate, if they had suitable dispersion and mobility, and the civilians in the towns would probably get the brunt of it. The chaos on both sides would be colossal, but as in the past, it seems that the only method of putting an end to it would be to occupy the enemy country with land forces, which would be assisted and linked-up by the R.A.F.

As a result of the inevitable dislocation of all essential services, not to mention the impossibility of dealing with the huge numbers of dead and wounded civilians—starvation, tremendous epidemics of disease, and general misery of the most sordid kind, would spread over all the countries involved, and the desolation left over at the end of the war would make the present not too happy state of the world seem enviable in the highest degree.

In such a war the British Empire would have the advantage of bases scattered over the world, which would probably not be attacked all at once, but this also implies the disadvantage of being unable to concentrate its forces quickly, while Britain, its heart, being so small and overcrowded, would form an exceptionally vulnerable target.

A likely development in a future war is the strategic bombing, by both sides, of the world's main oilfields and refineries.

It is quite possible to imagine that atomic bombs or missiles could put them out of action for a long period, and should this object be achieved, the consequences, after using up existing stocks of oil, would be extraordinary.

Machines of almost every type would either cease to function as soon as oil supplies gave out, or would rapidly deteriorate. Factory production would stop and transport would eventually have to rely on the small numbers of horses which have survived the process of mechanization.

Even bicycles would soon become inefficient and guns, rifles, etc., would not last long without lubrication and no spare parts could be made for them.

If the imagination is allowed to run on it is possible to visualize ultimately a return to the use of bows, arrows, and pikes! Oil substitutes would, of course, be produced, but it would probably be a long time before they could be sufficient to keep factory machines and railways working, leaving out any question of motor or air transport on any appreciable scale.

The most reliable remedy is for potential enemies to know that they will get worse than they can give, very quickly—from U.N.O., or from their intended victim. (The prospects from U.N.O. are not good, if it has to deliberate for several months before taking a decision which is then subject to the veto!) Until such arrangements have been made life must go on with an uneasy subconscious realization of these sinister possibilities.

REORGANIZATION

The present system of a period of compulsory service, followed by a period in the Territorial Army, is another radical change in the composition of the army. Recruits for regular engagements are not easily obtained in sufficient numbers, as although the British are the most disciplined and queue-minded civilians in the world, they never seem anxious to place themselves under military discipline in peace-time. Also the army has lost much of its glamour, and there are civilian jobs, with (at nominal value) very high wages. Another important reason is that a man feels that, after five or seven years' army service, he has little left from it except that amount of handicap in his civil occupation.

The result is that a regiment must consist mainly of temporary men, who can hardly learn to be soldiers before they are due for release—a problem which becomes more difficult owing to the ever-increasing number of technicians needed to man the complicated equipment and weapons now in use. This system makes the regular army into a training school for the T.A., and under these conditions it cannot be possible for its units to reach a standard even approaching that of a pre-war regiment.

The T.A., on the other hand, is expected to consist mostly of trained men and to be ready for service on mobilization, without having to spend several months, as they previously did, in completing the instruction of officers and men. The regulars' loss is supposed to be the T.A.'s gain, but considering the small amount of time the latter are able to spend in keeping themselves up to standard, the impression is that there will be no units of either force able to reach the state of smooth-running, self-reliant efficiency, which used to be the pride of a battalion when all the men had served together, in various parts of the world, for a number of years. In previous wars the regulars have trained the T.A. after hostilities began, and this is a reversal of the procedure, by doing it in peace-time, theoretically a wise and necessary change, but for the reasons given it seems a doubtful (as well as extremely expensive) method. But, probably, the ancient national prejudice against conscription will alter this before many years.

A possible solution seems to lie in making the army a life job —not five years' service, but perhaps twenty-five or thirty—the first part in fighting units, up to the age of, say, thirty-five, and afterwards in the numerous essential but only semi-combatant units, or as instructors with the T.A. After this a reasonable pension or government employment should follow, and there must be a great many men who would prefer service on these terms to civilian occupations.

Assuming that, under these conditions, the regular army could provide the necessary overseas garrisons and the backbone of a field army, the T.A. could then be made into a readily available reinforcement, by a much cheaper and less inconvenient method than the present conscription system.

Six to nine months in the regimental training centres, with a staff of regular N.C.O.s which could be greatly augmented under the above scheme, followed by say one month annually, ought to get the men up to a reasonable standard. Interference with industry would be reduced, the wasteful system of shipping short service men to far distant stations would be avoided and, with only regulars serving in them, those garrisons would be more efficient and there would be a corresponding gain in prestige abroad.

Each Territorial would be as carefully fitted into the right job as the regulars are and, up to the required numbers, each 'tradesman's' duties should be similar to his normal trade as a civilian.

Officers would need to do an additional course, on Sandhurst lines, and N.C.O's would also need longer training and refresher courses, but, given the will to make a success of it, these problems would be settled satisfactorily.

It would, of course, take time to build up both the regulars and the T.A. in this manner, and a transition scheme would have to be thought out.

REGIMENTAL TRADITIONS

Modern conditions of active service have resulted in so many transfers of men from one regiment to another, as well as conversions of whole units to different branches of the service, e.g. gunners to infantry, that the argument in favour of keeping unbroken the traditions and identities of the old regiments might appear to have received a setback. But the only method of judging correctly is by the results. There is now a trend towards the gradual amalgamation of groups of regiments, which is sure to be strongly resisted. It happened with pairs of regiments in 1881 and, in the Indian Army, between the two wars, groups of regiments with common associations were made into battalions of one regiment. In both cases it seems to have worked out satisfactorily. Something of this sort is becoming inevitable as, owing to the increasing proportion of technical and supply services now required, there is likely to be a considerable reduction in the number of permanent infantry battalions. The idea of 'killing' each one ('suspended animation') for a period, after every ten or fifteen years, and then reviving it later was not a good one and now seems to have been scrapped, but only to be followed by the more serious prospect that all the second battalions may disappear or be converted into units of a different type.

It is even possible that ultimately an entirely new type of composite unit might develop, which would be formed from all three services—a miniature expeditionary force in itself. It might contain mechanized cavalry and infantry, heavy tanks, self-propelled guns, and details of *R.E.*, *R.E.M.E.*, *R.C.S.*, *R.A.S.C.*, *R.A.M.C.*, etc., accompanied by aircraft, transports, landing craft and escort vessels. All these specialists would, of course, begin their service life in their own branches but, to increase efficiency in working together as a unit, speed-up mobilization, and facilitate independent action under the dispersed conditions of atomic warfare, the forces might at some future date be organized in permanently established units of this sort—probably with variations, according to whether their duties would consist of overseas offensive action or home defence, etc. This idea may be wide of the mark, but it seems that it would obviate the need for the distribution and movement of troops and supplies, to make up the necessary formations, after the chaotic conditions of atomic bombing had set in.

But there is no doubt that as much as possible of the old regimental spirit will be retained. What is so valuable is the element of rivalry and of pride in the long history and achievements of a regiment which permeates every thought of the trained soldier, giving him an ideal to live up to and a record which he must keep unblemished. 'We are not just a regiment or a battalion. We are THE ——, who were at Minden, who routed the French Guards at Waterloo, who led the attack at Alamein.' 'We are the only regiment allowed to wear roses on St. George's Day.' 'The —— do NOT have untidy men put on charges by the R.C.M.P.' 'On service the ——'s picquets are ALWAYS alert.' 'Men of the —— do NOT fall out on the march.' 'Who ever heard of the —— leaving their billets dirty?' Who can say that this is not the spirit which made history, or that it should be scrapped without very serious consideration indeed? Yet perhaps it can be broadened a little and still flourish.

> *But 'tis the talent of our English nation,*
> *Still to be plotting some new reformation.*
> (JOHN DRYDEN, 1631–1701)

APPENDIX I

1748: LIST OF REGIMENTS, AND COLOURS OF FACINGS

HOUSEHOLD TROOPS

The Life Guards (4 Troops)		Blue
The Horse Grenadiers (2 Troops)		Blue
Royal Horse Guards	Blue Coats	Scarlet
1st Foot Guards		Blue
2nd or Coldstream Regiment of Foot Guards		Blue
3rd Foot Guards		Blue

CAVALRY

1st, or King's Regiment of Dragoon Guards	Blue
2nd, or Queen's Regiment of Dragoon Guards	Buff
3rd Regiment of Dragoon Guards	White
1st Horse	Pale blue
2nd Horse	Full green
3rd Horse, or The Carabiniers	Pale yellow
4th Horse	Black
1st, or Royal Dragoons	Blue
2nd, or Royal North British Dragoons	Blue
3rd, or King's Own Regiment of Dragoons	Light blue
4th Regiment of Dragoons	Green
5th, or Royal Irish Dragoons	Blue
6th, or The Inniskilling Dragoons	Full yellow
7th, or The Queen's Regiment of Dragoons	White
8th Regiment of Dragoons	Yellow
9th Regiment of Dragoons	Buff
10th Regiment of Dragoons	Deep yellow
11th Regiment of Dragoons	Buff
12th Regiment of Dragoons	White
13th Regiment of Dragoons	Light green
14th Regiment of Dragoons	Lemon yellow

INFANTRY

1st, or Royal Regiment	Blue
2nd Tangier, or Queen's Regiment	Sea green
3rd Regiment	Buff

4th King's Regiment	Blue
5th Regiment	Pale green
6th Regiment	Deep yellow
7th Royal English Fuzileers	Blue
8th King's Regiment	Yellow
9th Regiment	Yellow
10th Regiment	Yellow
11th Regiment	Green
12th Regiment	Yellow
13th Regiment	Deep yellow
14th Regiment	Buff
15th Regiment	Deep yellow
16th Regiment	Yellow
17th Regiment	Light Grey
18th Regiment	Blue
19th Regiment	Pale green
20th Regiment	Pale yellow
21st Royal Scotch Fuzileers	Blue
22nd Regiment	Reddish buff
23rd Royal Welsh Fuzileers	Blue
24th Regiment	Green
25th Regiment	Deep yellow
26th Cameronians	Yellow
27th Regiment	Buff
28th Regiment	Yellow
29th Regiment	Yellow
30th Regiment	Bright yellow
31st Regiment	Buff
32nd Regiment	White
33rd Regiment	Red
34th Regiment	Yellow
35th Regiment	Orange
36th Regiment	Green
37th Regiment	Yellow
38th Regiment	Yellow
39th Regiment	Pale green
40th Regiment	Buff
41st Regiment	Blue
42nd Oglethorpe's Regiment	Green
43rd Highlanders	Buff
44th (1st Marines)	Yellow
45th (2nd Marines)	Green
46th (3rd Marines)	Yellow
47th (4th Marines)	White
48th (5th Marines)	Pale yellow
49th (6th Marines)	Green
50th (7th Marines)	White
51st (8th Marines)	Yellow
52nd (9th Marines)	Buff
53rd (10th Marines)	Yellow
54th Regiment	White
55th Regiment	Deep yellow
56th Regiment	Deep green

57th Regiment	Yellow
58th Regiment	White
59th Regiment	Buff
60th Regiment	Black
61st (Spotswood's) American Regiment	Green
61st Richbell's Regiment	White
62nd Batereau's Regiment	Yellow
63rd Trelawney's Regiment	Green
64th Loudon's Regiment (Highlanders)	White
65th Shirley's Regiment	Green
66th Peperell's Regiment	Green

Before the Royal Warrant of 1751, 'Royal' regiments did not necessarily have blue facings, and Standards and Colours often did not correspond with the facings.

It is interesting to compare the above list with the later ones, 1815 and 1914, and to notice how the number of 'Royal' regiments and of other titles has multiplied through the years, and how many of the titles and facings of 1750 can be easily recognized in the Army Lists of recent years.

There was, however, a certain amount of renumbering, disbanding, and raising of new regiments later in the eighteenth century, which is liable to cause confusion among some of the regimental numbers, unless one is aware of it. (See notes, Plate V [12].)

APPENDIX II

1815: LIST OF REGIMENTS, AND COLOURS OF FACINGS AND LACE

CAVALRY

	Coat	Facings	Lace
1st Life Guards	Red	Blue	Gold
2nd Life Guards	Red	Blue	Gold
Royal Regiment of Horse Guards	Blue	Scarlet	Gold
1st (or The King's) Regiment of Dragoon Guards	Red	Blue	Gold
2nd (or The Queen's) Regiment of Dragoon Guards	Red	Black	Silver
3rd (or Prince of Wales's) Regiment of Dragoon Guards	Red	White	Gold
4th (or Royal Irish) Regiment of Dragoon Guards	Red	Blue	Silver
5th (or Princess Charlotte of Wales's) Regiment of Dragoon Guards	Red	Green	Gold
6th Regiment of Dragoon Guards	Red	White	Silver
7th (or Princess Royal's) Regiment of Dragoon Guards	Red	Black	Gold
1st (or Royal) Regiment of Dragoons	Red	Blue	Gold
2nd (or Royal North British) Regiment of Dragoons	Red	Blue	Gold
3rd (or King's Own) Regiment of Dragoons	Red	Blue	Gold
4th (or Queen's Own) Regiment of Dragoons	Red	Green	Silver
6th (or Inniskilling) Regiment of Dragoons	Red	Yellow	Silver
7th (or Queen's Own) Regiment of (Light) Dragoons (Hussars)	Blue	White	Silver
8th (or King's Royal Irish) Regiment of (Light) Dragoons (Hussars)	Blue	Scarlet	Gold
9th Regiment of (Light) Dragoons	Blue	Crimson	Gold
10th (or Prince of Wales's Own Royal Regiment of (Light) Dragoons (Hussars)	Blue	Scarlet	Silver
11th Regiment of (Light) Dragoons	Blue	Buff	Silver
12th (or Prince of Wales's) Regiment of (Light) Dragoons	Blue	Yellow	Silver
13th Regiment of (Light) Dragoons	Blue	Buff	Gold
14th (or Duchess of York's Own) Regiment of (Light) Dragoons	Blue	Orange	Silver
15th (or The King's) Regiment of (Light) Dragoons (Hussars)	Blue	Scarlet	Silver
16th (or The Queen's) Regiment of (Light) Dragoons	Blue	Scarlet	Silver
17th Regiment of (Light) Dragoons	Blue	White	Silver
18th Regiment of (Light) Dragoons (Hussars)	Blue	White	Silver

	Coat	Facings	Lace
19th Regiment of (Light) Dragoons	Blue	Yellow	Gold
20th Regiment of (Light) Dragoons	Blue	Orange	Gold
21st Regiment of (Light) Dragoons	Blue	Black	Silver
22nd Regiment of (Light) Dragoons	Blue	White	Gold
23rd Regiment of (Light) Dragoons	Blue	Crimson	Silver
24th Regiment of (Light Dragoons	Blue	Light grey	Gold
25th Regiment of (Light) Dragoons	Blue	Light grey	Silver

FOOT GUARDS

	Facings	Lace
1st Regiment of Foot Guards	Blue	Gold
2nd or Coldstream Regiment of Foot Guards	Blue	Gold
3rd Regiment of Foot Guards	Blue	Gold

INFANTRY OF THE LINE

	Facings	Lace
1st, or The Royal Scots	Blue	Gold
2nd, or The Queen's Royal Regiment	Blue	Silver
3rd, or East Kent or The Buffs	Buff	Silver
4th, or The King's Own	Blue	Gold
5th, or The Northumberland Regiment of Foot	Gosling green	Silver
6th, or The 1st Warwickshire Regiment	Yellow	Silver
7th, or The Royal Fuzileers	Blue	Gold
8th, or The King's Regiment	Blue	Gold
9th, or The East Norfolk Regiment	Yellow	Silver
10th, or The North Lincolnshire Regiment	Yellow	Silver
11th, or The North Devonshire Regiment	Deep green	Gold
12th, or The East Suffolk Regiment	Yellow	Gold
13th, or The 1st Somersetshire Regiment	Yellow	Silver
14th, or The Buckinghamshire Regiment	Buff	Silver
15th, or The Yorkshire (East Riding) Regiment	Yellow	Silver
16th, or The Bedfordshire Regiment	Yellow	Silver
17th, or The Leicestershire Regiment	White	Silver
18th, or The Royal Irish Regiment	Blue	Gold
19th, or The 1st Yorkshire (North Riding) Regiment	Green	Gold
20th, or The East Devonshire Regiment	Yellow	Silver
21st, or The Royal North British Fuzileers	Blue	Gold
22nd, or The Cheshire Regiment	Buff	Gold
23rd, or The Royal Welch Fuzileers	Blue	Gold
24th, or The Warwickshire Regiment	Green	Silver
25th, or The King's Own Borderers Regiment	Blue	Gold
26th, or The Cameronian Regiment	Yellow	Silver
27th, or The Inniskilling Regiment	Buff	Gold
28th, or The North Gloucestershire Regiment	Yellow	Silver
29th, or The Worcestershire Regiment	Yellow	Silver
30th, or The Cambridgeshire Regiment	Pale yellow	Silver
31st, or The Huntingdonshire Regiment	Buff	Silver
32nd, or The Cornwall Regiment	White	Gold
33rd, or The 1st Yorkshire (West Riding) Regiment	Red	Silver
34th, or The Cumberland Regiment	Yellow	Silver
35th, or The Sussex Regiment	Orange	Silver

	Facings	Lace
36th, or The Herefordshire Regiment	Gosling green	Gold
37th, or The North Hampshire Regiment	Yellow	Silver
38th, or The 1st Staffordshire Regiment	Yellow	Silver
39th, or The Dorsetshire Regiment	Pea green	Gold
40th, or The 2nd Somersetshire Regiment	Buff	Gold
41st Regiment	Red	Silver
42nd, or The Royal Highland Regiment	Blue	Gold
43rd, or The Monmouthshire Regiment (Light Infantry)	White	Silver
44th, or The East Essex Regiment	Yellow	Silver
45th, or The Nottinghamshire Regiment	Dark green	Silver
46th, or The South Devonshire Regiment	Pale yellow	Silver
47th, or The Lancashire Regiment	White	Silver
48th, or The Northamptonshire Regiment	Buff	Gold
49th, or The Hertfordshire Regiment	Green	Gold
50th, or The West Kent Regiment	Black	Silver
51st, or The 2nd Yorkshire (West Riding) Regiment (Light Infantry)	Grass green	Gold
52nd, or The Oxfordshire Regiment (Light Infantry)	Buff	Silver
53rd, or The Shropshire Regiment	Red	Gold
54th, or The West Norfolk Regiment	Green	Silver
55th, or The Westmoreland Regiment	Green	Gold
56th, or The West Essex Regiment	Purple	Silver
57th, or The West Middlesex Regiment	Yellow	Gold
58th, or The Rutlandshire Regiment	Black	Gold
59th, or The 2nd Nottinghamshire Regiment	White	Gold
60th, or The Royal American Regiment	—	—
61st, or The South Gloucestershire Regiment	Buff	Silver
62nd, or The Wiltshire Regiment	Buff	Silver
63rd, or The West Suffolk Regiment	Deep green	Silver
64th, or The 2nd Staffordshire Regiment	Black	Gold
65th, or The 2nd Yorkshire (North Riding) Regiment	White	Gold
66th, or The Berkshire Regiment	Gosling green	Silver
67th, or The South Hampshire Regiment	Yellow	Silver
68th, or The Durham Regiment (Light Infantry)	Bottle green	Silver
69th, or The South Lincolnshire Regiment	Green	Gold
70th, or The Glasgow Lowland Regiment	Black	Gold
71st Highland Regiment (Light Infantry)	Buff	Silver
72nd Highland Regiment	Yellow	Silver
73rd Highland Regiment	Dark green	Gold
74th Highland Regiment	White	Gold
75th Highland Regiment	Yellow	Silver
76th Regiment	Red	Silver
77th, or The East Middlesex Regiment	Yellow	Silver
78th Highland Regiment (or The Ross-shire Buffs)	Buff	Gold
79th Regiment of Cameron Highlanders	Dark green	Gold
80th Regiment, or Staffordshire Volunteers	Yellow	Gold
81st Regiment	Buff	Silver
82nd Regiment, or Prince of Wales's Volunteers	Yellow	Silver
83rd Regiment	Yellow	Gold
84th York and Lancaster Regiment	Yellow	Silver
85th Regiment, or Bucks Volunteers (Light Infantry)	Yellow	Silver
86th, or The Royal County Down Regiment	Blue	Silver

	Facings	Lace
87th, or The Prince of Wales's Own Irish Regiment	Green	Gold
88th Regiment, or The Connaught Rangers	Yellow	Silver
89th Regiment	Black	Gold
90th Regiment, or The Perthshire Volunteers	Buff	Gold
91st Regiment	Yellow	Silver
92nd Regiment	Yellow	Silver
93rd Regiment	Yellow	Silver
94th Regiment	Green	Gold
95th Regiment (Uniform—green)	Black	—
96th Regiment	Buff	Silver
97th, or The Queen's Own Regiment	Blue	Silver
98th Regiment	Buff	Silver
99th, or The Prince of Wales's Tipperary Regiment	Pale yellow	—
100th, or His Royal Highness the Prince Regent's County of Dublin Regiment	Deep yellow	—
101st, or The Duke of York's Irish Regiment	White	—
102nd Regiment	Yellow	Silver
103rd Regiment	White	—
104th Regiment	Buff	—

The Army List of 1815 included also the Royal Regiment of Artillery, the Corps of Royal Engineers, and the Royal Waggon Train (which wore blue, with red facings and silver lace) a number of Colonial regiments, Garrison, Veteran, and Invalid units, Fencibles (Volunteers) and the King's German Legion, consisting of several regiments.

The facings, etc., of the 60th (now The King's Royal Rifle Corps) are not given above, as at that time there were some battalions dressed in red (Light Infantry), and others in green (Rifles).

The list had been greatly enlarged since the one of 1748, and it will be seen that few regiments now were without a special title in addition to their number. County titles were taken into use towards the end of the eighteenth century.

APPENDIX III

1914: REGIMENTAL TITLES AND UNIFORMS

Sc. =scarlet. Bl. =blue. Wh. =white. Gr. =green. Ye. =yellow. Blk. =black. Bu. =buff. Cr. =crimson.

Regimental Title	Tunic Facings	Head-dress	Forage Cap
HOUSEHOLD CAVALRY			
1st Life Guards	Sc. Bl.	Wh. metal helmet. Wh. plume	Bl., Sc. band
2nd Life Guards	Sc. Bl.	Wh. metal helmet Wh. plume	Bl., Sc. band
Royal Horse Guards	Bl. Sc.	Wh. metal helmet Sc. plume	Bl., Sc. band

Cuirass, Wh. leather breeches. Jacked boots. Stable jackets worn. Forage cap worn with Service Dress. Horses Blk., except trumpeters—greys. Trumpeters—Sc. plumes. Flask cord—1 L.G. and R.H.G.—Cr., 2 L.G.—Bl. Lambskins—1 L.G. and R.H.G. —Blk., 2 L.G.—Wh. Cloaks—1 and 2 L.G. —Sc., R.H.G.—Bl. Overalls. 1 and 2 L.G. —two Sc. stripes. R.H.G. one broad Sc. stripe.

Regimental Title	Tunic Facings	Head-dress	Forage Cap
CAVALRY OF THE LINE			
1st (King's) Dragoon Guards	Sc. Bl.	Brass helmet Sc. plume Band Wh. plumes	Bl., Bl. band
2nd Dragoon Guards (Queen's Bays)	Sc. Bu.	Brass helmet Blk. plume Band—Wh. plumes	Bl., Bu. band
3rd (Prince of Wales's) Dragoon Guards	Sc. Ye.	Brass helmet Blk. and Red plume Band—Red and Wh. plumes	Bl., Ye. band

Regimental Title	Tunic Facings	Head-dress	Forage Cap
4th (Royal Irish) Dragoon Guards	Sc. Bl.	Brass helmet Wh. plume Band—Blk. plumes	Bl., Bl. band
5th (Princess Charlotte of Wales's) Dragoon Guards	Sc. Dark Gr.	Brass helmet Red and Wh. plume Band—red plumes	Bl., Gr. band
6th Dragoon Guards (The Carabiniers)	Bl. Wh.	Brass helmet Wh. plume Band-red plumes	Bl., Wh. band
7th (Princess Royal's) Dragoon Guards	Sc. Blk.	Brass helmet Blk. and Wh. plume Band—Wh. plumes	Bl., Blk. band
1st (Royal) Dragoons	Sc. Bl.	White metal helmet Blk. plume Band—Wh. plumes	Bl., Sc. band
2nd Dragoons (Royal Scots Greys)	Sc. Bl.	Bearskin cap White hackle Band—Sc. hackle	Bl., Wh. zigzag band
3rd (King's Own) Hussars	Bl. Sc. collar	Busby. Wh. plume Garter Bl. bag	Red
4th (Queen's Own) Hussars	Bl. None	Busby. Sc. plume Ye. bag	Red
5th (Royal Irish) Lancers	Bl. Sc.	Lancer cap—upper part Sc. Gr. plume	Bl., Sc. band
6th (Inniskilling) Dragoons	Sc. Primrose	Wh. metal helmet Wh. plume Band—Sc. plumes	Bl., primrose band
7th (Queen's Own) Hussars	Bl. None	Busby. Wh. plume Sc. bag	Red
8th (King's Royal Irish) Hussars	Bl. None	Busby. Red and Wh. plume. Sc. bag	Red
9th (Queen's Royal) Lancers	Bl. Sc.	Lancer cap—upper part blue. Blk. and Wh. plume	Bl., Sc. band
10th (Prince of Wales's Own Royal) Hussars	Bl. None	Busby. Blk. and Wh. plume. Sc. bag	Red
Officers wear Sc. pantaloons, in levee dress. Officers' full dress horse furniture ornamented with cowrie shells.			
11th (Prince Albert's Own) Hussars	Bl. None	Busby. Cr. and Wh. plume. Cr. bag Band—grey fur busbies	Cr.
Cr. pantaloons and overalls			
12th (Prince of Wales's Royal) Lancers	Bl. Sc.	Lancer cap. Upper part and plume Sc.	Sc.
13th Hussars	Bl. Bu. collar	Busby. Wh. plume Bu. bag	Bu., Bl. band

Regimental Title	Tunic Facings	Head-dress	Forage Cap
14th (King's) Hussars	Bl. None	Busby. Wh. plume Ye. bag	Red
15th (The King's) Hussars	Bl. None	Busby. Sc. plume and bag	Sc.
16th (The Queen's) Lancers	Sc. Bl.	Lancer cap. Upper part Bl. Plume Blk.	Sc., Bl. band
17th (Duke of Cambridge's Own) Lancers	Bl. Wh.	Lancer cap. Upper part and plume Wh.	Bl., Wh. band
18th (Queen Mary's Own) Hussars	Bl. None	Busby. Sc. and Wh. plume. Bl. bag	Red
19th (Queen Alexandra's Own Royal) Hussars	Bl. None	Busby. Wh. plume and bag	Red
20th Hussars	Bl. None	Busby. Ye. plume. Cr. bag	Red
21st (Empress of India's) Lancers	Bl. French grey	Lancer cap. Upper part French Grey Wh. plume	Bl., French grey band

THE ROYAL REGIMENT OF ARTILLERY

Royal Horse Artillery	Bl. shell jacket Sc. collar	Busby. Wh. plume Sc. bag	Bl. Sc. band

Broad Sc. stripe on pantaloons and overalls.

Royal Field Artillery	Bl. Sc. collar	Helmet, with ball	Bl. Sc. band

Broad Sc. stripe on pantaloons and overalls. Girdle—Red with Ye. centre and two Bl. stripes.

Royal Garrison Artillery	Bl. Sc. collar	Helmet, with ball	Bl. Sc. band

Broad Sc. stripe on trousers. Equipment as for infantry.

THE CORPS OF ROYAL ENGINEERS

	Sc. Bl. velvet	Helmet, with spike	Bl. Red piping

Ye. cord on shoulders, collar and cuffs. Bl. piping on edge of tunic and skirts. Broad Sc. stripe on pantaloons and trousers. Band—bearskin caps.

FOOT GUARDS

Regimental Title	Tunic Facings	Head-dress	Forage Cap
Grenadier Guards	Sc. Bl. Buttons evenly spaced	Bearskin cap Wh. plume, on left	Bl., Sc. band
Coldstream Guards	Sc. Bl. Buttons in pairs	Bearskin cap Red plume, on right	Bl. Wh. band
Scots Guards	Sc. Bl. Buttons in threes	Bearskin cap No plume	Bl. Diced band
Irish Guards	Sc. Bl. Buttons in fours	Bearskin cap Bl. plume on right	Bl. Gr. band

INFANTRY OF THE LINE

Regimental Title Old numbers in brackets	Tunic Facings	Head-dress	Forage Cap
Royal Scots (Lothian Regiment) (1)	Sc. Doublet Bl.	Kilmarnock Bonnet	Glengarry Sc., Gr., and Wh. diced border
	Trews of Hunting Stewart tartan. Pipers' kilts of Royal Stewart tartan		
The Queen's (Royal West Surrey) Regiment (2)	Sc. Bl.	Helmet	Bl. Sc. band
The Buffs (East Kent Regiment) (3)	Sc. Bu.	Helmet	Bl.
The King's Own (Royal Lancaster Regiment) (4)	Sc. Bl.	Helmet	Bl. Sc. band
The Northumberland Fusiliers (5)	Sc. Gosling Gr.	Racoon-skin cap Plume Sc. over Wh. on left	Bl.
The Royal Warwickshire Regiment (6)	Sc. Bl.	Helmet	Bl. Sc. band
The Royal Fusiliers (City of London Regiment) (7)	Sc. Bl.	Racoon-skin cap Wh. plume on right	Bl. Sc. band
The King's (Liverpool Regiment) (8)	Sc. Bl.	Helmet	Bl. Sc. band
Norfolk Regiment (9)	Sc. Ye.	Helmet	Bl.

Regimental Title Old numbers in brackets	Tunic Facings	Head-dress	Forage Cap
The Lincolnshire Regiment (10)	Sc. Wh.	Helmet	Bl.
The Devonshire Regiment (11)	Sc. Lin- coln Gr.	Helmet	Bl.
The Suffolk Regiment (12)	Sc. Ye.	Helmet	Bl.
Prince Albert's (Somerset Light Infantry) (13)	Sc. Bl.	Helmet	Gr.
		Only non-'Royal' regiment with Bl. facings. Sergeants wear their sashes on left shoulders.	
The Prince of Wales's West Yorkshire Regiment (14)	Sc. Bu.	Helmet	Bl.
The East Yorkshire Regiment (15)	Sc. Wh.	Helmet	Bl.
The Bedfordshire Regiment (16)	Sc. Wh.	Helmet	Bl.
The Leicestershire Regiment (17)	Sc. Wh.	Helmet	Bl.
The Royal Irish Regiment (18)	Sc. Bl.	Helmet	Bl. Sc. band
Alexandra, Princess of Wales's Own (Yorkshire Regiment) (19)	Sc. Grass Gr.	Helmet	Bl.
The Lancashire Fusiliers (20)	Sc. Wh.	Racoon-skin cap Primrose plume on left	Bl.
The Royal Scots Fusiliers (21)	Sc. Bl.	Sealskin cap. Wh. plume on right	Glengarry Sc., Gr., and Wh. diced bor- der
		Trews of Sutherland tartan.	
The Cheshire Regiment (22)	Sc. Bu.	Helmet	Bl.
The Royal Welch Fusiliers (23)	Sc. Bl.	Racoon-skin cap Wh. plume on left	Bl. Sc. band
		Flash worn by officers.	
The South Wales Borderers (24)	Sc. Grass Gr.	Helmet	Bl.
The King's Own Scottish Bor- derers (25)	Sc. Bl. Doublet	Kilmarnock bonnet	Glengarry Sc., Gr., and Wh. diced bor- der
		Trews of Leslie tartan. Piper's kilts, Royal Stewart tartan.	
The Cameronians (Scottish Rifles (26) (90)	Gr. Gr. Doublet	Shako. Blk. plume	Gr. Glen- garry
		Trews of Douglas tartan.	
The Royal Inniskilling Fusiliers (27) (108)	Sc. Bl.	Racoon-skin cap Grey plume on left	Bl. Sc. band
The Gloucestershire Regiment (28) (61)	Sc. Wh.	Helmet	Bl.
		Small badge worn at back of head-dress	

Regimental Title Old numbers in brackets	Tunic Facings	Head-dress	Forage Cap
The Worcestershire Regiment (29) (36)	Sc. Wh.	Helmet	Bl.
The East Lancashire Regiment (30) (59)	Sc. Wh.	Helmet	Bl.
The East Surrey Regiment (31) (70)	Sc. Wh.	Helmet	Bl.
The Duke of Cornwall's Light Infantry (32) (46)	Sc. Wh.	Helmet	Gr.
The Duke of Wellington's (West Riding Regiment) (33) (76)	Sc. Sc.	Helmet	Bl.
The Border Regiment (34) (55)	Sc. Ye.	Helmet	Bl.
The Royal Sussex Regiment (35) (107)	Sc. Bl.	Helmet	Bl. Sc. band
The Hampshire Regiment (37) (67)	Sc. Ye.	Helmet	Bl.
The South Staffordshire Regi- ment (38) (80)	Sc. Wh.	Helmet	Bl.
The Dorsetshire Regiment (39) (54)	Sc. Grass Gr.	Helmet	Bl.
The Prince of Wales's Volun- teers (South Lancashire Regi- ment) (40) (82)	Sc. Wh.	Helmet	Bl.
The Welsh Regiment (41) (69)	Sc. Wh.	Helmet	Bl.
The Black Watch (Royal High- landers) (42) (73)	Sc. doub- let Bl.	Feather bonnet. Sc., Wh. and Gr. diced border. Sc. hackle	Bl. Glen- garry
Regimental tartan. Sporran Wh. with five Blk. tassels. Pipers—feather bonnets and Royal Stewart tartan.			
Oxfordshire and Buckingham- shire Light Infantry (43) (52)	Sc. Wh.	Helmet	Gr.
Essex Regiment (44) (56)	Sc. Wh.	Helmet	Bl.
Sherwood Foresters (Nottingham- shire and Derbyshire Regiment) (45) (95)	Sc. Lincoln Gr.	Helmet	Bl.
Loyal North Lancashire Regiment (47) (81)	Sc. Wh.	Helmet	Bl.
Northamptonshire Regiment (48) (58)	Sc. Wh.	Helmet	Bl.
Princess Charlotte of Wales's (Royal Berkshire Regiment) (49) (66)	Sc. Bl.	Helmet	Bl. Sc. band
The Queen's Own (Royal West West Kent) (50) (97)	Sc. Bl.	Helmet	Bl. Sc. band
The King's Own (Yorkshire Light Infantry) (51) (105)	Sc. Bl.	Helmet	Gr.

Regimental Title Old numbers in brackets	Tunic Facings	Head-dress	Forage Cap
The King's (Shropshire Light Infantry) (53) (85)	Sc. Bl.	Helmet	Gr.
The Duke of Cambridge's Own (Middlesex Regiment) (57) (77)	Sc. Lemon Ye.	Helmet	Bl.
The King's Royal Rifle Corps (60)	Gr. Sc.	Busby. Blk. plume, with Sc. base	Gr.
The Duke of Edinburgh's (Wiltshire Regiment) (62) (99)	Sc. Bu.	Helmet	Bl.
Manchester Regiment (63) (96)	Sc. Wh.	Helmet	Bl.
The Prince of Wales's (North Staffordshire Regiment) (64) (98)	Sc. Wh.	Helmet	Bl.
York and Lancaster Regiment (65) 84)	Sc. Wh.	Helmet	Bl.
Durham Light Infantry (68) (106)	Sc. Dark Gr.	Helmet	Gr.
Highland Light Infantry (71) (74)	Sc. doublet Bu.	Bl. shako. Gr. tuft Cr., Wh. and Gr. diced border	Gr. Glengarry
Trews of Mackenzie tartan. Bandsmen—feather bonnets. Sc. hackle. Gr., Cr., and Wh. diced border.			
Seaforth Highlanders (Ross-shire Buffs, the Duke of Albany's) (72) (78)	Sc. doublet Bu.	Feather bonnet. Sc., Wh. and Gr. diced border. Wh. hackle	Glengarry Sc., Gr., and Wh. diced border
Mackenzie tartan. Wh. sporran, with two blk. tails. Bandsmen—Sc. hackle.			
Gordon Highlanders (75) (92)	Sc. doublet Ye.	Feather bonnet. Sc., Wh. and Gr. diced border. Wh. hackle	Glengarry Sc., Wh., Gr. Diced border
Gordon tartan with Ye. stripe. Sporran Wh. with two Blk. tails.			
The Queen's Own Cameron Highlanders (79)	Sc. doublet Bl.	Feather bonnet. Sc. Wh., Gr. diced border Wh. hackle	Bl. Glengarry
Cameron-Erracht tartan. Sporran Blk. with two Wh. tails.			
Royal Irish Rifles (83) (86)	Gr. Gr.	Blk. fur busby. Blk. and Gr. plume	Gr.
Princess Victoria's (Royal Irish Fusiliers) (87) (89)	Sc. Bl.	Racoon-skin cap Gr. plume on left	Bl. Sc. band
Connaught Rangers (88) (94)	Sc. Gr.	Helmet	Bl. Gr. band

Regimental Title Old numbers in brackets	Tunic Facings	Head-dress	Forage Cap
Princess Louise's Argyll and Sutherland Highlanders (91) (93)	Sc. doublet Ye.	Feather bonnet Sc. and Wh. diced border Wh. hackle	Glengarry Sc. and Wh. diced border
Sutherland tartan. Sporran Blk. with six Wh. tassels. Sgts. and Officers—badger's head.			
The Prince of Wales's Leinster Regiment (Royal Canadians) (100) (109)	Sc. Bl.	Helmet	Bl. Sc. band
Royal Munster Fusiliers (101) (104)	Sc. Bl.	Racoon-skin cap Wh. and Gr. plume on left	Bl. Sc. band
Royal Dublin Fusiliers (102) (103)	Sc. Bl.	Racoon-skin cap. Bl. and Gr. plume on left	Bright Bl. Sc. band
The Rifle Brigade (The Prince Consort's Own)	Gr. Blk.	Blk. fur busby Blk. plume	Gr.

DEPARTMENTAL CORPS

Army Service Corps	Bl. Wh. collar	Helmet, with ball	Bl. Wh. piping
Two Wh. stripes on pantaloons and overalls. Girdle—blue with Wh. and Ye. stripes.			
Army Ordnance Corps	Bl. Sc.	Helmet, with spike	Bl.
Two Sc. stripes on trousers.			
Royal Army Medical Corps	Bl. Dull cherry	Helmet, with ball	Bl. Cherry-red band
Three cherry-red stripes on trousers.			
Army Veterinary Corps	Bl. Maroon	Helmet, with ball	Bl. Maroon band
Ye. shoulder cords. Ye. piping on collar cuffs and skirts. Two maroon stripes on pantaloons and overalls. Wh. sword belt over tunic.			
Corps of Military Police (Mounted and Foot)	Bl. Sc.	Helmet, with spike	Red Blk. band
Broad Sc. stripe on pantaloons and trousers. Ye. shoulder cords. Brown belts. Whistles and chains. M.M.P.—Wh. gauntlets.			
Army Pay Corps	Bl. Ye.	Helmet, with spike	Bl. Ye. piping
Two yellow stripes on trousers.			

APPENDIX IV

LIST OF AUTHORITIES

During the necessary research work a great deal of help has been obtained from the War Office library, the Prince Consort Library at Aldershot, the Royal United Services Institute, and other libraries and museums. The following are some of the numerous books, manuscripts, pictures, etc., to which reference has been made:

Army Lists.
General Orders.
Circular Memoranda.
Dress Regulations.
Clothing Regulations.
The Clothing Book. 1742.
Historical Records of numerous regiments.
The Journal of the Society for Army Historical Research.
King's Regulations.
The Dress of the British Soldier. Luard.
Standards and Colours of the British Army. Milne.
History of the Dress of The Royal Regiment of Artillery. McDonald.
A History of the Uniforms of the British Army. Lawson.
British Battles on Land and Sea. Sir E. Wood.
South Africa and The Transvaal War. Creswicke.
The Years of Endurance. Bryant.
English Saga. Bryant.
Sergeant Lamb of the 9th. Graves.
Armies of India. Lovett and McMunn.
India's Army. Donovan Jackson.
British Military History, 1660–1936. Cole and Priestly.
A Short History of the British Army to 1914. Sheppard.
Official War Publications.
Various publications by Messrs. Gale & Polden.
The Army Quarterly.
The Journal of the Royal Artillery.
The Great War. Churchill.
Heraldry in War. Cole.
The Great Civil War. Cattermole.
The Empire and The Army. Fortescue.
Following the Drum. Fortescue.
The Enemy at the Gate. Hargreaves.
Revolution in Warfare. Liddell Hart.
Battlefields in Britain. Wedgewood.
British Soldiers. Johnston.
The British Army. Graham Seton Hutchison.
Numerous other books and periodicals.

Drawings and prints by most of the artists who have dealt with the subject of uniforms, have been studied, of whom the following are a few:

Martens, West, Forster, Turner, Raeburn, Hayes, Rochard, Copley, Cosway, Grant, Jones, Heath, Morland, Clayton, Bunbury, Rowlandson, Brandard, Singleton, Alken, Porter, Hoppner, the Dightons, Wymer, Bartolozzi, Dubois, Drahonet, Campion, Manshirch, Simpson, Baxter, Newhouse, Shee, Mansion and Eschauzier, Hull, Hamilton Smith, Lynch, Houston, Stadler, Atkinson, Thomas, Morin, Ramsay, Tomkins, Morier, Hogarth, Granville Baker, Wollen, Holloway, Ibbetson, Chidney, Payne, Simkin, Reynolds, etc.

INDEX

Index

Printed by Lithography in Great Britain by Jarrold and Sons Ltd., Norwich